D0096466

THEATRE, THEORY, POSTMODERNISM

Drama and Performance Studies ▬▬ *Timothy Wiles, General Editor*

JOHANNES BIRRINGER

THEATRE, THEORY, POSTMODERNISM

Indiana University Press • *Bloomington and Indianapolis*

First Midland Book Edition 1993

© 1991 by Johannes Birringer
All rights reserved

No part of this book may be reproduced or utilized in any form or by any means, electronic or mechanical, including photocopying and recording, or by any information storage and retrieval system, without permission in writing from the publisher. The Association of American University Presses' Resolution on Permissions constitutes the only exception to this prohibition.

The paper used in this publication meets the minimum requirements of American National Standard for Information Sciences—Permanence of Paper for Printed Library Materials, ANSI Z39.48-1984.

∞ ™

MANUFACTURED IN THE UNITED STATES OF AMERICA

Library of Congress Cataloging-in-Publication Data
Birringer, Johannes H.
    Theatre, theory, postmodernism / Johannes Birringer.
        p.   cm. — (Drama and performance studies)
    ISBN 0-253-31195-0 (alk. paper)
    1. Theater. 2. Postmodernism. I. Title.
    PN2039.B57 1991
        792'.01—dc20   90-24442
    ISBN 0-253-20845-9 (pbk.)

2 3 4 5 6 99 98 97 96 95 94 93

For Dee Anna

Today, the virtues of exhaustion are caused by
the exhaustion of the land.
                              Bertolt Brecht, *Galileo*

The concept of progress is to be grounded in
the idea of the catastrophe.
That things 'just go on' *is* the catastrophe.
It is not that which is approaching but
that which is.
                              Walter Benjamin, *Central Park*

CONTENTS

Illustrations

Preface

The following essays are a series of attempts: _Versuche_ in the sense in which Brecht understood such writings as political/aesthetic experiments reflecting on the institutions and social conditions that provoke new artistic practices.

On the one hand, they attempt to come to terms with recent and current trends in the theatre and the performing arts. As I am unable to formulate a coherent and comprehensive overview of the many ways in which my understanding of theatre and performance has changed over these last ten years I have spent moving back and forth between Europe and the United States, I propose at least to share some of the ambivalent fascination I experience in thinking of theatre, and writing for the theatre. I dare to do this at a time when many among us would argue that theatre no longer has any cultural significance and is too marginal or exhausted to intervene in contemporary cultural-political debates.

But to describe it as marginal may not be so accurate. Consider for example, the highly subsidized and ponderously visible state theatre system in West Germany or the confusing proliferation of spectacles and images produced on the stages of the much larger and more pluralistic American performance industry. That practitioners and audiences perceive theatre exhausted may instead point to their refusal to acknowledge the increasingly complex relationship which has evolved between theatre/art practice (a theatre that can no longer be considered separate or autonomous from the other arts), a wide spectrum of contemporary speculative thought and theory, and the general cultural formation that has come to be named "postmodern", more and more unavoidably.

On the other hand, then, these essays seek to hold on to writing for and thinking through theatre precisely by recognizing the accelerating effect of recent theories of postmodernity and its modes of cultural reproduction, an effect through which the historical reality of a performance event, always already precariously ephemeral and subject to the vicissitudes of production and reception, is further diminished and rendered anachronistic within the postmodern consciousness of a technological society.

One could argue that the theatre itself, regardless of whether we now think of play-writing, theatre training or scholarship, dramatic performance or experimental forms of theatre scenography and performance art, has diminished its historical consciousness because it seems not to live within the image-ridden and hysterical world of postmodern consumer capitalism, at least not to the extent that it would have hastened to theorize its institutional status or the aesthetic and political ideas/strategies with which it wants to participate in the cultural struggle over images, values, or material conditions that shape our perceptions of a constantly mediated reality.

There is something charming about the theatre's resistance to being on the cutting edge of the discourses that have affected the other arts and cultural practices such as film, photography, television, advertising, architecture, popular music, literary theory, or the human sciences. But theatre's inertia is actually rather incapacitating since it prevents it from expanding, revising, and revisioning the theatrical knowledge derived from those earlier interventions into the order of representation (by, say, Brecht, Meyerhold, Artaud, Grotowski) that may have prepared both the radical energies of the 1960s and 1970s (an era marked as much by the nomadic Living Theatre or the "social sculptures" of Joseph Beuys as by the focused, formalist innovations of Robert Wilson) as well as the exhaustion of the "order" *and* of the avant-garde in the 1980s.

Today we are not sure whether Brecht or Beuys or Wilson could be considered a model or an art practice that offers a way of rethinking and analyzing the social and cultural conditions under which a dominant aesthetics of representation can be challenged in an act of performance that reinscribes the margins between theory and practice. Among actors, directors, and writers there is very little discussion about what a "postmodern theatre" might be, and we notice the same reluctance among drama critics and scholars who continue to write about a world of texts and performances that seems largely untouched by the debates on the politics of postmodernism or on the technological transformation of the late modern culture.

What is at stake in this transformation is neither a political nor an aesthetic problem that I would want to see reduced to a definition or a new model of postmodern performance. And certainly not to one that extends the male European-American lineage of models that seems safely embedded in dominant historical conceptions of the twentieth-century Western avant-garde (from futurism and Dada to current multimedia performance). Rather, in facing the future of theatre we are already facing conditions in which the very notion of a dominant or unified culture, a traditional notion traceable back to historical idealizations of the theatre of the Athenian *polis*, will become obsolete by the changing realities of our fundamentally multicultural, multilingual, and socially polarized societies.

In view of these realities, we must reinvent our cultural topographies and engage in collaborative intercultural art, media, and research projects. And in view of a "postmodern theatre," we need to accommodate the significant impact of women's performances, both on the stage and on feminist critical practices seeking to analyze cultural productions in regard to their constructions of identity, gender, race, and sexual preference. My own preferences as an interpreter are shifting. I have not succeeded, I hope, in determining a coherent model for experimental performance that could safely distinguish between male-identified realist or high-technological theatre and woman-identified ritual body art or performance art. Such lines of demarcation will be crossed in a more heterogeneous, repeated movement between positions identified, say, with Robert Wilson, Laurie Anderson, or Karen Finley. The challenge I see in this movement—a movement always detachable, connectable, reversible, modifiable and without beginning or end (as in the old drama)—will perhaps be formulated most clearly in the middle of this book, when I return to the German Tanztheater of Pina Bausch.

Toward the end, in "The Postmodern Body in Performance," I arrive at the very problematic question of how the contemporary body appears, not as a figure of dramatic theatre or performance theory (Artaud, Grotowski) but in new forms of performance art and multimedia performance that either foreground or displace the body in ways similar to its construction in the visual media, in music television, in aerobics and body building, and the promotional industries of fashion and advertising. In discussing the work of Laurie Anderson, Robert Wilson, John Jesurun and Karen Finley, I am therefore equally drawn to other models of posing the body (Calvin Klein ads, Madonna videos) because such models connect imaging technologies and artistic practices. In fact, in this open-ended essay I come closest to recognizing video as the paradigmatic postmodern medium indicating changes in cultural production that are not merely changes in technology but in aesthetic models and ideologies of the subject as well. The body is the site of these changes, and the dematerializing and dehumanizing effects of postmodern technologies provide perhaps the strongest argument for the reinvention of theatrical consciousness based on the experience of the dispossessed body. Linking this dispossession to a politics of resistance and revolution, the book explores the current interaction of cultures (in theatre anthropology and intercultural performance) through its own dialectical frame of reference, which brings the postmodern theatre of surfaces (Robert Wilson and the various avant-garde opera and dance concerts I discuss in chapters 8, 9, and 10) into collision with those practices in dance and performance art that refuse to neutralize and technologize the human body or to edit out its history. The erasure of specific histories, traditions, and cultural differences promoted by the globalizing spectacles of postmodern capitalism is one of my main concerns in chapter 10, which is about Wilson's *the CIVIL warS* and the 1984 Olympic Arts Festival, and in chapter 7, "Theatre Anthropology after Brecht," in which I examine how Brecht's Marxist "learning play" model might have influenced the politics of European theatre research (Eugenio Barba) or at least helped me to approach the current dialogue between Western performance traditions and the Asian and Latin American traditions. In resorting to Brecht's understanding of the role of theatre as a social learning process, I try to account for the deeply ambivalent and provocative pessimism in the recent work of East German playwright Heiner Müller. Chapter 2, " 'Medea': Landscapes Beyond History," explores Müller's postrevolutionary plays (or "synthetic fragments," as he calls them) not only against the background of the catastrophic history of the two Germanys but also in reference to the seductive ease with which they have become assimilated into Robert Wilson's architectural theatre scenography. The couple Müller/Wilson is one of the stumbling blocks in this book, since it exemplifies both the confluences between German and American experimental performance theatre in the 1970s and 1980s *and* the divorce between German dance-theatre and American postmodern dance that I discuss in chapter 6, "Pina Bausch: Dancing across Borders."

The same dialectic is at work in the museum exhibitions that are the subject of chapter 5, "Overexposure: Sites of Postmodern Media." The exiled Hungarian theatre company Squat plays an intermediary role in this chapter, which seeks to read Lyotard's staging of "Les Immatériaux" (Centre Pompidou) against the Whitney Museum's spectacular display of "Image World: Art and Media Culture." In a sense, this reading also reflects the transatlantic direction in which postmodern theories have traveled from France to the United States. In the course of tracing this movement of theory, I repeatedly arrive at the "America" projected in the ironically nihilistic sociological writings of Baudrillard. Without sharing Baudrillard's nihilism, I find my experience divided between my European commitment to a political and philosophical understanding of theatre, and my American interpretation of the expanding power of postmodern consumer capitalism and the spectacle of a culture dominated by the new electronic media. In my search for a theatre practice that has not been subsumed or marginalized by this culture, I encounter the "archaeological" work of Herbert Blau. The theoretical writings and experimental stagings of his KRAKEN company present a powerful model of *thinking through the theatre*. Though the impact of Blau's deconstruction of *Hamlet* on the American theatre may be minimal, the substance and depth of his thoughts create an important counterpoint to the on-going spectacle of postmodern art and commercial entertainment. In one sense, Blau's intellectual emphasis on *Hamlet* is a deliberate anachronism, and I discuss it in chapter 3, "Tracing the Ghosts in the Theatre," by interpolating the radical self-critique of Müller's *Hamlet-machine* and by adding a commentary on the most significant postmodern *Hamlet* production in an institutional theatre—chapter 4: "Self-Consuming Artifact: *Hamlet* in West Berlin". In order to recover the thought of theatre and its critical connection to postmodern culture, the long, introductory essay in chapter 1 sets the scene for the various leitmotifs of postmodernist philosophy and ideology that I discover in the contemporary space of culture. Before I even mention a particular theatre work or performance art event, I therefore concentrate, first of all, on architecture, urban space, and the visual mediation of late capitalist culture in order to explore the pervasive social and economic displacements that underlie this mediation. My own experience of the dispersion of local identity in the postmodern city leads me to see the city itself as the ultimate site of postmodernist theoretical debates, and I explain why this site became the focus of my own current theatre project, *Invisible Cities*.

Before I locate the emergence of postmodern performance from this space, I draw attention to Joseph Beuys's concept of "social sculpture"as a process of social transformation, to the intersection of cultural politics and theatre (in the case of Fassbinder's *Garbage, the City and Death*, a play halted by the city for/against which it was written), and to the situationist interventions of Krzysztof Wodiczko, whose "counter-projections" directly expose the architectural façades of late capitalist culture. These intersections help me to set the historical stage for the conjunction of theatre and postmodern culture that I will return to throughout the other ten chapters.

The essays that follow do not present a thesis but rather explore different ways of looking at contemporary modes of performance. At the same time they will bring some of the postmodernism debates into the focus of the theatre in an effort to reappropriate and reposition the theatrical metaphors that have been so widely used by other cultural discourses and practices. Perhaps inevitably, such an effort to theorize the historical conditions of contemporary theatre can only be tentative. If there is a limit to the theory and the future of theatre, however, it is most certainly related to the radical impoverishment of postmodern culture and to the "exhaustion of the land."

Having said this, I admit to the limitations of a book written by a male European displaced into the borderland of Texas. His struggle against the exhaustion of European-American culture may be self-contradictory insofar as it is waged with the languages and concepts it has internalized. A different language will become necessary, as Gloria Anzaldúa has suggested in her book on "borderlands," if we want to reverse the progress of history that has brought us to the current crisis. More realistically, perhaps we can acknowledge the crisis at the juncture of cultures as our common ground. La frontera es lo único que compartimos.

Houston, Texas
January 1990

Acknowledgments

Versions of some of the essays in this book have previously appeared in print. I wish to thank the editors of *Performing Arts Journal*, *The Drama Review*, *Theater*, and *Gestus* for their kind permission to let me use these materials.

Much of my thinking in these essays developed in response to performances and exhibitions I saw while traveling in search for a practice. While my critical debts will become obvious, I owe special thanks to those colleagues and practitioners who have encouraged my search either directly or indirectly. I would like to mention Robert Corrigan, Julian Olf, Herbert Blau, Michael Oppitz, Bonnie Marranca, Gautam Dasgupta, Rustom Bharucha, Heiner Weidmann, Frank Leimbach, Renato and Iris Miceli, Dawn Kramer, and Attilio Caffarena. Attilio's criticism was vital at a point when I lost faith in the theatre as well as in role of the director, and I also wish to thank Randal Davis, Cristina DeGennaro, Mya K. Myint, Laura Steckler, and Eoghan Ryan for their help in this transitional period. When I began to focus on the praxis of performance, I realized how much I had been moved, on a deeply personal level, by the experience of my frequent encounters with Pina Bausch and the dancers of her company. Working through this experience, I need to thank all the actors, dancers, and visual/performance artists who have collaborated with me over the past few years. Their generous encouragement has helped me to accept the painful loss that binds me to Houston.

The photographs used in the book are reprinted with the permission of the artists whose work I have reviewed. I am grateful to them. Several photographers and art galleries/museums have been very generous in allowing me to use their photographs. I regret that in a few instances the photographers are anonymous and I was unable to give proper credit to their work.

I also wish to thank the readers and editors of Indiana University Press for their expert advice and their trust in the frequently nomadic style and logic of my writing.

THEATRE, THEORY, POSTMODERNISM

1 ■ THE POSTMODERN SCENE

Exhausted Land/Exhausted Theory

> . . . the mental desert form, which is the puri-
> fied form of social desertion, expands visibly.
> Disaffection finds its purified form in the
> barrenness of speed. The inhumanity of our
> late, asocial, superficial world immediately finds
> its aesthetic and ecstatic form here. For the des-
> ert is no more than that: an ecstatic critique of
> culture, an ecstatic form of disappearance.
>   Baudrillard, *America*

Postmodernism has not yet taken place, although it is talked about as if it
were a central theme of contemporary theory and cultural practice. We
cannot dispute the term's use for a variety of cultural forms, from art to
advertising or from technology to everyday lifestyles. The inflationary use
of the term renders it sufficiently abstract and powerful, even though the
fascination for it, along with all the polemical debates, seems largely due
to the uncertainty we experience in our abstract relations to the changes
in our time, that is, our *imaginary* relation to time, to what is contemporary.

I grew up in West Germany shortly after World War II, and at that time I already found myself in a strange vacuum: the scenario of an unexplored and unspoken division between generations, one unwilling to confront its past and the other too young to understand why everything had to be new and different. The "new" social and economic organization, with its very palpable and visible progress of capitalist modernization, was to be called "reconstruction." The dead had been buried, the pile of debris cleared away, and the scars mostly covered over. I remember that when I was barely ten years old, my parents took me to the opera (Mozart's *Don Giovanni*). The building had been restored after the bombing; the huge crystal chandelier, a gift from Hitler, still hung from the ceiling. Later that year I saw my first American movie with Marilyn Monroe; it was the year in which John F. Kennedy proclaimed that he was a Berliner too.

By that time, other divisions had become more graphic and implacable. The ideological border between the capitalist world and the socialist world developed its Manichean architecture of entrenchment, and the cold war established its stone wall that cut time into two halves. It seemed a peculiarly fitting historical irony that the Wall, a belated symbol of an historical juncture and the separation of political and philosophical conceptions of history, cut its way straight through Germany and the middle of the Old World. On either side of this symbolic Wall (perhaps it could be called a monument) the revolution, and with it the entire tradition of modern rationality handed down from the Enlightenment, led its posthumous existence.

The Berlin Wall with its borderline, a fortified no-man's land that encloses and doubles the condition of the city, can be seen as a complex image of our postmodernity. The Wall constructs boundaries of difference but also contorts space in a way that postpones a clear territorial or categorial "break" as long as the city remains the east of the west and the west of the east. Thus it is also an image of the recent past and of the conjuncture of complementary fictions that refer back both to the bourgeois and the Marxist conceptions of the "project of modernity," as it has been called by the critical theorists of the dialectic of enlightenment. Postmodernism in this sense could be called a retrospective process in which a myth or imaginary construction as a mode of cultural (re)production is tied to the physiognomy of modern industrial society and to the historical trajectory of its political and aesthetic transformations. It is the trajectory of an historical tragedy. For somebody growing up in this divided postwar country, the new growth and prosperity of the one part of a defeated nation was always linked to the memory of its suppressed legacy: Prussian militarism, the failure of the Weimar Republic, Nazi fascism, and the Holocaust. The economic success of West Germany's capitalist modernization will determine the future of the other part now that East Germany's authoritarian party regime and its real existing socialism have collapsed. The disappearance of the Wall after the November revolution of 1989 will only intensify the problems of coming to terms with the double past. At this early point in 1990 one cannot foresee the results of a rapid process of political and economic unification. But if one walks across the no-man's land of Berlin's border and watches the removal of the Wall, one already knows that it will remain a part of the collective psychopathology. Christa Wolf, in her newly published book *Was bleibt*, was the first East German writer to pose the question of the "remainder," of the residue of guilt and self-oppression, and she was immediately attacked for posing it. The question, however, will not go away.

As I continue with this introduction, which is not about theatre, I realize that I am only interested in writing about the theatre and its condition within the postmodern scene because I appreciate its absolute dependence on the past (the history of drama and the cultural history of interpretation mediated through techniques of acting) as well as its structural dependence on the current institutions and conventions of representation. This, I believe, has forced the theatre into a contradictory space and gives it a certain ghostliness within the cultural formations of modern societies predicated on technical and scientific progress.

More precisely, I am interested in the disappearance of theatre from the evolving debates on, and the theories of, postmodern art and culture, especially as these theories no longer debate the possibility of revolutionary change in the West. In considering contemporary theatre within the confluence of political neoconservatism and the phenomenon of postmodernism in the 1980s, as well as of the pessimistic, terminal pronouncements of the Left on the "obsolescence of the avant-garde,"[1] the "end of humanism,"[2] and the "end of art theory"[3] during the same years, I want to explore the specific boundaries (implicit in the idea of the *end of history*) that relate to the theatre.

Since my earliest encounters with theatre performance (mostly the classical repertoire of Greek plays, Shakespeare, Goethe, Schiller, Ibsen, and Chekhov, which in the later 1960s was presented in "revisionist" stagings), I had always thought of theatre artists as historians, archaeologists, and time travelers. Or, borrowing a comic figure from Shakespearean tragedy, they might perhaps be called "grave-diggers," working on the edge of the two extremes of destruction and preservation, throwing up the skulls of history and transforming them. Each rehearsal, each night of performance is a new beginning that preserves what comes back, each act an affirmation (which makes it institutional) whose consequences cannot be "saved" or guaranteed. When I spoke of the contradictory space of theatre, I meant to refer to the different realities—the simultaneity of the unsimultaneous—present in theatre productions that take place *in* time and *through* time, on either side of the existing or invisible wall.[4] Unlike literature, film, painting, or the popular mass media, the theatre must show its physical, bodily existence and its "liveness," the volatile progress of its human labor, the contingencies of the space in which it labors, and its schizophrenic awareness of its own unreality.

This awareness results from the temporal structure of performance: the work on stage and the process of its creation are suspended and then disappear. This suspension of the time-space or "world" of performance divides the theatre from itself. It cannot hold on to the reality it imagines and produces, and the lived body of work becomes a fiction the moment it vanishes. What remains is the "hidden scene of production" (Marx), not so much the functional normality of the conceptual and technical processes of rehearsal (beginning again) as rather the unconsciously produced image the theatre has of itself and conveys to its culture.

Theatre's self-image permutates under the pressures of experience, the changing focus of cultural and art critical discourse, and the exigencies of the political economy of which the theatre is a part. There will be different images within the same space of a culture, and they will differ again from those produced in other cultural spaces of the global west/east schism. To invoke the notion of difference is troublesome today, because the old languages of cultural and political discussion seem to be falling by the wayside. The classical modernist dichotomies of subject/object, high/low, left/right, mainstream/oppositional, rational/irrational, elite/popular, and so forth, become useless in the face of the phantasmagoric "global American postmodernist culture."[5] The distorted expressions of this phantasmagoria are appearing everywhere in the Western centers of advanced capitalism, where our abstract vision of the world is shaped by a massive mediation of products/commodities. When Christopher Columbus left Italy and Spain some five hundred years ago to discover the New World, "America" was an image of the future, of distance. That distance has collapsed. We may not have a future anymore, and certainly the idea of a global American postmodernist culture, with Universal Studios and Disneyland as late museums of frontier's end, suggests a profoundly antitheatrical conception of empty space.

A global culture would be a culture without a perspective. We would be trapped in a perpetual present, in the same space, circulating the same cultural products over and over. The way in which a new "cultural logic" of the "postmodern condition" is invoked by the founding texts of postmodern debate[6] makes one wonder what critical perspective is claimed by theories that speak about the inability of positioning ourselves in an homogenous cultural space. They may not have found a critical perspective because the dissolute phenomenon of contemporary postmodernisms is not yet fully visualized.

But the questions that are asked, if we were indeed at the end of history, are well worth asking as we try to cultivate our complex cultural landscapes. A lot of examples readily come to mind. For instance, the contemporary city, such as Dallas or New York, is perhaps the most complex spatial figure of our time. The fragmented surfaces and the delirious, discontinuous fabric of its sights, signs, and sounds are infinitely difficult to describe. If we analyzed them in terms of the changes, redevelopment, destruction, and gentrification that have occurred over the years since, say, the presumed spatial revolutions of modernist architecture, the dreams of the Modern Movement would no longer be legible between today's broken sightlines. The visions of Le Corbusier, Mies van der Rohe, Gropius, Taut et al. would disappear among the gigantic emblems of economic power—the gold, silver, or emerald green glass box skyscrapers of banks, oil companies, or multinational corporations—and the overcrowded freeways, crumbling factories, cheap convenient stores, and decaying urban ghettoes.

The dehumanizing, dystopian reality of the contemporary city has been imaginatively portrayed in cynical futuristic films such as *Blade Runner* or *Repo Man* that seem to mock the phallic and mythic architectonics of industrial technology in Fritz Lang's *Metropolis*. The reflecting mirror facades and glazed transparencies of postmodern architecture could refer back to the other reality of a provocative specular scene of desecuring trompe l'oeil effects and disembodied spaces that announce new immaterialities and imaginary urban perspectives while their stylishness merely accentuates the disproportion between such design and the total crisis of political, social, or ecological responsibility in urban planning. The first discussions about postmodernist "free styles" (Charles Jencks) began in the late 1960s among architects little concerned with the intricacies of urban planning or the politics of strategic destruction and reconstruction played out on the unstable infrastructures of the city's collective body. They were intent on superseding the transparent functionalism of International Style Modernism with their own brand of a self-assertive, stylistic eclecticism. With the most symbol-laden public structures of corporate towers, convention halls, museums, hotels, and super malls, they created spectacular images of themselves. Architects such as Philip Johnson, Michael Graves, Robert Stern, and Paolo Portoghesi now appeared on the covers of *Time* and *Newsweek*. Their bold buildings, with their histrionic facades and picturesque effects, not only *were* sublimely useless but pretended to be *fashionably* so.

Such stylishness also pretends to be free from the burden of historical reflection and present repercussions of inner city crises. The low comedies of public notoriety (as in the case of Johnson's Chippendale ATT Building in New York or Charles Moore's Piazza d'Italia in New Orleans) were never questioned. Did the fashionable posturing beyond failed utopian aspirations of the functionalist austerity of High Modernism express a new "cultural logic" or an embarrassing disarray of values or both? One perhaps needs to look more critically at the equation between postmodernism and the conditions of a degraded pluralism under late capitalism than is suggested by Fredric Jameson's speculative insight and self-incorporation into the "originality of postmodern space."[7]

I am sympathetic, since I stumbled into the same confusion at the same MLA conference in Los Angeles in 1982. I am less inclined, however, to follow Jameson's elaboration on John Portman's Los Angeles Bonaventure Hotel. He assumes the spatial dislocations and the bizarre and bewildering perceptual teasing of this hotel's interior need to be considered a particularly fascinating postmodern architectural analogue to the ecstatic dispersions (of the body, of thought, of images, of capital, commodities, values) experienced at the edge of our late culture. For Jameson, it is the edge of a panic that keeps us immersed in a "hyperreality" that he links to the "great global multinational communicational network," the "hyperspace of capital," and the "space of postmodern warfare." It seems that Jameson is caught up in the *spectacle* of the dizzying "hyperspace" and the milling confusion he describes as the "complete world" or "miniature city" of the Bonaventure's interior. He starts out to criticize the depthless, placeless autoreferentiality of a hotel architecture that attempts both to create fantastic spatial and perspectival ambiguities inside its monumental and mannerist atrium (where you are dazzled by spaceship elevators shooting up and down but cannot find the way out of its multistoried dome) and a radical dissociation of its closed structure from the downtown neighborhoods (via hidden entry-ways and aggressive mirror glass surfaces). He ends up instead focusing on the kinaesthetic excitement that this "new total space" might induce for those prepared to congregate in it. Congregating in the Bonaventure's miniature city, Jameson argues with obvious references to the populist "consumption" of the Beaubourg in Paris,[8] ought to result in a "new collective practice" of experiencing mutated leisure-time space and of the bodily perceptions needed to grasp—and actually find your way through—this designed ambience.

Even as Jameson knows it impossible to gain a total vision of this new space, he insists that there must be a cultural politics and a radical aesthetic that can invent ways of cognitively *mapping* this new totality. This radical aesthetic must be able to interconnect a wide range of cultural phenomena (as he considers the Bonaventure connected to current writing, film, music and painting) with relations between multinational capitalism, new technology, and postmodernism as the dominant "cultural logic" in this new "world space." But unlike Walter Benjamin who in the *Passagenwerk* attempted to reconstruct the prehistory of capitalist modernity and commodity production out of a topography of concrete urban images (the "scene" of the capital of nineteenth-century France), Jameson's theoretical constitution of a hegemonic postmodern space articulates itself aesthetically without "prehistory," so to speak. It is as if the older idealism of an autonomous culture of modernism, or the revolutionary avant-garde's project to transform art and society were exploded.

Jameson locates this rupture in the 1960s and implies that what found cultural expression through the desire for an uninterrupted present or the polymorphously perverse theatricalization of everyday life in the 1960s, eventually collapsed into an ever-expansive commodity system where the polymorphous fetishism of Andy Warhol's soup cans or Marilyn Monroe portraits is the order of the day.

This dissolution into the as yet unrepresentable totality of the postmodern capitalist scene, "where our now postmodern bodies are bereft of spatial coordinates and practically (let alone theoretically) incapable of distantiation,"[9] is analyzed negatively as the end of critical distance and the final dispossession of the subject as it has been endlessly elaborated in the antihumanist body of poststructuralist discourse. But Jameson's essay does not claim to attack postmodernism from a historical or Marxist position that would, first of all, have to defend its discredited logic and, second, need to distinguish itself from currently fashionable attacks by conservative critics who are driven by their own nostalgia for a lost ideal of modernist culture. Rather, Jameson prefers to engage his totalizing logic positively. He cannot but recuperate, albeit with an insufficiently postmodern body, the polymorphous perversity of the Bonaventure Hotel as the "norm" of the cultural space of postmodernism. He does not comment on the *excess economy* of this architecture, on its wanton diversions and hyperbolic collages of neorational rigor, baroque pomposity and surrealist optical effects, on its labyrinthine mixture of parody and kitsch that distracts from one's radical disorientation inside the simulated landscape complete with lush vegetation, a miniature lake, and bridges. (In this landscape of virtual perspectives, virtual volumes, and virtual mobility, walking is displaced into escalating and "flying" in the space shuttle elevators). As a purely aesthetic technoscape of designed overaccumulation so abstract that the architect had to add information booths and guidance color codes, the Bonaventure turns architecture and property development into aestheticized commodities that participate in the postmodern economy of signs. Of course, equally disorienting designs of perceptual experience abound in fashion, music video, film, and advertising.[10] Finally, the Bonaventure successfully demonstrates how capital is reinforced by elevating the commodity form into an abstractly selfreferential and excessive site of power.

When Jameson praises the space shuttle elevators as spectacular, gigantic "kinetic sculptures," he refers to them as "virtual narratives" or paradigms of trajectories and movements that are inscribed on our postmodern bodies. Such an inscription of power calls for a specific analysis. But Jameson then refers to them as machines *replacing* the movement of the body since they can act as pure, self-reflexive signs. His thought breaks off here, and he seems still preoccupied with the qualitative changes in the habits of bodily perception when he, several pages later, comments on the "unimaginable quantum leap in technological alienation" produced by the "new machines" which no longer represent motion (like older automotive machines) "but which can only be represented *in motion*."[11] He then shifts into "a very different area, namely the space of postmodern warfare," quotes from Michael Herr's *Dispatches,* a book on the Vietnam War that Jameson claims breaks with all previous narrative paradigms, since that "first terrible postmodernist war" is no longer representable in the older languages of the war novel or movie. It is worth repeating the excerpt from Herr's text:

He was a moving-target-survivor subscriber, a true child of the war, because except for the rare times when you were pinned or stranded the system was geared to keep you mobile, if that was what you thought you wanted. As a technique for staying alive it seemed to make as much sense as anything, given naturally that you were there to begin with and wanted to see it close; it started out sound and straight but it formed a cone as it progressed, because the more you moved the more you saw, the more you saw the more besides death and mutilation you risked, and the more you risked of that the more you would have to let go of one day as a "survivor." Some of us moved around the war like crazy people until we couldn't see which way the run was taking us anymore, only the war all over its surface with occasional, unexpected penetration. As long as we could have choppers like taxis it took real exhaustion or depression near shock or a dozen pipes of opium to keep us even apparently quiet, we'd still be running around inside our skins like something was after us, ha ha, La Vida Loca. In the months after I got back the hundreds of helicopters I'd flown in began to draw together until they'd formed a collective meta-chopper, and in my mind it was the sexiest thing going; saver-destroyer, provider-waster, right-hand-left-hand, nimble, fluent, canny and human; hot steel, grease, jungle-saturated canvas webbing, sweat cooling and in the other, fuel, heat, vitality and death, death itself, hardly an intruder.[12]

This horrific narrative of the fantasized "meta-chopper" as an eroticized machine of death and survival follows in brutal juxtaposition to the admiring exposition on the entertaining "leisure-time space" of the Bonaventure. Jameson apparently wants us to think of his examples of "technological alienation" in a dialectical way that could unite the catastrophic and progressive aspects of postmodernism. If that reminds us of the familiar metanarrative of the "dialectic of enlightenment," it also of course opens out on different perspectives that are suppressed by Jameson's narrativization of postmodern space.

    In particular, I am thinking of the significant work of Paul Virilio[13] whose "aesthetics of disappearance" evolved from his studies of urban space, the history of warfare and technology, and the evolving relations between speed, transportation, film, and politics. What strikes me as crucial in this context is the *image* or *sign of dislocation*—and its larger implications as an ideological expression for advanced capitalism—not captured by Jameson's glowing description of the Bonaventure elevators. Both the space shuttle elevators in their delirious verticality and the helicopters are hardly machines of "technological alienation." They are technologies that facilitate speed and movement that participate in the general formation of "territories of time and space."[14] At the same time, if we think of them in their real and fantasized environments, the Bonaventure Hotel and the war machine in *Dispatches*, they become indispensable to the operation of an excessive and absolutely offensive economy, an economy of "death itself," to extrapolate from *Dispatches* as well as from the theoretical fictions of Georges Bataille and Jean Baudrillard.[15] But how much excess can be accumulated, toward the exhaustion of death and the inertia reached at the limit of movement, in an aesthetic mode parading as "floating signifiers," as meta-choppers or metaelevators, in a hallucinatory territory where all external referents (to the body, to transportation, speed, mobility, attack-force, surveillance, and so forth) are extinguished or, rather, suspended within a pure, symbolic exchange, an endless cancellation of the real? How deadly erotic can an elevator or a helicopter be once it is abstracted from its technical functions into a quietly terroristic sign that simulates motion "in motion," in purely imaginary relationships to the body and the eye, circulating in the void?

The economy of death that comes into play here revolves around the convergence of *seduction* and *power*. It is analyzed by Baudrillard—in his most excessive and dramatic formulations—as the postmodern apotheosis of simulation in that the circular floating of images (the "saver-destroyer, provider-waster" in *Dispatches*) cancels all dialectical positions (subject/object, cause/effect, active/passive, sender/receiver, and so forth). And as it cancels perspective, depth of field, and real space between sign and referent (what I would also call the *embodied experience* of space and time), it brings the localization of any specific term of a power relation to an end. This model of postmodern power is experienced as fascinating and seductive, Baudrillard argues, because the only "information" of its simulated expressions lies in their cynical display of *effects* (optical illusions) that no longer belong to any rational or representational order constituted by systems of economic power (Marx) or sociological and political power (as delineated, for example, in Foucault's normalized society of the panoptic). No longer a rational foundation or a principle of organization of knowledge and experience, simulated power appears like a figure in an absurdist play, an "endgame" operation in blind laughter covering up the loss of meaning in its endless recursiveness.

> The universal fascination with power in its exercise and its theory is so intense because it is a fascination with a *dead* power characterized by a simultaneous 'resurrection effect,' in an obscene and parodic mode, of all the forms of power already seen—exactly like sex in pornography.[16]

Perhaps the parodic excess of the Bonaventure's simulation of a "hotel"—of a place of necessary regulations of traffic, exchange, communication, accommodation, departure and arrival—makes it an interesting architectural example of the question whether the "logic of postmodernism" can be examined exclusively under the sign of the final abstraction of capitalism's commodity forms.[17] Perhaps instead such an isolated instance of the "overexposed city" (Virilio) needs also to be seen in the context of the very contradictory and shifting fashions in which the largely unresolved physical and perceptual transformations of an advanced technological culture have the power to *affect* people and their actual relations to the perceived environment.

I do not think, for example, that the Bonaventure's space shuttle elevators, sublimely hyperreal as they are, need to be seen as a "resurrection effect" covering up disappearing social and political realities with a "desperate staging"[18] of mobility. The false conquest of space that they simulate—and we are painfully reminded of the fatal explosion of a real space shuttle, the Challenger, in 1986—rather indicates the building's internal struggle to overcome the contradictions between the milling diffusions of its overdesigned ambience, meant to arouse excitement and consumer receptivity, and the practical necessities of regulating the exchange and accommodation of customers who actually choose, and can afford to choose, to sleep in the hotel. Portman's designed postmodern ambience stages a scene built for the heightened aesthetic reception of a commercial business space that would otherwise be as bland and mediocre as the innumerable motels and Holiday Inns across the country. The spectacular architecture of the Bonaventure also embodies the political spectacle of dislocation unrelated to Baudrillard's cybernetic and implosive model of the hyperrealization of "dead power." Rather more concretely, it unleashes the power and the antiurban real-estate speculations of foreign investors and local, downtown interest groups. This dislocation or disappearance, in the context of the downtown redevelopment in Los Angeles, is not yet the replacement of built structures and older urban forms of demarcation projected by Virilio's account of the "overexposed city" (in which a new synthetic time-space is ruled by the interfaces of electronic communications). Rather, a transfer of corporate headquarters and foreign investments (the Bonaventure was financed by the Japanese) into the older inner city residential areas around Bunker Hill has since the 1960s led to the displacement of poor Asian-Hispanic neighborhoods by the sky scrapers and multiblock structures of the new downtown financial district.[19] What is so striking about this pattern of urban redevelopment (with parallel cases in Houston, Detroit, Atlanta, Dallas, and other major cities) is the violence with which such a financial district invades and segregates ethnic inner city neighborhoods. Such a concentration of economic power and high property value in the reckless overconstruction of commercial space, with the simultaneous decay of adjacent areas "designed" to disintegrate or to be taken over for strategic gentrification, does not reflect a homogenizing logic but a territorial economy that we remember from the political, religious, racial, and class segregations of divided cities like Berlin, Belfast, Beirut, or New York.

The territorial demarcations reflect a war machine that has begun its postmodern collapse of economic and military spaces of accumulation. Absolute collective violence—the total nuclear destructibility of the world—could be seen as a heightened expression of the continuous destructions and rearrangements of the cities.

> The so-called "technocrats" are very simply the military class. They are the ones who consider rationality only in terms of its efficiency, whatever the horizon. The negative horizon's apocalyptic dimension doesn't strike them. It's not their problem. . . .

The great stroke of luck for the military class's terrorism is that no one recognizes it.[20]

The technocracy of urban architecture, as it designs its Bonaventure Hotels and Trump Castles into seductively disorienting aesthetic wonderlands, need not fool itself into believing that its violent invasions of social space are not recognized. Surpressing this violence compromises Jameson's account of the Bonaventure, and doubtless those who lack access to its upper-class leisure space or who have been hit hard by housing shortage or the general deterioration of urban communities and social relations will be affected differently by the "originality" of postmodern architecture's restricted enclaves. These enclaves of corporate power are not a cultural dominant that could actually subordinate the city's inhabitants, or their heterogeneous cultural practices and social networks, to the enormity of their images and global fantasies. Rather, they are paradoxical private/public territories, both expansive and threatening and claustrophobic. And it is hardly ironic, in the light of the historical continuity of First World capitalism's imperialist, racist, and colonial evolution that commercial megastructures of the Los Angeles downtown come to look like a *besieged site*, formed in the very same "protective maze of freeways, moats, concrete parapets, and asphalt no-man's lands" that Mike Davis traces back to Portman's Hyatt-Regency built for Atlanta's Peachtree Center in 1967:

> Downtown Atlanta rises above its surrounding city like a walled fortress from another age. The citadel is anchored to the south by the international trade center and buttressed by the municipal stadium. To the north, the walls and walkways of John Portman's Peachtree Center stand watch over the acres of automobiles that pack both flanks of the city's long ridge. The sunken moat of I-85, with its flowing lanes of traffic, reaches around the eastern base of the hill from south to north, protecting lawyers, bankers, consultants and regional executives from the intrusion of low-income neighborhoods.[21]

Davis suggests that the "fortress function" of these "centers" within the decentered and sprawling postindustrial city reveals the coercive intent of metropolitan elites to polarize urban spaces. One could also argue that the displacement of marginalized, adjacent ethnic communities within the lateral sprawl of Los Angeles has created constantly migrating and proliferating strategies of intrusion that keep the vibrant expressions of various black, Asian, Hispanic, or Chicano minority culture alive even as the white dominant mass media pretend they are not or carry on their mainstream homogenization of the world through television. Like the highly mobile and visible force of the illegible graffiti language that defaces the New York subway cars and travels permanently through the underground of Manhattan and the adjacent boroughs, multiethnic popular culture and art in Los Angeles have created interreferential gestures (as in Chicano music addressing and fusing different inherited styles and languages) and activities (street festivals, craft fairs, communal projects, street theatre, graffiti, posters, murals, alternative video, and community access cable) that use the communal body as material for performance art, and the city and its human movements (traffic, zones of everyday social practice) as material support for a kind of inverse appropriation of the urban landscape. This subversion both interferes with and by-passes the protected and institutionalized spaces of "legitimate culture."

In writing about East Los Angeles Chicano music, George Lipsitz explains that many of the bands have developed their own forms of "postmodern cultural manipulation" by treating ethnic identity and musical genres as plastic and open-ended, creating a *bricolage* of eclectic styles and cultural fusions: Mexican folk music, polkas and corridos, Afro-American rhythm & blues, white rockabilly and country, pop, jazz, and punk. Simultaneously, street slang, folk dancing, clothing styles, car customizing and wall murals become sources of community subcultures.[22] The Chicano band Tierra, which became the favorite band of the Mexican-American low rider subculture in the 1970s, is a good example of such cross-overs. The car customizers themselves play with established codes when they "juxtapose seemingly inappropriate realities (fast cars designed to go slowly, 'improvements' that flaunt their impracticality [and] make ironic and playful commentary on prevailing standards of automotive design)"[23] and name their low riders after songs or political and historical incidents of the past. When low rider events incorporate Chicano music and other performances of local culture that deal with collective history and social communication, and when their parade of redesigned, "slow" cars cruises down the L.A. main thoroughfares, we can speak of a "social sculpture" or an "action" in the sense in which Joseph Beuys described such a creative process as an activation, by means of intervention, of our time and space. When Beuys spoke about basic human energies and used for art ordinary objects and materials of our everyday collective reality, (milk, fat, water, felt, wood, soil) he meant to show how a specific movement can bring dead, elemental material into a form of *social architecture*. He demonstrated a chemical process that was always also a political process of participation, of an opening to a collective consciousness for social change. Shortly before his death in 1986, Beuys refered to himself not as an artist, but as somebody trying to intervene in the structures of society to help building a new world that might be finally inhabitable (directly quoting André Breton's vision of *"un monde enfin habitable"*).

If this is one of the unaccomplished projects of the historical avant-garde, it also of course is a project that postmodern art inside institutional spaces cannot accomplish. We have also seen how quickly the underground graffiti of the New York subways can end up as "art works" in fashionable new wave galleries of the East Village. It is of particular consequence, then, to remember Joseph Beuys's contention that art (whether inside or outside of institutions and the commodity market) does not exist yet, and that his "social sculptures" are directed toward the future.

Beuys's action events, installations, environments, sculptures, and teachings themselves perform a movement that constantly shifts and crosses the boundaries of what the dominant culture (mainstream and academic) defines as "inside" or "outside" and consecrates as natural rituals of perception: consider the way architecture relates to property value, or museums exhibit art objects, or media and art critical discourses represent those art objects, and so forth. Praising or ridiculing Beuys as a prophet and shaman, the media in Germany were quite unable to assimilate the work that he built and lived. Nor did they seem to realize, when they attacked him as a charlatan, that they were discrediting their own aesthetic value systems and norms that could not contain the flux of ever-changing categories of identity, both in Beuys's life and in the materials he treated.

I remember vividly how stunned I was when I first encountered Beuys and saw how he invaded the protected space of institutionalized "high art." During his action event *Iphigenia/Titus,* staged in Frankfurt in 1969, Beuys sat inside an enclosure with a white horse that quietly ate hay and gazed at us. The only other objects he had on stage were a tape recorder playing monotonously recorded readings from Goethe's *Iphigenia* and Shakespeare's *Titus Andronicus,* and diverse materials including sugar, margarine, iron, fur, and a huge pair of orchestra cymbals. There was no recognizable connection between these heterogeneous action components, yet the scenic allegory of Beuys's gravitating position in between the dead texts of cultural tradition and the living horse gradually crystallized into a richly associative confrontation between inert material and organic life. Beuys repeatedly described his interaction with materials that provide warmth or are sensitive to heat as a "methodical" confrontation with the elements of death in an environment of death that must be overcome.

I had not known then how sensitive to heat classical literary texts can be, and I experienced Beuys's intervention—in the presence of the quiet vitality and indifference of the animal—as an attempt to bring each participant into crisis with his or her aesthetic complicity in the mutilation and violation of our lives, symbolically represented in the idealized metaphysics of sacrifice in *Iphigenia* and the unredeemable brutality in the scenes of treachery, rape, and slaughter in *Titus.* No theatre production of these classic dramas could avoid reproducing the ideology of an autonomous art that can be aesthetically appreciated and that severs the audience from any social responsibility. Beuys's shift toward a pedagogical action or sculpting process demonstrates different positions of understanding our implication in a violent and indifferent organic system. In 1976 Beuys addressed the violation of the social body in a haunting installation entitled "Show your Wound," which clearly referred to the destructiveness of the concentration camps and the Holocaust under the German fascist regime. Perhaps Beuys's entire lifework after the war has been an effort to keep visible what is disappearing from our consciousness, and what has certainly disappeared from an art that speaks only about itself or fawns upon the market place.

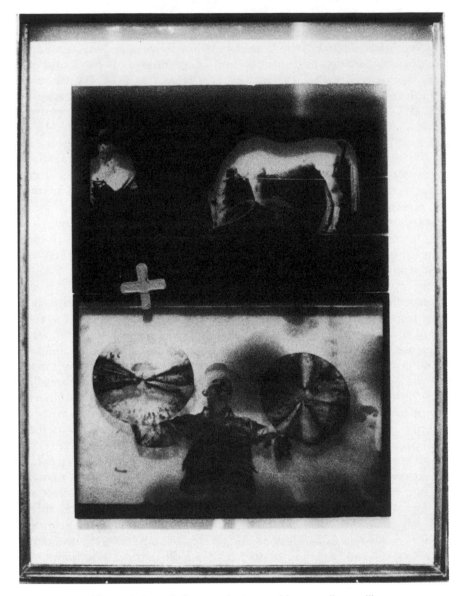

Figure 1. Joseph Beuys, photographic negatives with brown cross, from the action "Iphigenia / Titus Andronicus," Experimenta 3. Frankfurt, 1969. Courtesy Davis/McClain Gallery, Houston.

Most of contemporary art does not wish to be reminded of its failure to accomplish the project of the historical avant-garde. It is disconcerting to think that those of us who write about what is considered avant-garde art today contribute to its failure. Joseph Beuys had always been associated with major museums and art exhibitions in Europe and had made significant contributions to the public visibility and international status of the documenta exhibitions, acting out, for example, his three-month-long "Organization for Direct Democracy" piece in 1972. But later he once again took a position completely at odds with the lavishly promoted "art about artists" scene of documenta 7 in 1982 (focusing on neoexpressionist painting) when he initiated the long-term project of the planting of seven thousand oak trees in the city of Kassel, West Germany. Directly related to Beuys's participation during the early 1980s in the ecological and peace initiatives of the Green Movement in Europe, his invitation to the public to help plant trees (at a time when the disastrous effects of chemical pollution and acid rain on the environment were becoming clearly visible and threatening the destruction of the forests, a symbolic part of the historical landscape) in the dreary, grey, and faceless cityscape of Kassel was also meant to provoke a conscious act of *communal healing*, of bringing new organic life to a dead, fragmented, functionalized city. Kassel, a typical mid-size provincial city that was an important center of military industries under the Nazis, was severely devastated during the bombings at the end of the war. With major automobile and chemical industries continuing operation, Kassel quickly went through postwar reconstruction that left it anonymously resembling other cities reconstructed in the same faceless, utilitarian-modern style, divided up into suburban shopping malls compensating for the gradual loss of a vital public center. No riots here in the 1960s; not even a small sign of the grass roots civilian protests that flared up in Frankfurt at the same time, which turned the social-democratic city government's grand designs (supported by a business consortium and the major banks) for urban modernization into a highly politicized battle over the "Manhattanization" of the West End. A spontaneous coalition of diverse left-wing, feminist, and countercultural groups, with ideological ties to the urban guerilla movements of the Italian *lotta continua* and *autonomia* as well as to the militant antiimperialist interventions of the RAF (Baader-Meinhof Group), fought a battle that became known as *Häuserkampf* ("squatters movement"). They began to occupy and renovate those empty buildings that had been bought by real estate speculators. The city was trying to purge the West End population—mostly students, foreign workers, and low middle-class families—in order to transform the old residential neighborhood into a commercial district. After buildings bought were left to deteriorate or to be demolished, the squatters moved in to repossess the site of eviction. It took several years, until the early 1980s, for tactical police forces to clean up the scene. The end of the squatters movement, however, did not end an increasingly diverse and "situationist" development of cultural-political resistance to the hegemonizing tendencies of late capitalist urban ("postarchitectural"?) *erasure*. This erasure that has less to do with modernization and urban planning than with a wholesale speculative real estate competition for images and commercial clients, in an exchange with political interest. But besides the new twin skyscrapers of the Deutsche Bank in Frankfurt, a virtual replica of the World Trade Center in Manhattan, there are other images burnt into the public consciousness: for every fence erected to protect a new demolition site or the construction work on a new airport runway, there is a new civilian protest group that gathers in front of the fence and forces the metropolitan police to reveal the powerful antisocial and anticommunal interests at stake. The puppet Hitler in Hans-Jürgen Syberberg's *Hitler: A Film from Germany* (1978) declares at one point: "And yet did I not win after all? And are the cities not more destroyed today than they ever were as the result of my bombing?" His posthumous comment may be superbly cynical and appropriate to the postmodern condition of our cities, but it does not fully capture the escalating and highly volatile forms of countercultural and anarchistic resistance growing out of the unresolved contradictions of Germany's on-going postwar reconstruction.

Rainer Werner Fassbinder's play *Garbage, the City and Death* (1975) still awaits its first production, since all previous attempts to stage it had to be cancelled because of public protests in Frankfurt. In it Fassbinder tears open the wounds and the guilt of the city by exposing the disastrous impact of corrupt political and real estate speculation on both victims and victimizers alike. He moves the ambiguous role of Jewish speculators and bankers into the foreground, painfully entangling the violence of technocratic capitalism with the catastrophic history of German antisemitism. Fassbinder's complex portrayal of the "city" and its deformations (for example, the human waste it piles up as it tries to erase the historical core of its political legacy) breaks the taboo suppressing the issue of anti-Semitism that allowed state bureaucracies to bury the ghost of postwar guilt and self-laceration[24] under a process of "normalization." Fassbinder's concern with the city's destructiveness articulates itself from the position of the exploited and "unreconstructed" minorities—the Jew, the woman prostitute, the homosexual, the disabled, and the poor—trapped in a system that instrumentalizes guilt in order to reproduce exploitation and self-oppression. The relationship between the prostitute and the Jewish real-estate developer is paradigmatic for the play's insistence on their "otherness": both are outsiders in an inherently fascist state that distorts the reality of its "reconstruction" by employing the labor of those whom it has already forgotten or "designed" as casualties.

"From day to day the city's growing bigger. The people in it are getting smaller and smaller," says Miss Violet, one of the street prostitutes, in scene 3 of *Garbage, the City and Death*. This is the third scene that deals with the physical suffering, the self-degradation, and dehumanization of the women who sell their bodies as commodities on the streets of a city that has become uninhabitable. The atmosphere of destitution is very concrete in these scenes, and so is the sexual sadomasochism that Fassbinder will treat obsessively later in his films. The images of the city remain largely abstract, however. It is with the figure of the "Rich Jew," who arrives to solicit the prostitute Roma B., that the narrative and historical scenes of victimization are tied together:

Rich Jew. Do you know that sometimes I'm afraid? You don't know, and why should you. Business is going too well, which is asking for trouble. That plainly yearns to be punished. But, instead of receiving the punishment, it punishes the frightened one—me. Me: nothing more than me. No freedom, no desire. To me you are beautiful. But it is irrelevant. You could be however you want to be. Beauty, for whom is that enough?

I buy old houses in the city, tear them down, build new ones and sell them for a profit. The city protects me. It has to. I am, first of all, a Jew. The Chief of Police is my friend, for what it's worth; the Mayor invites me over. I can count on the City Council. To be sure, none of them particularly likes what he is allowing, but it's not my plan, it was there before I came. I have to be indifferent if children cry, if the old and the feeble suffer. I must be indifferent. And when some people scream in a rage I quite simply ignore it. What should I do otherwise? Burden my hunched back with a bad conscience?[25]

The rhetorical question about "bad conscience" hits hard. Fassbinder will portray himself with the same analytic coldness in his relations to his lover and his mother during the most traumatic phase of RAF terrorism in 1977 (in his contribution to the collectively made film *Germany in Autumn*). Here the allegorical figure of the "Rich Jew" asks the cynical question that recalls the mass deportation and extermination of the Jews and other minorities. This question must not be asked under an administration trying to return its city to a "normality" requiring the same popular indifference that enabled the Nazis to carry out the "Final Solution."

It is the fatal absence of this question—and the total absence of Jews and mention of the local concentration camp—that completely compromises Edgar Reitz's nostalgic return to the lost cultural history of German home life in his sixteen-hour film and TV series *Heimat* (1984). This much-publicized media event reached the United States in the spring of 1985, when Ronald Reagan was preparing his reconciliatory speech for the Bitburg visit:

The German people have very few alive that remember even the war, and certainly none of them who were adults and participating in any way . . . [They have] a guilt feeling that's imposed upon them. And I just think that's unnecessary. . . . Some old wounds have been reopened, and this I regret very much because this should be a time of healing.[26]

Reitz's sentimental, revisionist film is an embarrassing example of an apologetic postmodern aestheticism that plays into the hands of conservative "normalizers" who claim that its homemade "regionalism" would reconstruct what the American *Holocaust* TV series had "expropriated" from German history. While President Reagan's frighteningly ignorant remarks abuse historical memory, I do not want to argue that Fassbinder's unperformed play successfully penetrates the repressed trauma and the historical contradictions that have created the destructive normalization through which the "city" tries to change its image. Fassbinder's identification with the victims blinds him to the mechanisms of false reconciliation and exclusion produced by his allegory, which rehabilitates the unreflected polarization between abstract power and its "other." His insistence on exposing the repressed prehistory of contemporary power relations has managed nonetheless to lay open the painful deficits of postmodernism. In its constructions of the world, postmodern theory generally proceeds as if contemporary reality had already been aestheticized to the point where history (and its representation) has fallen outside of the system of cultural reproduction. The German version of the "postmodern condition," Baudrillard and Lyotard might argue, would then merely display a general amnesia and inability to "come to terms" with a lost past that can only be dissimulated in the discourses of racial, sexual, and ideological stereotypes already appropriated by the hegemonic media industry. For Baudrillard, this dramatization can only be a nostalgic way of helping the postmodern consciousness to forget that it is only confronted with pseudoevents or, as Lyotard argues, with a multiplicity of different and incommensurable "language games" predicated not on truth or historical knowledge but on "performativity."

French postmodern discourse, in trying to escape from the nostalgia for a time when modernist and avant-garde resistance to commodity mass culture was not yet a parody of its own dead labor, embraces an aesthetics of indifference which (if we are to believe Lyotard) is the consequence of the self-destruction of reason in history. That self-destruction, exemplified by the "annihilation named Auschwitz,"[27] leads Lyotard to perceive postmodernity as an antirationalist free-play world of agonistic language games that invent their own rules and strategic definitions of reality. For the aesthetics of postmodernism Lyotard is then able to claim the same posthistorical break: the postmodern escapes the temporal structure of modernity (history, capitalism, the technoscientific system, institutional discourses, and so forth) if it invents its own rules and seeks "to present the unpresentable."[28]

By invoking the terror of the sublime, Lyotard seems to think of postmodernism as a paradoxical and continuous displacement of reference and identification with a single master discourse: the "unpresentable" as a continuous break. All paradoxical moments of rupture, however, are the same according to Lyotard's scheme. Because all the different language games are absolutely equivalent, they are therefore inconsequential, like so many sudden changes in fashion and advertising which are our solemn caricatures of the eternal recurrence of the new. Everything is fair game: anything goes.

This probably sounds like a good slogan for the parodic language games of contemporary architecture which have such privileged status in most postmodernism debates. This same slogan also disguises the reality, not only of the very consequential territorializing logistics of an urban architecture which, as I tried to show in my previous example of Kassel, seeks to absorb all contradictions, but also of *unequal* and underrepresented languages within the general field of contending cultural relations. Lyotard would like to see the postmodern condition be the site of radical experimentation after the "master discourses" of rationality (the French tradition of Enlightenment) and totality (the German Hegelian/Marxist tradition) die and *before* the failure of the political illusions of aesthetic modernism, i.e., before the repetition of such a failure.

The aesthetic languages of avant-garde experimentation, however, seem as stuck in their illusions as the polluted postmodern body is stuck in some of its old habits, even though fashion and high technology invent newly designed bodies all the time. The theatre, in this respect, tends to confirm the failure more concretely than the other arts since its inventions take more time. It is reassuring, then, that Lyotard's diagnosis of the postmodern condition fails to understand, for example, how complex dialectical relations between aesthetics and ideology, economics, politics, and culture could come to a momentary standstill over *Garbage, the City and Death* in Frankfurt, precisely because one group, in this case the Jewish community, did not play the language game of "normalization" and refused to forget history or the political fact that references to a shared reality do matter.

The Fassbinder controversy involved not only the very concrete frustration of the squatters movement and their battle against the master rhetoric of the city administration's reconstruction plans, but also a whole cluster of issues raised by the conservative government's "normalization" policy and the way that policy affects the question of Jewish identity in Germany and the latent or inverted anti-Semitism among the various conservative, liberal and left groupings in the population. Linked to the defensive anti-American bias that emerged once again during the discussions over the Bitburg spectacle, the protests against Fassbinder's play in Frankfurt quickly developed into a nationalist polemic over the terms for a reconciliation with the German past, far exceeding the aesthetic dimension within which the merits of *Garbage, the City and Death* were initially discussed. These discussions included exaggerated concerns about artistic freedom and morality (in reference to the latent obscenity and homosexuality in Fassbinder's play) that reflected a paranoia similar to the one troubling the various factions of the German Left that wanted the play performed. While sympathizing with the Jewish intervention, the Left was struggling with its own confused sense of cultural identity in relation to the reconstructed Germany. This relation, incidentally, is very appropriately disfigured in Fassbinder's play. The only father figure in the text, Herr Müller (the father of the prostitute Roma), turns out to be a transvestite hiding his fascism under a constant change of clothes.

The transvestism of Germany's economic and political recovery after the war and the massively mediated ideology of "normalization" for a new, cleaned-up cultural facade are precisely the intervention targets for both

Fassbinder's and Beuys's demand to "Show your Wound." Perhaps it is the inability or unwillingness to see such interventions that proves the impoverishment of much postmodern discourse. The response of *Art in America* to documenta 8, for example, included a reference to the exhibition's promotional literature ("For those who want to experience contemporary art as a souluplifting adventure—documenta 8 offers every opportunity"), which was then used to deride Beuys's "7000 Oak Trees" project as a self-indulgent piece of "nostalgia" and "art-as-magical-healing."[29] Completely in line with Jameson's "cultural logic" of postmodernism and a nostalgic euphoria for dead styles and simulated experiences, such criticism enacts a defensive recoding of Beuys's insistence on the "wounds," which only heightens the cynical despair on this side of postmodernism. This criticism never negotiates the other sides of an on-going cultural struggle over the space and rhetoric of images and their real stakes—stakes that scarcely involve the "souluplifting adventures" promised by promotional culture but rather the unpromised survival of human lives and human cultures as such.

What is also at stake is the extent to which we allow a general critique of contemporary culture to thrive on ideological constitutions of the postmodern that move back and forth between apocalyptic, cynical, and affirmative diagnoses. Such a critique may implode into purely rhetorical games with cynical affirmations of the kind we meet in a recent Canadian book, *Excremental Culture and Hyper-Aesthetics*, or in Baudrillard's speculations on the American desert.[30] Baudrillard's speculations, in spite of their perverse insinuation that we (Europe? the West? America?) have already reached an irreversible condition, bear on the description I tried to bring to postmodern urban scenarios in Germany and the United States.

> The inhumanity of our late, asocial, superficial world immediately finds its aesthetic and ecstatic form here. For the desert is no more than that: an ecstatic critique of culture, an ecstatic form of disappearance.

Traveling across the vast empty spaces of the American West, Baudrillard claims to discover the "completed catastrophe," our future-in-the-present, of a culture that already *is* a desert of undifferentiated surfaces and pure expanse where all the traces of history and all vital and theatrical forms of social relations are erased. The speed and fluidity of traveling across a nonreferential space suggest to Baudrillard a movement of abstraction and disappearance: an endless voyage that ends (predictably) in Los Angeles, a city that is not a city. Los Angeles mirrors Baudrillard's ecstasy: "all depth is resolved there, you are delivered from it—brilliant, moving, superficial neutrality, a challenge to sense and to depth, a challenge to nature and culture, farthest hyperspace, without origin, without reference."[31]

This is a description of a cultural landscape, which describes the distance it claims to have traveled. It is already there. Baudrillard's ecstasy is in itself terminal; travelogue and sociological analysis end, before they even start, in descriptions of placeless, neutral fictions of "America" or "Los Angeles." They are the same as the fatal descriptions he has offered us about the ubiquity of the media and the transpolitical universe of nuclear deterrence (the latter seen in terms of a neutralizing, implosive violence that cancels the possibility of any atomic war ever taking place). The scene is empty, not because there is nothing there but because the "desert" of American culture, like the TV screens of the mass media and the perfectly masterful imaginary version of "America" on display in Disneyland, is *too much* and more of the same, all too visible and endlessly reproducible, obscenely banal, gloriously affectless and absolutely powerful all at the same time, with nothing there to oppose it. Above all, Baudrillard's description of the "desert" always supplements and fulfills *his* inexhaustable model theory of hyperreality ("the precession of simulacra") which is self-descriptive and circular. Since there is nothing outside of the model that has not already disappeared into it, or is made to disappear lest it disturb the model, "America" or "Los Angeles" or any other example—"anything goes"—falls readily into (the same) place.

Installing this model in the place of the social and cultural realities he has left behind, deserted and ghostly, Baudrillard effectively neutralizes himself, since there is nothing more to say once the theory—or the desert—can go on quoting itself. There is a crucial difference, then, between the way Baudrillard sees "disappearance" without acknowledging any stakes, and the strategies of urban intervention (or reappearance) employed by those perhaps less ecstatic citizens, artists, and communities who live in cities like Los Angeles and directly confront the overexposure of the "desert" or "Bonaventure" models (even if this is not what they would call them). The superficial signs of a homogenizing mass society fail to overinscribe the urban landscape of the postindustrial "diffused metropolis" (Virilio), because the very diffusion and deterritorialization of the city's multiple currents, including the different temporal orders stretching from futuristically constructed "downtowns" and shopping malls to the decaying warehouses and wastelands around the next block, have only reinforced an ethnic, culture-geographical, and aesthetic plurality not easily subsumed under a postmodern global logic.

If there is such a global logic that projects one form of concentration, information, and visibility, and that were to succeed, say, in reproducing identical "Galleria" shopping malls, identical fashions and styles, identical soundscapes and television sightscapes in every city, the relationship between the visible and the invisible would still be one of constantly shifting boundaries across which the local meanings of social and cultural "architectures"—*as boundary spaces*—are articulated. The current interest in the theory of margins and the cultural "other" reflects the need to contest a vision of the "global process of capital" as an increasing abstraction of social relations and a general aestheticization of life lacking regard for centers and margins. But in order to locate and distinguish the superimpositions of such a cultural imaginary within the broader mediascape and the dominant ideology of consumption—for which the border between image and reality, identity and difference, mainstream and margin, the global and the local has become a matter of indifference—it is necessary to ask whether margins are not as artificially constructed as the assumed homogeneity and domination of mass culture. Postmodern theorizing about "hegemonic space" (First World global mass culture) and its margins is subject to the same contradictions we have found in the landscapes of the metropolitan centers of the West. Such theorizing originates and collaborates in the marketable success of a postmodern art that seeks to authenticate itself through a regressive cynicism about its very lack of originality, subjectivity, and distinctness.

Much of this art cannot articulate its privileged, fashionable visibility in the art market except in the terms of a fashionable discourse that pretends to deny any politics or economy of domination. In the words of one of the New York simulationist painters, such art participates "in a context of collapsing social hierarchies, social values, social realities—not to mention the collapsing of abstraction itself."[32] While it apparently enjoys the paralyzing irony of being grossly parasitical of a Baudrillardian discourse that has actually proclaimed the disappearance of art, such art also shares an ideological context of *appropriation* in which an exploitative rationality operates on the basis of its own denial—thus affirming and preempting the critique of its montrosity.

Another simulationist painter has this to say about a culture confused by its own afterimages of denial:

> Likewise, the poles of life and death collapse into a state of non-life and non-death. No one either lives or dies. The possibility of life is negated by the imposition of mechanical time and by regimentation, both physical and temporal. Meanwhile, death is replaced by disappearance and is negated by manipulation of time within the recording media.[33]

Appropriating "abstraction" for the postmodern theory/painting of a technologically dependent, prerecorded, and disembodied information society, such speculation necessarily acts as if the death of art, finally, were as infinitely reproducible as abstraction itself. The fate of contemporary art, in this sense, would be the overexposure of all the dead styles and, consequently, the indifference between the fake posturing of painterly neoexpressionism and the quotational remake of readymades or serial images.

"Dead issues are reopened . . . .: artists become transvestites and viewers voyeurs watching history become less alien, less authoritarian."[34] The arrogance of this transvestism shows the absolute complicity of this manufactured art with the very real economic function of fashion and commodity production, perfectly visible in the successful packaging of "simulationist art" for upwardly mobile collectors. Further, the repression and bracketing off of history reach their most disturbing dimension in the idea that aesthetic abstractions ("voyeurism" of "history"?) can mask the immediate urban context of death, disease, homelessness, poverty, violence, and waste.

Surely it must have occurred to Peter Halley that death in New York and elsewhere, whether it results from destitution, child abuse, rape, racial violence, crime, or contracted disease, is too present and too obscene to be called hyperreal. The increasingly terrifying presence of the AIDS epidemic has created widespread anxiety in our culture, beyond the so-called risk communities of ever more stigmatized sexual and racial minorities. And even as information about AIDS transmission is variously manipulated by the dominant media and public institutions, the death of a friend or acquaintance from AIDS is not "disappearance" but a real experience of loss. Inevitably, the finality of the AIDS virus will generate hysterical reactions across the boundaries of ideological definitions of "normalcy" and "deviance," and also within the boundaries of the "general public," which now experiences the subordination of the "postmodern body" to a volatile and contradictory political process of postprevention risk control (e.g. mandatory testing for pregnant women; diverse "safe sex," condom, and celibacy campaigns; policing of cities and premises, and so forth). Nowhere will anyone agree on what constitutes "public health" or safe sexual behavior.

The dirty reality of death and of the surveillance technologies installed to control it does not indicate to me a collapse of social hierarchies or normative definitions, nor an abstraction of the body as the site on which powerful symbolic inversions of cultural values and roles are acted out. Are all our bodies "hyperrealized" by panic discourses and sign systems of "disease control" and case statistics? Or are some bodies overexposed to medical and legal practices of control, constraint, information, and care, while others remain underexposed, isolated, and forgotten? Are there not different realities we have to account for if we want to speak about the increasing concern over the body in postmodern times marked by uneasy crossovers between global fantasies of nuclear destruction, the grittier individual fear of death, and the ambiguous engagement of death and violence in the ghostly appearance of urban punks flaunting their self-disfigurement?

Are we to consider the abstract geometric simulation-paintings of Halley, Bleckner, and Taaffe symptomatic of anything but the most callously reductionist style productions and "language games" (representations of abstraction that are abstractions of representation) that disintegrate in the very instant they *deny* the social and technological realities they pretend to mediate?

I am vividly reminded of the messy collage of theory and political rhetoric in the face of the Chernobyl nuclear disaster in April 1986. As the clouds of invisible radiation spread over Europe, the diverse and contradictory cosmetic responses of government experts to control damage and maintain "acceptable tolerance levels" remained sublimely irrelevant throughout the crisis to entire populations shocked into recognizing the fragile boundaries of their bodies, their homes, their individual liberties. It was finally something as banal and primary as food, once vegetables and milk were thought to be contaminated, that threw the media into disarray, exploding the image of a pacified, homogenized consumer consciousness drawn by postmodern theory.

Chernobyl was not a floating signifier or a seductive media event. A plethora of contradictions in the highly theatricalized political and compassionate but inefficient local crisis management split apart the theoretical entity of the Common Market. Contaminated Italian lettuce was sold in France, where people were told that the winds blowing the lethal rain clouds across Germany and Belgium had somehow stopped at the French border. At the same time, the ideological margins of safety, in the debates on communist and capitalist nuclear reactors, shifted around so widely at variance with what the irradiated audiences themselves cared to believe that one could feel very succinctly, on an untheorized, ontological level, how the social body resisted this new map of body invasions. For many people, especially those on the social and technological periphery, the fall-out of Chernobyl constituted a concrete moment of rupture in which the real scope of those devastations usually hidden by cultural and humanist ideologies of science, technology, and economic progress became visible for a short time. All of our lives had been rendered grotesquely precarious and vulnerable.

As I am writing this, I see in the *New York Times* that public health experts from New York, Houston, San Francisco, Los Angeles, and Miami have mapped the demographic statistics of AIDS cases in order to "track its destructive path." One expert asserts that "in this epidemic, geography is destiny," and goes on to explain that (through their breakdowns of cases and death tolls by residence, gender, race, age as well as "risky behavior,") the maps chart the relative growth of "devastation" in specific areas and neighborhoods. The militaristic language notwithstanding, the article describes the public health officials' belief that the surveillance maps will help to predict the risk to residential areas. What is not spelled out is the underlying assumption that heterosexual neighborhoods (New York's Staten Island, for example) and the "general public", must be warned away from the disproportionately affected communities of gay men, blacks and Hispanics, drug users, and other "physiologically and economically depressed subgroups."[35]

The possibility that such mapping could also encourage racism and homophobia while innocently perceived as a strategy of creating outcast AIDS zones, raises the dark specter of abject displacement. One thinks of walls and barbed wire, of apartheid and other "white mythologies" that emerge in paranoid postmodern warfare splitting at so many levels into sites of violence, sites of profit and exploitation, and sites of expendable people.

When I commented on Jameson's agenda for a mapping of the new logic of postmodernism, I meant to suggest that his inscriptions of "cultural dominants" contribute to displacing the less visible and less easily absorbable. Not to mention the "badlands" of East Los Angeles, which resist the defensive corporate space of the Bonaventure Hotel, is to efface the context that produces the resistance to the apparent centrality of corporate structures. As we experience how postmodern capitalism generates its own contradictions, the idea of a *cultural politics* becomes increasingly important the more we actually see the political masquerade as aesthetic, and the more we recognize the difficulty of creating an aesthetics of negation that could express itself without being subverted into a fashion. And if we were to argue, using our Los Angeles example one more time, for a contextual criticism that does not isolate the Bonaventure Hotel as more visible than other "local" interventions for visibility, such as the breakdancers on Figueroa or the enormous murals facing the downtown sidewalks and freeways (by Willie Herron, Carlos Almaraz, Kent Twitchell, and many others), we would then need to explore the specific relations between the social and aesthetic performance of breakdance or mural art, and the socioeconomic and aesthetic function of the building within the larger urban processes of architectural production and cultural counterperformances.

Much of postmodern theory seems to travel a lot yet belong nowhere in particular. Some of it spreads out because it seeks to be as enormously visible as the Los Angeles murals and as publically successful as the antiaesthetic, political art it chooses as its privileged examples of cultural critique (when it doesn't choose the Julian Schnabels and John Portmans of the chic avant-garde). But how successful are the mixed medium installations of a Hans Haacke (exposing corporate investments in art patronage and military dictatorships) or the photo silkscreens of a Barbara Kruger ("We don't need another hero"; "I shop therefore I am") in their attempt to criticize the commodification of art in our consumer society and the site of their own production?

Since these representations about the position of art in the market system function very well, they garner high visibility because they present their political critique in familiar media images. What gets buried is the question of whether critical-intellectual or aesthetic work can transform or liberate the social imagination in our culture. The radical social and political activities of the 1960s are now already of a past that seems all but forgotten, and late capitalism does its best to incite our imaginations all the time (Mastercard ad: "Master all the possibilities"). In these conditions we must wonder about the survival of an art or a radical culture practice that could imagine itself to be radical, unfashionable, and able to modify the conditions of its production/consumption. Postmodern theory, in spite of its insistent chatter about transgression and desire (a fallout from Deleuze and Guattari's anti-Oedipal schizo-analysis of "desiring-productions" and "bodies-without organs") has largely failed to account for its disinterest in the human condition and in the different physical and geographical realities of the distressed map of contemporary culture it draws.

The success of postmodern thought in a neoconservative, crisis-ridden and scandalized political era reflects its distance from the concrete and unresolved cultural formations-in-process that resiliently struggle to emerge from the bleak ghettoes and divided territories of our existence. That it is so remote from any real stakes and any political practice of consequence makes its theoretical monologues about the current, gradual catastrophe of our fin de siècle culture appear about as ambivalent and voyeuristic as, for example, the exhausted "Scenes Before the Eye" painted by one of the heroes, Eric Fischl. These "Scenes" of a naked and oblivious American middle class suspended in its incestuous world of anxious leisure, fatally attracted to its own bigotry and moral confusion, as evidenced most recently in the national spectacle of a presidential candidate's adultery, have a strange, unresolved uneasiness about them. In an interview made in the early 1980s Fischl explained this condition of unease as follows:

> One truly does not know how to act. Each new event is a crisis, and each crisis is a confrontation that fills us with the same anxiety that we feel when, in a dream, we discover ourselves naked in public.

Before I turn more concretely to the practice of theatre, I want to make a transition from the city to performance that I hope can illuminate my position on cultural politics and on the struggle for visibility, and which can connect the culturally marginalized work of the theatre to other forms of enactment addressing the social imagination (and social unease) from under- or untheorized places on the postmodern map.

Counter Projection

> The plague as a form, at once real and imaginary, of disorder had as its medical and political correlative discipline. Behind the disciplinary mechanisms can be read the haunting memory of 'contagions', of the plague, of rebellions, crimes, vagabondage, desertions, people who appear and disappear, live and die in disorder.
> Foucault, *Discipline and Punish*

Returning to Europe is a kind of disciplinary mechanism for me. On each return I imagine a further reconciliation with the past and experience a transitory ritual of confrontation with the spaces, institutions, and formations of knowledge that informed my relationship to the world I grew up in. Each return is a visit to a disordered memory that functions without certainty yet holds on to my body. I feel a fatal attraction to familiar ground even though the old unities of time, place, character, and language of the once familiar landscape have disintegrated. In the oldest cities of my past the ruined aura patiently awaits the visitor. The old monuments are now joined by new shopping centers, and the traffic-free pedestrian precincts allow for a comfortable circulation of consumption. The streets are perfectly paved, no beach visible (*"Sous les pavés, la plage"* was a dream back in 1968). In between the monuments and the shopping centers is a vast aggregate of images and physical appearances offering themselves to the perceptions of the customers and the milling crowds of the urban environment.

The older the city, the more one senses its exhaustion, driven underground, buried under the complex surface collage of architectural, commercial, and symbolic images, and mixed media (words, pictures, sculptures, light, sound, decorative design, and all the signs of destruction/preservation in progress).[36] This repressed exhaustion generates a constantly splitting and fracturing text seemingly divorced from any origin of production. This divorce *is* the spectacle. Its consumable surface turns me into a tourist, shopping for a past either contained and hidden or exploded out into so many collectible items of present everyday experience. Yet the perceptual experience of the disorder and contagion of the urban spectacle is already produced for me and takes possession of me as if I had returned too late to reconstruct a time that has disappeared. The spectacle does not offer itself to be reconstructed. Contemporary theory's obsessive speculations on disembodiment and disappearance are perhaps only the reverse image of our visualized and projected culture.

Returning home, however, is not a theoretical project, even though I am intensely aware of the possibility that I may only be crossing a fictional boundary between my homeless existence in Dallas, Texas, and my lost home and former language in Germany. The boundary between homelessness and origin, between exile and belonging, is not fixed but subject to a permanent process of deterritorialization. Dallas, certainly, eludes not only the theory but also the visual experience of "home." Nobody pretends that there is a community, a graspable center or identity to hold on to, or a meaningful ground for a relationship between part and whole. The "metroplex" is a construct dissipated around the Dallas/Fort Worth International Airport in an experimental arrangement. Nobody walks in this sprawling, sunlit landscape without borders or sightlines; the forgotten sidewalks are replaced by billboards and pictures framing the freeways like giant screens. The pictures do not refer to the city or to any buildings; they just flash up and disappear, more or less instantly depending on the speed of your car. People are attached to each other by telephone answering machines and by roads, though even these are unreliable; a friend of mine who has lived there for fifteen years still gets lost regularly and needs to consult a map to find her way home. But the map is not the territory. One learns to live without a sense of place under an infinitely vast sky that mirrors the memoryless flatness of the land.

Perhaps it is preferable to get lost sometimes and not to have a map at hand. I remember my long visit to Venice in the summer of 1985. I had not come to Venice for the seductive historical atmosphere of its medieval palaces, piazzas, and canals. Nor was I particularly attracted to the literary myths attached to this floating city, where the stench of rotting water punctures the fetishized romantic surface that hungry tourists come to photograph. Looking at the canals I can barely make sense of the aesthetic metaphor of the "plague" used in Thomas Mann's *Death in Venice*. Plague came to represent the collapse of the moral order brought about by the pursuit of the city's beauty and sensuousness, which turns out to be a study in self-degradation. Today the marketing of the city's beauty for mass tourism and its multiple economies is so pervasive that the idea of an aesthetic or moral crisis seems utterly incongruous with the festive spirit that turns Venice into a carnivalesque theatre of attractions and ostentatious rituals. The self-dramatizing city tempts you to become absorbed, to drift along with the flow of sights and sensual stimuli, to play your roles as spectator and actor, to touch and be touched by the promiscuous gratifications of its physiognomy.

Sometimes such drifting can bring about a different form of crisis. I have followed the twists and turns of a canal too far into the normally concealed spaces or corners of the city; I misunderstood a gesture or a sign and now suddenly notice the prohibitions and perceptual barriers that govern my own body now out of place. I want to experience a new way of seeing or imagining at the moment that I discover my body in relationship to a particular space or object. This relationship opens up an infinite number of associations, but it also restricts the tourist body to familiar defenses. When I travel I become more sensitive to the restricted economy of the defenses. Each crisis provokes me into being "naked in public," so to speak, and to look for the mechanisms and imaginary sublimations that conceal such nakedness. A mere moment in the everlasting cultural production of the urban geography of the Imaginary, the unconcealed body does not stand opposed to the scenes of the city. Instead, it finds its position shifting (in place/out of place) within the discursive sites and the canals of meaning that regulate or affect the drifting of identities. But the sites of the city themselves are not immutable or "just there." Like the traveling body which thinks itself lost in between places, they do not escape the mutability of the boundaries and hierarchies that connect or separate the cultural contents we find in them. Similar to the way art or fashion constantly resurrects and rearranges histories and cultures, so does the rethinking of our bodies and our visions imply a rethinking of our social and symbolic topographies. If we were to lose our body, as postmodern theory has argued, we would no longer be able to imagine a city or culture in which to live.

What I am describing here became the subject of a research and theatre project that began in Venice and Genova in 1985, moved back and forth between Dallas and Genova, and ultimately culminated in two performance works staged in Dallas in 1988 and in Genova in 1989. Entitled *Invisible Cities*, the project developed out of my encounter with Genovese theatre artist Attilio Caffarena who had worked with Jerzy Grotowski in the 1970s and then founded his own experimental theatre company, Teatro dell'Orrore, in Genova. There he directs a performance research center located in the annex to an old psychiatric hospital. Caffarena's deep identification with the historical and cultural predicament and psychic topography of an old seaport city (built quite literally onto the edge of a mountain range that descends deliriously into the Mediterranean) and my own equally deep sense of homelessness in Dallas was the starting point in a series of experiments that used theatrical languages and theatrical thinking as a basis for exploring the visible and concealed textures of the urban spaces in Genova and Dallas. Working on location with a joint group of artists from both cities meant also that we had to ask ourselves to what extent performers can travel and speak across the boundaries of cultures and specific historical, social, political, and aesthetic spaces. Even more importantly, we asked ourselves whether theatre, which is of course always located inside the city, can *perform* excursions, misplacements, interruptions and rediscoveries of the perceptual process itself that defines (inside and outside the theatre) how we see, what we might be prepared to see, or what we imagine we should or should not see, according to the conventions and boundaries of our pictures of reality.

The question of whether theatre can *produce perception* and intervene in the ideological repetitions within the relationship of the perceivers and the perceived was raised insistently by Bertolt Brecht in his theoretical notes (with passing references to Galileo and Einstein) toward a new "theatre of the scientific age." We still wonder what it would look like, with our scientific age progressing ever more visibly. And yet our most self-conscious postmodern experimental theatre, dance, multimedia and performance art would be inconceivable without the continuing search of those who—in the shadow of Brecht and Artaud—continue to reflect on the place of the theatre's perception of life in the culture, and on the shifting scenes of exchange between the performers and the audience. I am thinking of such important texts as Grotowski's *Towards a Poor Theatre,* Peter Brook's *The Empty Stage,* Augusto Boal's *Theatre of the Oppressed,* Herbert Blau's *Take Up the Bodies,* Richard Schechner's *Between Theatre and Anthropology,* or Eugenio Barba's *Beyond the Floating Islands,* but also of many other, less widely known experiments that question the familiar territories and "closed circuits" of the theatre's system of representation. Consider Laurie Anderson's song "Lighting Out for the Territories" at the end of her *United States* performance:

> You can read the signs. You've been on this road before. Do you want to go home? Hello, excuse me, can you tell me where I am? You can read the sign language. In our country, good-bye looks just like hello. This is the way we say hello. Say hello. Hello, excuse me, can you tell me where I am?[37]

Laurie Anderson's map of the United States, projected onto a large screen behind her, turns out to be a rather flat grid of electronically produced images that unfold into each other, turn over and over, without end, returning to the same ambiguity of the "sign language" that is her performance medium. Her high-tech apparatus of feedback loops, echo effects, and circulating sounds and images trace the outlines and directions of our looking and reading. The work is as much about the "United States" as it is about the mediation and (re)production of looking (the signs that show up) in a performance that frames her body (where she is) and her gestures (this is the way we say hello) with the imaging systems of postmodern technology and mass culture. The attention stays on the surface of the staged signs, and as Anderson manipulates the media that can alter her appearance (e.g. switching the tonality of her voice so that she can project both a feminine and a masculine "vision"), she becomes another surface in a visual-aural design across which indefinite meanings traverse and cancel each other out. There are no new departures. Her theme songs about travel, money, social life, love, and politics tell the same story of contemporary experience, here presented as an experience of technology *as* the determining language and space. Both saturated by and reduced to mechanical repetitions and self-interferences, that experience is also subjected to the constant trafficking through a space that depends on our transitory and unthinking relation to it. All the visual information in Anderson's performance, including the signs and the words of her body outlined and mirrored on the screen, moves around as if we could not perceive anything, anyplace, except in passing, as we try to keep up with the transitional ready-made images from the postmodern media that "work us over completely," as Marshall McLuhan predicted (in *The Medium is the Message*). We are kept from knowing that this completeness would also be frighteningly banal, an environment of a luminescent emptiness. A televised space and its double.

If Anderson's *United States* presents itself as an extended meditation on a technological scene that reduces itself to a mere surface of shifting information, it does so as a performance so connected with mass media culture that it cannot produce a perception or critical knowledge of its own. It confirms that we are already fully enveloped by a technoscape that has become the limit of our experience. At the same time, Anderson's use of the media is often flippant and ironic; her mimicry of technological experience in a sense depends on our recognition of its limits, as well as on the exploitation of our defenselessness against the violence and seductive power advanced media technologies use to transform reality.

When we were working on *Invisible Cities* we became aware of the problem of recognizing our limits in a different way. The realities of the two cities we explored clearly exceeded any form of theatrical representation that would map or document or dramatize a condition of being and a space neither fully present (as a closed, finite unity) nor ever completely visible. The more one tries to reproduce or project a city's multiple identities, the more they elude the grasp of a description. The city, in this respect, is like a performance without a beginning and an end, as in the old drama. A city, unstructured, fragmentary and discontinuous, is composed of overlapping layers and elements that might change independently from each other, and lacks a central perspective. Thinking of urban space as a terrain of economic, social, and cultural processes that constantly produces disparate viewpoints of the city's conditions, we began to see that our own city project had to take into account not only the postmodern fascination with compulsively visible aesthetic surfaces, but the very proposition that a contemporary theatre can break the deep surface of its own appearances (the text, the actors, the images, the sound, the gestures, and so forth) that cover the invisible performances it wants to understand.

"Invisible Cities" was our metaphor for the breaking of expected visibilities and credibilities, though when we started out we did not always know what we were looking for. Our second metaphor of the "journey" became important, therefore, because it was out of the distance and the dialectic between Genova and Dallas that we developed our own set of references to the fictions, myths, and ideological operations we found in each "theatre of the city." The performance, in turn, was to question the references and challenge the mediums of the city themselves, which foreground certain physical appearances and sensory perceptions while hiding and displacing others.

I am not suggesting that our performance journey is a model for contemporary experimental theatre. But I believe that any theatre practice worth thinking about in the context of postmodern culture has been fundamentally concerned not only with recovering the meaning and boundaries of performance in the theatre (in distinction to what is meant by "performance" and "theatricality" just about anywhere else in contemporary mass culture) but, specifically, with the *transformation of visual space* and the difference in attention to the perceptual process produced by scenographies of visual and acoustic images that no longer recreate the appearance of dramatic realism. This difference in perception (in our case of the city *and* of the theatre and its visual space) relates back to my initial question about the possibility of imagining a self-subverting artistic practice that could reinvent a radical and unfashionable vision at a time when conventional wisdom and postmodern theory would maintain that that is no longer possible. But such wisdom forgets that the theatre, to a large degree, is a very old-fashioned medium (almost to the point of being radically anachronistic in comparison, for example, to the "theatre of technology," as the MacIntosh/MacWorld Magazine describes its latest updates in computer software and designs). Its inertia is an advantage, since even with the inclusion of film and video in recent experimental performance, the stage is always a concretely physical space where temporal and spatial perceptions are shaped by what comes physically into the space. But the self-evidence of this space, and of the mechanics of the live body of the performer, is precisely what the theatre can defer and speculate on by making us apprehend its relationship to the not-seen and not-heard, to the out-of-place and the forgotten. Perhaps it is also an advantage that the theatre has become eccentric to mainstream culture: it no longer needs to pretend (as Broadway still does) that it must entertain the obvious illusions of the familiar.

I want to conclude this brief journey into the theatre with a few notes that were composed at the end of the first rehearsal workshop on *Invisible Cities*. These notes reflect our approach to the conceptual work of the performance.

Nearly 500 years ago Christopher Columbus left Genova and the Old World to cross the ocean in search for the yet unknown "America," the abstract continent of a "New World" that was the frontier or horizon of discovery. The discovery of unknown territory was not merely a form of geographical exploration, however. It was also a political, economic, and technological process (accompanied by religious justifications) directed at the future of an abstract potential (a utopia) outside of the boundaries of the mapped and enclosed European space of towns and kingdoms.

But exploration is always also a projection of the known and a carrying-over of familiar relations to, and mental images of, one cultural space into an other. Regardless of the specific economic motives for the exploration, the discovered territory is already a product of *cultural displacement* tied to the imaginary geography of representations and narratives which, ever since the times when emperors and kings sent out their ships and their conquerors, have covered foreign space by asserting, measuring, describing and inscribing reality.

This process could be called "cultural speculation": the unknown is made visible. Or, in theatrical terms: it can be made visible if it can be *staged*, recollected into a memory and history not of its own.

The performance of the theatre collage *Invisible Cities* reenacts a process of "geographical exploration" into a contemporary American metropolis of the late 20th Century. The focus of the journey is on the urban space of the postindustrial city of DALLAS. The performance is nondramatic, but the journey reflects the changes that have affected our perceptions of what a city is, in the sense in which we can say that, as we have reached the limits of the known, explored and mapped world, our conception of the limits and dimensions of our city has collapsed and shifted towards hallucinatory scenarios of unknown territory.

The idea for this performance originated from our frequent travels between Genova and Dallas. Genova, one of the oldest cities in the Old World, offers the fascinating case of a place both overwhelmed by the past and, at the same time, dreaming of a future (the new electronic and technological capital of Italy). Dallas, on the other hand, is a city almost already consumed by its future and no longer "visible" in terms of classical perspective, or through stable images of the past, through monuments or an architectonics of order and cohesiveness.

Yet like any major city, Dallas is an intercultural scenario: its territories bear, superimposed, different and polyvalent orders of time and space. Its concentration of images and messages along the freeways emphasizes the permanent transit between territories (and image-spaces)—a transit that is temporal and spatial. The performance of *Invisible Cities* is a journey or a translation, a "carrying-over" of audio-visual impressions experienced within the territorial systems of transit and transfer between imaginary and real scenes of urban life in Dallas.

Invisible Cities probes the imaginary readings or projections of the metropolis, in response to the transitory ways in which it faces us, so to speak, as a city-collage itself, as a screen of appearing and disappearing images. Created by an intercultural ensemble of visual and performance artists from Dallas and Genova, *Invisible Cities* explores the different effects of the city-collage on human behavior and perception, and on the physical and emotional experience of inhabiting the temporal space of the nervous system of urban images.

The actors work from within this nervous system: performing in front of and against projected and filmic images of Dallas, their movements, gestures, and expressions traverse the terrain between the "body of the city" and the "city in our body," a journey across surfaces and boundaries that are in constant mutation, like the fictional text (Italo Calvino's *Le città invisibili*) from which the performance draws its inspiration. The Calvino novel is a sequence of allegories or projections: Marco Polo, the constant traveler and nomad, invents the scenarios, the landscapes, and the archaeologies of the cities he describes to the Kublai Khan (who remains at home in his sky scraper). Marco Polo is a cartographer of myths and a semiotician of the geometries of cities that may or may not exist.

The performance of *Invisible Cities* is acted out as a movement towards the limits of myth (the limits of the map?), and in terms of the historical connection with Columbus mentioned in the beginning, this implies that the theatrical journey through Dallas is also a return to an American cultural imagination that is separated from the history and the representational order of the Old World.

The Info-Mart (a museum of future computer technologies), the Galleria (a super mall, not an art gallery), or Las Colinas (a complex of studios and a miniature city built for future film production) in Dallas are postmodern architectural symbols at the far end of the journey or immigration across the plane of water or the great plains of the American continent. "The sky is our ocean," they say in Dallas. The long distance to an erased past that is not remembered constitutes the particular fascination of the immense land of Texas and the inhuman dimensions of the expanse of the Dallas metroplex. This space is transreferential and perhaps incomprehensible in terms of European aesthetic and metaphysical culture. But since the past in postindustrial society has itself become a collection of photographic, filmic, and televisual images, the performance of *Invisible Cities* will explore the vertiginous mobility of the images and signs produced in a spectral city which seems built without a recollection of human scale.

The cinematic presentation of this mobility will be increasingly interrupted up to the point where we are solely interested in the missing matter of the human scale, in the physical and emotional depravations of the body caused by a mythic urban space that projects future development in a constant denial of present social impoverishment and paranoia. What the actors show about this defeated body, in the end, becomes a matter of recollection: not a mimicry of shadows of the past but intimations of a struggle against a diminished

Figure 2. Attilio Caffarena, rehearsal scene from *Invisible Cities*. Dallas, 1987. Photo: J. Birringer.

Figure 3. Attilio Caffarena, rehearsal scene from *Invisible Cities*. Dallas, 1987. Photo: J. Birringer.

(shadowless) present, of a hole in the wall, or of a gesture of life not taken from the surface of fact as we know it.

I might add that the performance of *Invisible Cities* does not claim to reinvent a Dallas we do not know, even though it searches for the missing shadows invoked by Artaud when he wanted to push through the deadly surface:

> Our petrified idea of the theatre is connected with our petrified idea of a culture without shadows, where, no matter which way it turns, our mind encounters only emptiness, though space is full.[38]

The cinematic images we use to construct Dallas on the screen of the stage do not imitate postmodern strategies of "quotation" or "appropriation"; the theatre cannot "decontextualize" or "dematerialize" its connection with the city by adopting and reframing pictures of the city's real-estate architecture or everyday commodity signposts in its own exhibitional format. But it can project a fullness of space against which the

Figure 4. Attilio Caffarena in "Blind City," a scene from *Invisible Cities,* Lawndale Art Center, Houston, 1989. Photo: J. Birringer.

alien, isolated human figure emerges as from the grave, signalling through the screen.

The moments of rupture in this performance lie in the contradiction between the human body and the screen. I remember that we started working on this contradiction in an early rehearsal in which we looked at a "scene" from Melville's *Israel Potter*, where he has Benjamin Franklin pose before a large map on which everywhere the word "desert" is crossed out. Our contemporary culture has quite reversed the confidence of this pose; we now live in those crossed-out zones.

By the time we completed final rehearsals for the Houston performance of *Invisible Cities* in October 1989, the "Franklin scene" had been replaced by a section entitled "Blind City." In this scene the performers crisscross the triangular playing area several times. Each physical movement expression was chosen by the performers individually. All of the gestural sequences shared the same gestus of constriction, however, as if these women and men were locked into their own private territorial zones that separate them from each other even as they appear together. Attilio Caffarena sits on a chair near the center, reading a white book that could also be a map or a tourist guide. He observes the three huge screens placed at the corners of the triangle. Two of the screens show projections of still photographs of the reflecting glass facades of enormous downtown skyscrapers in Houston. On the third screen you see a film shot in an abandoned and decaying parking lot on one side of the Southwest Freeway. An Anglo-American woman, an African-American man and an Asian-American man (Wendy Aldwyn, James Martin, Brian Liem) rummage through the debris in this vacant lot and discover strange discarded objects. At one point they come together after having found bits and pieces of broken glass, which they lay on the ground in the shape of a jigsaw puzzle. The camera goes up over their heads as they bend down to study the puzzle. What appears in the frame are the broken faces in the broken mirror.

Meanwhile, Caffarena has unfolded the open book he was holding: it transforms into an open cube which he places over his head. Blinded and suddenly dislocated, he stubbornly tries to regain his sense of balance and walks very slowly into a direction he seems to remember. Perhaps he is walking toward the sound he hears from this corner. A recorded voice recites a text from Baudrillard's *America*; the voice speaks softly about the silent surface of the desert, a visual silence produced by "the gaze that stares out and finds nothing to reflect it." Caffarena walks very slowly toward the second screen with its large image of a blue glass facade. During the time it takes him to reach the screen, small-scale slide images begin to appear on the vertical skyscraper image. These smaller images show a row of tiny, dilapidated wooden shotgun houses from Houston's Fourth Ward, a shockingly impoverished black ghetto that borders directly on the downtown financial business district. (During the months we were working on the scene, we learned that the city plans to demolish the

Fourth Ward, historically known as "Freedmen's Town"—Houston's old-est black settlement which has enormous emotional value for its elderly residents—and replace it with commercial development.)

When Caffarena reaches the screen, the images from the historical black community disappear, the lights fade out, and his body disappears from sight. The only part of him that remains visible is his cubical head, a white body that catches the light from the skyscraper image. His "head" dissolves into the screen projection. Throughout the performance, the audience is made aware of urban architecture and of the urban design and zoning of human experience. Although held together by a constant acous-tic and electronic soundscape ("found sound," music, and percussion arranged and performed by Mark Goolsby and Yiannis Efstathiou), the accumulation and dispersion of stage images, screen images, and video monitor images make it impossible for the viewer to have a unified per-spective on the city. We incorporated the fragmentation and segregation of community in contemporary cities into the visual design. The spectator comes in from the outside into the huge, cavernous space of the gallery, with the giant screens marking the corners of the triangular playing area,

Figure 5. Wendy Aldwyn, Emmanuel Woodward, and Sandy Marcello in "Blind City," a scene from *Invisible Cities.* Lawndale Art Center, Houston, 1989. Photo: J. Birringer.

and the small monitors ringing the black flats for seating. The flats are arranged in an angular fashion all around the playing area, so that each viewer's experience of the live and filmed images (in front, behind, to either side) is unique and separate. It makes a difference, for example, to watch the scene I just described from a position that brings the viewer into close physical proximity with the interracial couple locked in a contradictory movement configuration. The male performer's body (Emmanuel Woodward) is gripped by an intense emotional quality. Torso arching forward, he seems ready to take immense steps in order to move across the space. But the woman (Wendy Aldwyn), whose hands he had gently and carefully attached to his ankles, lies on the floor behind him, heavily weighted down by the rock she had dropped on her stomach. Her unnatural weight pulls the man back and reins him in. His energy is not neutralized, however, since he visibly persists in his effort and struggles for every inch he can gain. The painful irony in his struggle is as unrelieved as Caffarena's seduction by the Baudrillardian voice that travels across the visual silence of the projections.

The more I think about the work as it progressed, the more I see it as an architectural exhibition, an installation of architectural images and metaphors that hide the human struggle and the human costs. The architectural silence screens historical space, community, and living tradition. Against this screening we wanted to throw the movement of actual bodies to recreate everyday urban life, from the internalized violence, and from our imaginary responses and physical resistance to the violence we see written on us. In this respect, our performance has something in common with the counterprojections of Krzysztof Wodiczko. His work has created a form of traveling urban intervention that addresses human dispossession and displacement disguised by the seemingly autonomous and symbolic function of public monuments, architectural structures, and aesthetic designs. As in his recent Union Square "Homeless" Project, or in the Duke of York Column Projection in London (1985) and the Astor Building/New Museum Projection in New York (1984), Wodiczko's unusual slide projection performances "mobilize" buildings and monuments and modify public perception of the ideological use to which they are put within the broader urban context of a city's social and economic politics.

Projecting gigantic images of objects and body parts onto the facades of monuments, corporate towers and museums, Wodiczko can create montage effects that bring the building's "institutional body" into collision with its shadows, which are those less visible functions of the architectural screen inherent in city planning schemes, real estate speculations, preservation and redevelopment designs, zoning and property regulations, and so forth. Wodiczko developed "The Homeless Projection" for Union Square Park in New York at the same time the park's buildings and monuments underwent a process of calculated restoration and gentrification. The urban site is transformed from a spectacle of cultural landmarks into a grueling "architectural real-estate theatre," as Wodiczko calls it. Restoring the public monuments (Abraham Lincoln Monument, Lafayette Monument, George Washington Monument, Mother and Child Fountain) for the gentrified park is part of a much larger scheme of real-estate interests, in the course of which a decaying area with its obvious share of social problems (poor housing for low-income tenants; deteriorating neighborhoods with homeless people and drug traffic) is to be "cleaned up" and transformed into luxury office spaces and condomini-

Figure 6. Krzysztof Wodiczko. Proposed Projection, Abraham Lincoln Monument, Union Square Park. Photo: © K. Wodiczko.

Figure 7. Proposed Projection, George Washington Monument, Union Square Park. Photo: © K. Wodiczko.

Figure 8. Proposed Projection, Mother and Child Fountain, Union Square Park. Photo: © K. Wodiczko.

Figure 9. Proposed Projection, Lafayette Monument, Union Square Park. Photo: © K. Wodiczko.

ums. Wodiczko's projections enact a counterrestoration that visually exposes not only the false idealism in the aestheticized symbolic monuments (the neoclassical facade of American civil liberty), but also the very concrete social consequences of the mass evictions of the city's poorest residents.[39]

What Wodiczko's projected images achieve is a dismantling of the authority of architectural forms. The four Union Square monuments no longer stand aloof as enduring symbols and repositories of collective memory. They can be read as "actors" in the present drama of redevelopment in which they decorate an unacknowledged and aggressive aestheticization of homelessness and poverty. Grafting slide images of crutches and a bandaged leg onto the statues of Lafayette and Lincoln, a wheelchair onto Washington's horse, and a bag lady's shopping cart onto the Mother Figure, Wodiczko's visual montage disrupts the heroic postures of the monuments with embarrassingly familiar images of the contemporary urban poor.

The monumental language of public art and architecture itself begins to slide, and Wodiczko's temporary superimpositions provoke us into reading the contradictory political perceptions of the exhibited monuments simultaneously, as well as in their relationship—in their "union"—with the social urban fabric threatened by neocolonial real-estate development enforcing the dislocation of the underprivileged. This dislocation, acted out directly on the bodies of the homeless and the poor (who, in Mayor Koch's latest public campaign, were to be forcefully "evacuated" from the streets), marks significant changes both in economic and class relations under late capitalism. Our postmodern downtowns now often appear like crossed-out graveyards of an older, heroic industrial modernity. But the relations between the graveyard and the new financial economy are made invisible by the promotion of restored patriotic statues. These images of patriotism have not only become instantly manipulatable in postmodern corporate architecture; they also surface more and more frequently in the aesthetic productions of the postmodern culture industry. Examples flourish: from state and corporate-sponsored museum exhibitions and art festivals, or the increasing presence of the military in commercial television advertising, or the current obsession with *Rambo* and Vietnam war movies; down to the blatantly nationalist propaganda employed in such media spectacles as the 1984 Olympics or the 1986 Statue of Liberty Weekend Celebrations.

The grim irony in this nationalist mobilization is not commonly perceived, even at a time when criminal abuse of power can make Oliver North a national hero and President Reagan an innocent survivor of the Iran-Contra scandal. This is perhaps a measure of the forces determining the use and appearance of public symbols. But an enforced aesthetic perception of the restored Union Square monuments must necessarily neutralize their content, since as institutions of memory they mock the social ideals they embody. Indeed, New York's actual inner city violence, squalor and racial discord directly contradict any such mystifying pretensions. We are left with so many contradictions that it is unclear whether the architecturalization of the social body and the decorative use of aesthetic and symbolic images in the service of postmodern corporate power can be unmasked and subverted.

Wodiczko's projections of the bodies of the homeless map counterimages onto the surfaces of hyperbolic monuments. The flagpole plaque in the center of the park reads: "This monument setting forth in enduring bronze the full text of the immortal charter of American liberty was erected in commemoration of the 150th Anniversary of the Declaration of Independence." It is a very small plaque, hardly read by anybody. Across the street we see a gigantic billboard announcing the promise of the new luxury buildings: "The Shape of Things to Come." The superimposition of Wodiczko's slide images, themselves gigantic in size (as in the case of the hand pledging allegiance which appeared on the AT&T Building during the month of Reagan's reelection in 1984), creates an alienation effect that gives depth to the surface of an enduring structure. But as in the theatre, with its enduring architecture of perception in the divided house, the afterimage with which Wodiczko disturbs the surface is in effect a performance of artificial light, a temporary and ephemeral contradiction that appears and disappears like so many other images (and billboards across the street). Something is happening here absolutely crucial to our understanding of the *expansion* of the postmodern scene: as it becomes increasingly difficult to *interpret* the rupture of aestheticized surfaces and screens (the constant cinema in our heads), the continuum of culturally and technologically produced images of reality is perceived as a constant *substitution* of and by images.

In this sense we live in a fully visible world, but it is a continuum of the "shape of things to come." Again I want to invoke *Blade Runner* as a paradigmatic film for the totally designed perceptual experience in which bodies themselves (human/non-human/"replicant" images) are no longer distinguishable if we allow images to substitute for the work of interpretation. The critical edge that the theatre could have lies in its remembrance of its own threatened existence and also of its considerable power in refusing to show everything it remembers. Since the classical tragedy of the city-state, and more directly since the Renaissance theatre's involvement in the politics of city and state, public performance has always been conflicted with the power of the visible and the shadows of the invisible. If the theatre today seems to have disappeared from the center of postmodern thought, it may be because of the critical impoverishment of its own work at a time when culture itself, having lost historical consciousness and an understanding of art's critical relationship to politics and the community, proceeds to "theatricalize" all its surfaces.

Theatre/Postmodernism

▐ . . . make the visible a little hard
To see.

Wallace Stevens

If "theatricality" continues to be a diffuse idea in postmodern culture, it has much to do with the unthinking connections that the mass cultural and entertainment industries make with "performance" without necessarily knowing anything about the particular transformations that have occurred on the stage over the three decades. Even after the radical energies we connect with the Living Theatre and other avant-garde projects had dispersed or been assimilated into mainstream fashion and media, the theatre as well as the new performance art continued to experiment both with the new forms that had sprung from collaborations between visual artists, musicians, dancers, video/film makers and performers, and with the aesthetic and political positions of a body of work quickly developed but also quickly forgotten in the margin of postmodern commercial culture.

The lack of any sustained critical attention to these experimentations is perhaps easily overlooked in light of the pervasive interpretive efforts with which the theoretical disciplines (literary theory, psychoanalysis, anthropology, semiology, philosophy, sociology, and so forth) approached their own epistemological searches and introspections in terms of the "model of theatre," or the "phantom of theatre" as Roland Barthes called it, remembering Francis Bacon.[40]

Annexing the theatre as an integrative frame of reference for interpretation and, specifically in the case of deconstructionist and feminist theory, for a critique of representation and patriarchal power structures, has contributed to the further marginalization of new experimental theatre work not perceived within this frame of reference. At the same time, however, a discursive theatricalization of postmodern models of thought valorized and even privileged performance while reducing it to a purely rhetorical operation. The rhetoric of performance in contemporary theory, consequently, acts out its generalized projections of the "phantom" without closely examining how its metaphors of representation, narrative, textuality, and writing/reading are related to the mise en scène of different modes of dramatic/mimetic and nondramatic/nonrepresentational theatre. Barthes's early work on Brecht, and Derrida's and Kristeva's reflections on Artaud are exceptional insofar as they recognize the historical, speculative critique of representation formulated by theatre theory and practice themselves. Brecht and Artaud have by now come to constitute perhaps the single most important (if paradoxical) confluence of ideas shadowing diverse recent stage experiments in dance, theatre, and performance art.

What postmodern theories of textuality and visual representation (and the spectating subject examined by film theory) lack is a more concrete historical understanding of the complex and conflicted relations of text and language to performance and space in the theatre. Even more importantly, they lack a concrete theatrical knowledge of the reconceptions and revisions of various approaches to the acting in, and staging of, textual and nontextual (scenographic, choreographic and musical) work carried out by several generations of avant-garde artists in this century.

Current cultural discourses concerned with the postmodern aesthetics of the surface have drawn on metaphors of staging that invoke the projection of spectacle, immediacy, presence, and transparence as if the exhibitionism of technologically reproducible and interchangeable visual images in our mass-mediated culture could be readily compared to the visible presence of a performer, a visual design, or a stage image in the theatre. The theatre's production of visible presence, however, is less a question of the *projection* of character (as it is called in Stanislavski-influenced acting) or image (as it is called in postmodern multimedia performance) than one of the temporal presence of fluid and changeable elements (visual, auditory, kinetic) and objects that constitute the physical and imaginary spaces of a performance. In this respect, the theatre is precisely not interested, and has never been, in the "flatness" of the visible or in the formal structure and qualities of its materiality, at least not in the sense in which a very influential modernist art criticism in the 1960s sought to define the "specificity" of artforms. This project was to become the unfulfilled dream of theatre semiologists in the 1970s who wanted to delimit the "theatrical object" by means of elaborate categorizations of its signifying system, its codes, and its processes of meaning production and communication.[41]

In writing on experimental theatre groups of the 1970s (Mabou Mines, the Wooster Group, the Ridiculous Theatrical Company, etc.), Ellen Levy makes a very curious analogy between flatness and liveness that might, however, illuminate our perspectives on postmodern tendencies in recent performance art and multimedia theatre. She argues that the group theatres "in turning away from mass culture chose to resume what Clement Greenberg identified as the modernist artist's proper task, 'the use of the characteristic methods of a discipline to criticize the discipline itself—not in order to subvert it, but to entrench it more firmly in its area of competence.' Much as Greenberg's modernist painter emphasized painting's flatness, the quality distinguishing it not only from sculpture but also from inherently illusionistic media like film and photography, so the groups drew attention to theatre's *liveness,* the volatile quality of the relationship between the members of the audience and their 'representatives' onstage."[42]

To claim that theatre's specificity is its "liveness" (if we overlook, for a moment, the illusionistic aspects in the performance or representation of such liveness) is to remind us of the enthusiasm and aggressiveness with which the Living Theatre generation aimed at a participatory and communitarian reality of action events and happenings as if they were able, through the most volatile enactments of revolutionary desire, to sweep away the deadening repetition of the old drama in the repertoires of the established theatre identified with the repressiveness of the dominant political culture. Breaking drama's limits or the ceremonies of psychological realism in acting, was not an area of particularly firm competence, however; nor did avant-garde theatre turn away from mass culture, since it never belonged to a mass culture in the first place.

Levy's breathtaking analogy to the Greenbergian aesthetics of a high modernism striving towards complete self-referential, formal autonomy almost entirely misses its point. The radical theatre groups of the 1960s as well as the conceptual and performance art experiments of the 1970s moved away from the proscenium stage to other spaces (lofts, galleries, streets, factories) precisely because any normative aesthetics founded upon notions of territoriality and discipline (see Michael Fried's wonderfully appropriate denigration of the theatre and of anything "theatrical" that has no clear place and lies "between the arts") were considered as repellent as the formalist presumption of an artistic purity somehow separate from the everyday world of social and political life.

But the theatre experiments of the avant-garde that emerged among other adversarial cultural practices in the political arena fell victim to the same disillusionment and exhaustion that we have come to see as part of our postmodern condition. The history of the Living Theatre is a good example of how the transgressive politics and antiaesthetics of avant-gardism gradually ended up in exile or in that state of confused anachronism easily exploited by a postmodern culture industry looking for *styles* and *postures* of radicalism marketable as sentimental or ironic fashions.

Neither in America nor in Europe did experimental theatre have any impact on the cultural formations of postmodernism. Perhaps the theatre is indeed the perfect "phantom" between the arts and between cultural discourses, since not even the idea of "liveness" and the rituals of the body (championed in performance art that wanted to extend Artaud's and Grotowski's radical insistence on the physical presence of the actors) seem to have survived all that well into the 1980s. I say this even though performance art, under the influence of experimentalists and theatre directors (Richard Foreman, Robert Wilson, Lee Breuer, Philip Glass, Steve Reich, Trisha Brown, JoAnne Akalaitis, Lucinda Childs, among others), is an established presence at the institutionalized and highly fashionable "Next Wave" festival series sponsored by the Brooklyn Academy of Music and Philip Morris Companies Inc., or on the international circuit of theatre festivals (from Avignon to PepsiCo Summerfare).

I do not think we can locate a historical moment of transition to postmodernism in theatre and performance art. Unlike architectural or fashion discourses, the theatre never advertised or formulated the changes that it overtook. I suspect that a lot of theatre work, impatient with the increasingly ineffectual political strategies of the 1960s avant-garde and excited by the increasingly less minimalist and antiaesthetic performance experiments that became possible with the help of new, sophisticated video, film, and playback technologies, made its way into the 1980s without knowing the discourses of postmodern theory. Practitioners of such theatre work had no critical understanding that it was becoming a visible symptom of the changed cultural conditions under which the margin of survival for radical and disruptive experimentation has disappeared to the extent that we perhaps no longer recognize a radical performance even if we were to see one.

Since the theatre does not seem to join contemporary discussions about the problems of "affirming" or "repudiating" the postmodern, is this simply a sign that it has become expendable? Or has late capitalist society exiled its unconscious desire for liveness (not just in the relationship between the audience and its representatives) because of the almost total alienation in the body-politic?

A radical theatre practice always wanted to abolish the margin of pretense, appearing and pretending to be alive and present to itself. Contemporary practitioners who have returned to the proscenium do not exactly know whom they represent, even as they prodigiously show the theatre's "formalist apparatus as representational device" and its shifting inscriptions of the "spectating subject" in the visual field.[43] What distinguishes the experimental theatre of today from other artistic productions (including conventional drama) created for at least a potential mass audience is not so much its liveness, which is in any case barely visible in a lot of work that depends heavily on technological scenography and audiovisual media. Rather, its bad conscience makes it behave as if it needed to replay the struggle with representation and with the limits of the visual field in ever more obsessive ways.

I admit that I am attracted to the struggle and to the theory of the struggle. What I had conceived of as a widening circle of reflections on theatre and theory perhaps inevitably turned into a more narrow field of vision in which I return to the same questions I saw raised by the performances I found meaningful to understand the theatre's bad conscience. At the same time, I am aware of the obsessions and frustrations. Perhaps there comes a point at which I need to stop investigating the relentless unmasking of the body in Pina Bausch's choreographies, or the explosive rewriting of history and myth in Heiner Müller's "synthetic fragments," or the perversely fascinating landscapes in Robert Wilson's operatic "theatre of images," or the insubstantial and entropic phantoms of performance art.

But these investigations, to which I shall return throughout the book, encompass several characteristic directions in contemporary theatre, which in my mind reflect a similar if differently expressed fear of repetition, a fear and suspicion of *this culture* that pretends to be "postmodern" yet piles up more and more ruins of the elapsed consciousness of our humanity. The fear is also performed *as* repetition, in the self-consuming depressions, destructions, and manipulations of the body (danced out to the point of exhaustion in Pina Bausch's theatre); in the murderous images of an excremental history running its terminal course against all forgetting (envisioned in the antitheatrical theatre collages of Heiner Müller). Or the softer American versions that disguise the horror: in the autistic and trancelike dream surfaces of Robert Wilson's technological landscapes; or in the warped quasiautobiographical sketches and short-circuited anecdotes of the dispossessed self in performance art that goes out of sight so quickly if it does not reappear on the movie screen (Laurie Anderson's *Home of the Brave;* Spalding Gray's *Swimming to Cambodia;* Eric Bogosian's *Drinking in America*) or on prerecorded "live" TV talk shows ("Alive from Off Center"). In another sense, my writings are often too close to the work they address. Therefore I cannot claim a comprehensive perspective on all the reasons why the postmodern return of the body (a highly ambivalent return if we see, for example, how the body in American postmodern dance moves and moves like a high-wired marionette while in German and Belgian dancetheatre it often barely moves at all) coincided with the return of a technological-formalist aestheticism that simulates the reproduction of disembodied desire. Or why has an anthropological concern returned, not with the dispossessed self that is learning to speak again (in the chatter of the solo performance artists), but with more "primitive," i.e., primarily non-Western behavioral and ritualistic cultural performances and physical training processes?

These coincidences, however, turn up in the larger context of "global American postmodern culture." Although my introductory essay gives no answer to the complex and diversified exchange mechanisms in this contemporary scene, it attempts to connect the theory and practice of experimental theatre to those cultural processes that we have already accepted as normal, everyday coincidences. For example, it is possible to see on the same day and on the same block in the East Village or in Dallas or in Paris the perfectly slick and empty facsimiles of simulationist art side by side with a convulsive performance of painful body transformations in a Japanese butoh dance depicting the eternal human voyage from birth to death. If the exhibit and the butoh dance are radically different from each other, how can they appear on the same scene?

Reflecting on these cultural processes, Bonnie Marranca has spoken of the "fetishization of the body" in recent intercultural anthropology and performance studies. She very adroitly links the interculturalist, all-encompassing infatuation with body techniques and rituals to deconstructionist theory's obsessive focus on intertextuality and the "writing of the body."[44] I want to add another link to what I would call the fetishization of the contentless aesthetic surface in the theatre of images (Wilson), and then repeat Marranca's critical question:

[These are] different versions of the same distaste for theatre as representation, and more extremely, theatre as theory, its original root meaning. It is clear now that Artaud not Brecht has triumphed in our century as myth and ritual grow more attractive than history and its possibility of adversary cultures. How will theatre react to this attack on the text?[45]

The irony is, of course, that Artaud and Brecht, as well as anthropology and deconstruction, belong to the same tradition and history of the dialectic of enlightenment and that enlightenment's self-deconstruction. Myth and ritual in this tradition (Marranca calls them "antirational") keep returning to the surface where they can appear as a new logic of exchange with the revenging force of the plague, whose disordering power Artaud celebrated.

I am not sure that we have already seen the end of representation, which would be a truly fearful event, not only for the theatre, but for the historical conscience that still allows us to perceive the critical and conceptual impoverishment *in* the geometric abstractions of simulationist art, or in the *jouissance* of the body in writing or performance, or in the seductive amnesia of a theatre of images that discarded text and language but actually needed to bring them back when the images began merely to conceal the lack of thought.

I have never been much interested in a theatre that believed in, or subscribed to, the authority of the text and the authenticity of the body. Such belief quite naturally tends to reaffirm conservative cultural values and exchanges of meaning which, as feminist critics have insistently pointed out, serve to cover up how power relations, desire and the representation of sexuality, and authority itself are culturally constructed and reconstructed. The experimental performances I write about in the following essays belong to a history of what one could call avant-garde rituals of attack against the institutions and conventions of authority, textual and otherwise. At this point in postmodern culture, the fetishization of the image and the fetishization of the body (or its gradual disappearance in multimedia performance) perhaps reflect the inevitable aftermath of a radical suspicion of authority *and* of theory. Much of the rhetoric of performance in postmodern discourse has contributed to the theatre's failure to take stock of its critical achievements, which I believe have fundamentally altered our perception of the traditional dichotomy of text and stage, and of the whole structure of relationships (between actor, character, script, space, time, narrative content, image, design) implied by that historical dichotomy.

And if performance today, whether in theatre, dance, performance or multimedia art, is perceived as "postmodern," we may want to ask how its current practices on the critical margin of the body and the image can be reconstructed, not in terms of a distrust of history and its possibility of adversary cultures, but with an understanding of why the theatre's negation of its own history is always an unfinished and unfinishable experiment.

NOTES

1. Peter Bürger, *Theory of the Avant-Garde,* trans. Michael Shaw (Minneapolis: Univ. of Minnesota Press, 1984). See also *Postmoderne: Alltag, Allegorie und Avant-Garde,* ed. Christa and Peter Bürger (Frankfurt: Suhrkamp, 1987).
2. Richard Schechner, *The End of Humanism* (New York: PAJ Publications, 1982).
3. Victor Burgin, *The End of Art Theory: Criticism and Postmodernity* (Atlantic Highland, NJ: Humanities Press International, 1986).
4. Jean Baudrillard's ruminations on the expanding desert form of (American) postmodernity, from which I quoted at the beginning, presume the absolute voiding of historical contradictions in our collective indifference to the political development of societies. This has lead him to argue, in a 1986 symposium held in New York, that the Berlin Wall, too, has become merely a nostalgic sign or fetish of history, an "anorexic ruin." As I finish proofreading these pages, the "anorexic ruin" between the two Germanys has come down after the hard labor of a revolutionary double movement (internal resistance/exodus) in the GDR. The process is extremely volatile, and I fail to see the end of the contradictions that will now become quite obvious and forceful in the simultaneous presence of the two time frames. Different realities exist, and will continue to do so long after the Wall has disappeared, or been turned into a museum, or been sold as so many pieces of nostalgic kitsch, to American supermarkets and museum gift shops.
The proceedings of the New York symposium have been published under the title *Looking Back on the End of the World,* ed. Dietmar Kamper and Christa Wulf (New York: Semiotext(e), 1989).
5. The term "global space" frequently crops up in discussions of the world market, the dominant production systems (capitalism and socialism), and their political, economic, and military relations. According to American Marxist theorist Fredric Jameson, multinational capitalism may be understood as a cultural politics struggling to dominate markets and control space. Distinguished from the "colonized" or "imperialized" formations of the so-called Third World this "global American postmodernist culture" seems to arise at a moment when the homogenizing force of such a logic would seem to require the greatest possible (global?) resistance. See Jameson, "Third-World Literature in the Era of Multinational Capitalism," *Social Text* 15 (Fall 1986): 65–88. Jameson's position on Third-World "nationalist" cultures has already come under attack by Pakistani writer Aijaz Ahmad ("Jameson's Rhetoric of Otherness and the 'Nationalist Allegory,' " *Social Text* 17 (Fall 1987): 3–25) and by the Chinese critic and translator Rey Chow ("Rereading Mandarin Ducks and Butterflies: A Response to the 'Postmodern Condition,' " *Cultural Critique* 5 [Winter 1986–87]: 69–93). Yet the question whether there is a unifying force of contemporary history and/or postmodernist culture has only begun to be raised. Current technological transformations of culture itself raise this question most forcefully. Another indication appears in the global conceptions of current blockbuster museum exhibitions that claim the "universality" of art at the very moment when the final and irreversible disappearance of its "aura" has evened out the distinction to other objects and spectacles of consumption. In his critique of the "Primitivism" show at the Museum of Modern Art, Hal Foster comments on the Hegelian aftermath of a universalizing logic in the West that had sought to incorporate what was different: "Though presented as art, the tribal objects are manifestly the ruins of (mostly) dead cultures now exposed to our archaeological probes—and *so too are the modern objects.* . . . Against its own interests, the show signalled a potentially postmodern, posttribal present; indeed, in the technological vacuum of the museum space, this present seemed all but

posthistorical." (Cf. *Recodings: Art, Spectacle, Cultural Politics* [Port Townsend, WA: Bay Press, 1985], 190–91).

     6. See especially, Jürgen Habermas, "Modernity: An Incomplete Project," in *The Anti-Aesthetic,* ed. Hal Foster (Port Townsend: Bay Press, 1983), 3–15; Jean-François Lyotard, *The Postmodern Condition: A Report on Knowledge* (Minneapolis: Univ. Of Minnesota Press, 1984); Fredric Jameson, "Postmodernism, or the Cultural Logic of Late Capitalism," *New Left Review* 146 (1984): 53–92, and Andreas Huyssen, "Mapping the Postmodern," *New German Critique* 33 (1984): 5–52. The American discussion of postmodernism in literature and architecture started almost a decade earlier, in the early 1970s, but the actual "inflation" (an economic term used by Charles Newman to describe the acceleration rate of theoretical fictions about the cultural dissolution of late modernity; cf. *The Post-Modern Aura: The Art of Fiction in an Age of Inflation* [Evanston: Northwestern Univ. Press, 1985]) of broader, interdisciplinary theories of the social reality and the culture of postmodernity only began with the confrontational debate between German social theory (Habermas) and French poststructuralism (Lyotard, Derrida, Foucault, Baudrillard, et al.) in the early 1980s. Most of the journals engaged in critical theory have published special issues on the postmodernism debate; see especially "Modernity and Postmodernity", *New German Critique* 33 (Fall 1984); "Debates in Contemporary Culture," *Telos* 62 (Winter 1984/85); "Modernity and Modernism/Postmodernity and Postmodernism," *Cultural Critique* 5 (Winter 1986/1987); "Burnout," *Art & Text* 16 (Summer 1984). Although most critical journals devoted to studies in art and architecture, film, literature, mass media, technology, ideology and institutions, social history, economics, politics and culture have been suffused with poststructuralist and postmodernist perceptions, the leading theatre journals and the professional theatre reviewers in the U.S. and Europe have shown little interest in entering the debates or even acknowledging their relevance to the condition of contemporary theatre and performance. *Performing Arts Journal* (over the last ten years) and, more recently, *Theatre Journal, The Drama Review, Théâtre en Europe, Theater Heute, TheaterZeitSchrift* and *Patalogo* have increasingly situated their focus on traditional and experimental performance within the context of cultural theory.

     7. "The Cultural Logic of Late Capitalism," 80.

     8. Cf. Jean Baudrillard's fascinating and thoroughly cynical praise of the self-consumption built into the simulacrum of transparent cultural space in the Centre Pompidou that had a mass appeal outside of the art exhibitions it was meant to house: *L'effet Beaubourg. Implosion et dissuasion* (Paris: Editions Galilée, 1977).

     9. "The Cultural Logic," 87.

     10. For an important study of the science-fictional design of the audiovisual ambience in films *(Liquid Sky, Looker, Blade Runner)* that deal directly with technological landscapes, fashion modeling, computer simulation, genetic engineering and the aesthetic imaging of "virtual" sexual difference, see Janet Bergstrom, "Androids and Androgyny," *Camera Obscura* 15 (1986): 37–65.

     11. "The Cultural Logic," 84–85.

     12. Quoted in "The Cultural Logic," 84–85.

     13. Although I cannot precisely estimate the influence of Virilio's "aesthetics" on my own theatre work, I certainly am deeply indebted to his theoretical studies on technology and the formations of speed and territorial space. Most of his major books have only been published in Europe, including: *L'insécurité du territoire* (Paris: Stock, 1976); *Esthétique de la disparition* (Paris: Editions Balland, 1980); *L'espace critique* (Paris: Christian Bourgois, 1984); *Guerre et cinema* (Paris: Editions de l'Etoile, 1984). English translations by Mark Polizzotti were published under the titles *Speed and Politics* (New York: Semiotext(e), 1986), and *Pure War* (New York: Semiotext(e), 1983).

     14. Virilio, *Pure War,* 4–6 and 67–71.

     15. See Georges Bataille, *Visions of Excess: Selected Writings 1927–1939* (Min-

neapolis: Univ. of Minnesota Press, 1985). Baudrillard's important critique of the political economy of the commodity form, *Pour une critique de l'économie politique du signe* (Paris: Gallimard, 1972), offers a rhetorical and analytical break with the Marxist categorical dialectic of production. Since *L'échange symbolique et la mort* (Paris: Gallimard, 1976) and his later, obsessive theorization of simulation, the concept of production in capitalism is shifted entirely into modes of *cultural reproduction* in postmodernity. Baudrillard dwells on the crucial relationship between the sign/image and the real, suggesting that the accelerated and excessive floating of signs in postmodern capitalism creates a hyperreality of aesthetic abstraction that is catastrophic and fascinating in its nihilistic indifference to actual events and referents of the real. Cf. *Simulations* (New York: Semiotext(e), 1983), and *In the Shadow of the Silent Majorities, or the End of the Social* (New York: Semiotext(e), 1983).

16. Jean Baudrillard, *Forget Foucault* (New York: Semiotext(e), 1987), 61.

17 I am here referring to Guy Debord's observation, made in the late 1960s before the appearance of Baudrillard's theory of "simulation," that the final form of commodity capitalism is experienced as alienation to such a degree of abstraction "that it becomes an image." Cf. *The Society of the Spectacle* (Detroit: Black & Red, 1983), paragraph 34.

18. Cf. *In the Shadow of the Silent Majorities*, 85.

19. See Mike Davis, "Urban Renaissance and the Spirit of Postmodernism," *New Left Review* 15 (1985): 106–13

20. Virilio, *Pure War*, 18–19.

21. Carl Abbott, *The New Urban America* (Chapel Hill: Univ. of North Carolina Press, 1983), 143. Cf. Davis, "Urban Renaissance," 112.

22. George Lipsitz, "Cruising around the Historical Bloc: Postmodernism and Popular Music in East Lost Angeles," *Cultural Critique* 5 (1986/87): 157–77.

23. Ibid., 170.

24. The severe controversy that arose over the planned staging of *Garbage, the City and Death* at the Frankfurt Schauspielhaus in October 1985 led to its cancellation and subsequently to a heated debate over issues of aesthetic freedom and censorship. Members of the Jewish community occupied the stage at the Frankfurt theatre to protest the play in spite of the artistic director's contention that the "Schonzeit" (closed season) of tabooed relations between Jews and non-Jews was over now, and that nobody could claim a special "guilt bonus." The irony in this demand for the opening of a closed season has to be perceived in the full context of the growing sentiment, across a wide spectrum of political opinion, for a final return to "normality." That return found its epitomizing spectacle in the carefully planned reconciliation ceremony uniting President Reagan and the conservative German chancellor Helmut Kohl in a symbolic handshake over the graves of the military cemetery at Bitburg in May 1985.

25. References are to Rainer Werner Fassbinder, *Plays*, ed. Denis Calandra (New York: PAJ Publications, 1985), 168–71. I have slightly modified the translations.

26. The first quotation is from President Reagan's last press conference before his departure for West Germany. The second quotation is from his speech at Bergen-Belsen. By the time Reagan stood in front of the SS graves in Bitburg, he no longer referred to the Jewish or American dead but exonerated the German war dead as victims "crushed by a vicious ideology."

27. Jean-François Lyotard, *Le différend* (Paris: Minuit, 1983). Interestingly enough, Lyotard's reference to Auschwitz as an unspeakable event takes up Adorno's well-known claim that Auschwitz represents a categorical break in the flow of history and the ideology of modern progress. See *Minima Moralia: Reflections from Damaged Life* (London: Verso, 1978), 234ff.

28. Lyotard, "Answering the Question: What Is Postmodernism?" Appendix

to *The Postmodern Condition*, 81. See also "Presenting the Unpresentable: The Sublime," *Artforum* (April 1982): 64–69, and "The Sublime and the Avant-Garde," *Artforum* (April 1984): 36–43.

29. Nancy Marner, "Documenta 8: The Social Dimension?" *Art in America* (September 1987): 128–39; 197–99.

30. See Arthur Kroker and David Cook, *The Postmodern Scene: Excremental Culture and Hyper-Aesthetics* (New York: St. Martin's Press, 1986), and Jean Baudrillard *Amérique* (Paris: Editions Grasset & Fasquelle, 1986).

31. I have translated these passages from the German edition, *Amerika* (München: Matthes & Seitz, 1987), 15, 171.

32. Ross Bleckner, "Talking Abstract," *Art in America* (July 1987): 84.

33. Peter Halley, "Notes on Abstraction," *Arts Magazine* (Summer 1987): 37.

34. This is a reference to Philip Taafe's painted duplication of sixties paintings made by another simulationist painter/writer (Ross Beckner, Pat Hearn Gallery Catalog, January 1987, 7).

35. "Health Experts Map the Devastation of AIDS," *The New York Times*, December 13, 1987. See also "The Truth about AIDS: Dread Disease Is Spreading Rapidly through Heterosexual Population," *Ebony* (April 1987): 130.

36. Robert Venturi, in describing such megastructures as "eclectic accumulation" of styles and signs, characterizes the desert town of Las Vegas as the prototype of postmodern architecture based on communication and not on space, structure, form, or historical context. Cf. Venturi, Brown, Izenour, *Learning from Las Vegas* (Cambridge: MIT Press, 1972).

37. Quoted from the opening section, "Say Hello," of Laurie Anderson's *United States*. She repeats the same questions at the end of "Lighting Out for the Territories." The record was released by Warner Brothers in 1984.

38. Antonin Artaud, *The Theatre and Its Double* (New York: Grove Press, 1958), 12.

39. See Rosalyn Deutsche's penetrating study of the complex political and economic issues involved in the Union Square redevelopment scheme in "Krzysztof Wodiczko's *Homeless Projection* and the Site of Urban 'Revitalization,' " *October* 38 (1986): 63–98.

40. *Roland Barthes by Roland Barthes*, trans. Richard Howard (New York: Hill and Wang, 1977), 177.

41. The most comprehensive collection of studies in theatre semiology dealing with theatre's "signifying practices" appeared in a special issue of *Poetics Today* in the spring of 1981. They extend the earlier failure of the Prague School's linguistic and semiotic descriptions of the theatre as a formal system of signs and functions. Cf. Ladislav Matejka and Irwin R. Titunic, eds., *Semiotics of Art: Prague School Contributions* (Cambridge: MIT Press, 1976).

42. Ellen Levy, "Individuals and Autonomists," *Dissent* (Fall 1987): 587–88.

43. Cf. Timothy Murray, "The Theatricality of the Van-Guard: Ideology and Contemporary American Theatre," *Performing Arts Journal* 24 (1984): 93–99.

44. Bonnie Marranca, "Acts of Criticism" in the introductory essay to the 10th anniversary issue of *Performing Arts Journal* (1985): 36–39.

45. Ibid., 38.

I own the images of those
Who have been slain the screams of all the tortured
Since I left Colchis left my home to follow
Your bloody tracks . . .

I want to break mankind apart in two
And live within the empty middle I
No woman and no man. . . .

Now it is all quiet
The screams of Colchis silenced too
And nothing left
                              Heiner Müller, *Medeamaterial*

2   "MEDEA": LANDSCAPES BEYOND HISTORY

Argonaut-landscapes

Berlin: a deterritorialized city trapped between different historical times and political systems, walled into the schism between East-West, over-charged with the seductiveness of its schizophrenic space and the negative suspense created by the no-man's land that runs along the Wall. The void of the death strip and the visible decay of the vacant lots bordering the wall were watched over by armed border guards who had to prevent Germans from escaping into Germany. The present seemed overdetermined: this was the ruined capital, Pale Mother of Germany's self-divisions. The future of Berlin after the November revolution of 1989 will be built on the imaginary borderline that the Wall leaves behind.

When Bertolt Brecht looked down onto the streets of the May Day demonstrations in 1929, he watched with horror how the Berlin police, led by Social Democrats, fired at the crowd of unarmed Communist workers. The failure of the proletarian revolution in the face of emerging Hitler fascism and Stalinist terror intensified the contradictions inscribed into the frightening comedies of the early avant-garde. Walter Benjamin, brooding expert in the allegorical German *Trauerspiel*, was referring to Brecht's "new human type" in *A Man's a Man* when he remarked that the joyful transformation of Galy Gay can be accomplished because Gay is wise enough to dedramatize his individual identity: he becomes the "perfect empty stage" for the collective will.[1] The disturbing ironies in this proposition are obvious if we remember that Galy Gay surrenders his "private person" (he becomes "strong in the mass," as Brecht himself wrote in his program notes for the Berlin production) in order eventually to turn into a "human fighting machine" for the British colonial army. In a complementary act of caricatured self-abandon, Sergeant Bloody Five conquers his overbearing sexual desire by castrating himself with a pistol.

The joke, of course, is not on the revolutionary clown but on colonizing bourgeois history whose ghost fathers and ghost writers haunt the family romance of heroic manhood. For Marx, this anxiety of influence perpetrated a fictional model that required sons and nephews to repeat farcically the historical tragedies of their forefathers, strengthening the illusion that enlightenment's progress through disruptions/revolutions was in fact an emancipation *from* history.[2]

In Brecht's new theatre for the scientific age, the idea of progress was not allowed to make a fool of itself. It seems another radical political illusion, however, to find him stage a series of theatre experiments (*Versuche*) that had the actual contradictions within the Weimar Republic play themselves out toward the self-castration of bourgeois idealism that would allow for a future epic history without heroes. This was all the more suspicious at the very time when the protofascist climate in Berlin began to produce the new mythic gestures of hero worship that would lead to Hitler's Thousand-Year Reich.

The castration took place, but with the horribly destructive violence and savage logic that Heiner Müller tried to capture in *The Slaughter: Scenes from Germany* and *Germania Death in Berlin*. These two plays from the early 1970s announced Müller's subsequent preoccupation with the ruined promise and the catastrophic paralysis of modern revolutionary history (and all modern revolutionary theory, one should add).

In the following, I shall speak about the ruins and the standstill of history, with Benjamin's materialist and messianic perspectives on "petrified landscapes"[3] in mind. As well, the distance between Brecht and Müller, which for my purposes here (as well as for my own theatre practice) indicates the distance we have traveled from Brecht's *Lehrstücke*, which demonstrate a revolutionary consciousness within "learning" scenarios that stage critical thought and action, to the postrevolutionary nihilism in Müller's recent "synthetic fragments."[4] These texts, ostensibly written for the theatre, are rather more significant as *scenographies* of implosive thinking that describe the necessary disappearance of theatre.

In that sense, Müller's scenographies reflect a self-destructive energy that continues to exert a very strong, perhaps brutal pressure on a historical consciousness and critical reflection of our modernity. At the same time, they produce an aesthetic fascination with death and finality that seems to place them into the mainstream of apocalyptic postmodernist thought and art under advanced capitalism. Müller's "Landscape with Argonauts" is a recognizably postmodern scene of a culture suffused with self-hatred *and* an ecstatic consumption of the technological violence that brings the colonization of the lifeworld to its end.

> Figures among the rubble
> Natives of the concrete Parade
> Of Zombies perforated by TV spots
> In the uniforms of yesterday morning's fashion
> The youth of today ghosts of
> The dead of the war that is to happen tomorrow
> YET WHAT REMAINS IS CREATED BY BOMBS
> In the splendid mating of protein and tin
> The children lay out landscapes with trash[5]

The one who speaks this phantasmagoria is someone without a clear identity:

> Shall I speak of me I who
> Of whom are they speaking when
> They do speak of me I who is it[6]

The text assigns no one in particular to the speech; an anonymous discourse enacts a flight across space into which it will ultimately dissolve. Beyond fear, which has no individual name, lies a silent landscape that receives the disembodied discourse.

> A fluttering
> 'Tween nothing and no one provided there is wind
> I scum of a man I scum of
> A woman Platitude piled on platitude I hell of dreams
> Called by my accidental name I Fear of
> My accidental name[7]

But who or what completes this "reeling flight" which results in a suicided fusion of body and landscape?

> I felt MY blood come out of MY veins
> And turn MY body into the landscape
> Of MY death[8]

If the topography in this landscape betrays a striking relationship to the transmutations of the flesh in Kafka's hell-dreams of reality, it does not, however, share that painful blindness exposed in the Kafkaesque body's hopeless resistance against an impersonal, institutionalized system of dependency (for example, Joseph K's loss of orientation in *The Trial*). Unlike the still-expressible terror of the endless victimizing trials of the tortured individual vis-à-vis an abstract yet clearly totalitarian apparatus of disciplinary power in Kafka's parables,[9] Müller's theatre already assumes the identity of the subject, the subjected body, and the technological landscape. Or, consider this image from Müller's translation of the mythic labors of Herakles, who dissolves into "the personal union of enemy and battlefield" as he is desperately trying to locate the monster.[10]

There is a difference, however, between the suicidal union of Herakles and the Hydra, between the laborer and his task, and the dissolution of body and self into landscape. The differences between the imaging of "landscapes," functions of discourse, and the scenography that describe relationships ("Jason"/"Medea") to stages and landscapes of *history* is crucial for an understanding of the ambivalent political and aesthetic position that Müller's theatre assumes within the context of the postmodern decomposition of both politics and art that we experience in the culture of late capitalism.

A significant aspect of this ambivalence may lie in the well-publicized ease with which the plays of a Marxist writer travel from Berlin and the GDR to New York and the US, where they seem to have been seamlessly assimilated into the advanced capitalist formalism of Robert Wilson's lavish "theatre of images." Wilson's global multimedia opera, *the CIVIL warS*, to which Müller contributed the texts for the German section, has itself turned into something of an synthetic fragment. Rather than a Wilsonian collage of beautifully fused images drawn from myth, history, folklore, dreams, and literary narratives, we see a hyperserial that can now recurrently present installments of a never-completed totality (the entire work has not been staged yet because Wilson did not—perhaps did not want to—raise enough capital support to cover the $6.5 million production costs).

The perversion of previously resistant theatre and acting experiments in both Müller's and Wilson's work ended in simulacra of avant-garde theatre (staged, for example, at BAM's NEXT WAVE Festival) that fully participate in the fashion and commodity industry's colonization of social imaginary space. In the perfect union of Müller and Wilson, by which American reviewers presumably mean that Müller's complex texts give the necessary "weight" to the giant puppetry and the magic lighting in Wilson's impalpable stage pictures,[11] one can see the effacement of history and cultural difference that is a major ideological force in postmodernism. The political content in Müller's material strains against the images that seek to contain them, but if those contradictions erode, then the logic of Wilson's theatre of images unites with the market imperative of late capitalism to produce aesthetic indifference or, rather, to reproduce the fascination of consumption without regard to any particular content or meaning or historical reality.

Wilson's "civil wars" are a mythic construct. The picturesque abstractions—an astronaut hanging from the ceiling, or an oversized puppet Abraham Lincoln slowly slowly floating from stage left to stage right, or a female Frederick the Great dancing with a polar bear—complement quite precisely the theoretical gestures of Jean Baudrillard's discourse on "cynical power" and the "end of history" (the Real).[12] For Baudrillard, we have left the stage of history with a vacant look in our eyes; there is no more history because there is no historical subject. In the postmodern culture of abstract semiological reproduction, the fate of the subjective and the humane (a fate already sealed by structuralist theory) has become irrelevant within an immobilized universe of empty symbolic exchanges. The processing of image, spectacle, and information in the simulated reality of the electronic mass media neutralizes all social energy or political conflict.

What is most remarkable about French posthistorical theory is its joyful Nietzschean affirmation of this obsolescence[13] of political and dialectical reason. If the current exchange of theory in Paris begins to appear, in the fashion of postmodern architecture, as a titillating parody of masterful thinking (mixing Nietzsche with Bataille, Lacan, Derrida, Foucault, Lyotard, et al.), then the obsolescence of critical theory has announced itself too. We are no longer shocked to hear Baudrillard argue that finally even *death* itself, as catastrophe, although "fascinating as a necessity" (nuclear catastrophe and terrorism are offered as postmodern paradigms, but undoubtedly we shall see AIDS added to the list of fascinating necessities),[14] is not real but figurative, a mythic future-in-the-present, a sublime event that has already colonized postmodern consumer culture even though it cannot have happened except as a disembodied aestheticized *image* of disaster. Disaster as daily hit parade; daily murder as television. Baudrillard of course knows that he cannot surprise us because he has already affirmed the irreality of his own theory.[15]

All of this seems to me to resemble Jason's "reeling flight" enacted in the fantasy of the speaker in *Landscape with Argonauts*. It is a death wish fantasy of mythical proportions since it attests to an all-embracing wish to forget. The flight is in fact a forgetting of origins and destinations ("With the horizon the memory of the coast slips away. . . . But the voyage had no arrival"). It has already entered the terminal, frozen state of the uncompleted "project of modernity."[16]

This incompleteness, which includes the catastrophic horizon of modernity's progress, the high frontier of "Star Wars" weaponry, and the final, destructive colonization of the planet, indicates for Heiner Müller a standstill of time, a kind of death that is in one sense the final liquidation of the human subject unable to "look history in the eye."[17] In another sense the endpoint of a process of *inner colonization* (humankind turning into landscape) is necessarily incomplete as long as it does not produce revolutionary change: a "new human type." Müller's refusal to write drama rejects Brecht's optimistic belief that the theatre can represent the dialectical process that will produce the new. Müller's scenographies of history's "standstill" allegorize this production at the exact point of crisis where traditional theatre *and* Brecht's didactic theatre are no longer possible.

> The Theatre of the White Revolution is over. We sentence you to death, Victor Debuisson. Because your skin's white. Because your thoughts are white under your white skin. . . . Because you are a property owner, a master. . . . Whoever owns nothing dies more easily. What else belongs to you. Say it quickly, our School is Time, it doesn't repeat itself and there's no breathing space for didacticism.[18]

The black slave Sasportas, who thus indicts the revolution of European Enlightenment, describes the fate of Debuisson, son of a plantation owner, who betrayed the bourgeois revolution after it had already betrayed itself. But Debuisson, who might have been a hero in the old drama, is like the theatre he stands for: he cannot quite die. He is afraid of his death, which makes him seek for oblivion in the embrace of his FirstLove and the return to his father's plantation. This betrayal and return is naturalized in Müller's scenographies as a regressive movement typical of the male white intellectuals who represent the failure of revolution in their failure to destroy the continuity of privilege and property, of the institutions of power, knowledge, and oppression. Debuisson's refusal to die for revolutionary change ends in his returning home. Müller's text, however, does not end with an act of returning: it ends with a highly ambivalent sexual dream, during which Debuisson fantasizes dissolving into the feminine body of FirstLove. This body is both seductive and threatening as well as symbolic of the sensual power and transgressive desire of revolution itself.

> Debuisson closed his eyes against the temptation to look at the face of his first love who was Treason. Treason danced. Debuisson pressed his hands against his eyes. He heard his heart beat in the rhythm of the dance steps. They grew faster with his heart beat. Debuisson felt his eyelids twitching against his palms. Perhaps the dance had already ended and only his heart was still booming while Treason, her arms crossed perhaps over her breast, or her hands placed on her hips or, by this time, grabbing her crotch, her vulva probably quivering already with lust, looked with swimming eyes at him. . . . He opened his eyes. Treason smiling showed her breasts and silently spread her legs wide open, her beauty hit Debuisson like an axe. . . . Then Treason threw herself upon him like a heaven, the bliss of the labia a dawn.[19]

I am not sure whether a "dream" scenario such as the above can be acted or represented in our theatre. I want to argue that Müller's writing—the imaginary space (*Bildraum*) of the writing—is incompatible both with modernist forms of realist theatre and with postmodernist practices of the theatre of images or performance art.

The homelessness depicted in Müller's writing may bear traces of the utopian struggles of the historical avant-garde, the aporias of modernist literature (e.g. Kafka, Beckett), or the Marxist aesthetics of Brechtian theatre with its learning techniques (*Verfremdungseffekt*, montage, gestus, epic acting) for a new history of humankind not yet begun. But unlike Brecht, who returned home after his exile to become institutionalized with the Berliner Ensemble, and more like Artaud whose theatre never existed except in the metaphors and poems he wrote, Müller writes with a destructive impulse (*"Schreiben aus Lust an der Katastrophe"*)[20] that continues to disturb the inherited models and definitions through which existing theatre understands the staged relationship between words and images.

Perhaps comparable to the uncanny, surrealist "Elevator"-monologue that suddenly appears in *The Task* as if the ground had shifted and we were listening to a Kafka parable about the loss and disappearance of all possible tasks, Debuisson's dream cancels the realism of the theatre. Treason's dance, described by Debuisson in the third person and in past tense, cannot be staged literally. Nor is the projection of "Treason" onto the feminine body a hallucination that could be *acted out* by a performer, since it is not written as an internal monologue. Nor could a disjunction of text and images (e.g. staged/filmic/photographic images that project beauty or seduction or violence without duplicating the gestus of the text) be presented without losing the collapsing difference between subject and object theatricalized in the writing. What Debuisson describes is not what he sees. He cannot see his death for himself: the landscape of betrayal (the home of FirstLove) is inside him. Yet it is also on the other side of the shattered integrity of the self whose boundaries (the white skin, the mark of property) have already dissolved. Debuisson describes the blinding shame of a dissolution he cannot face.

Treason's dance anticipates a landscape after Debuisson or, rather, a landscape in the moment of his disappearance. But the moment's connection of sexuality and death (a positively validated union for Müller) is embodied in the woman-body. And that embodiment, although it perhaps signals the end of male occupation/colonization of *Lebensraum*, is an allegory, or an image of a "frozen dialectic," as Benjamin would call it, that is ultimately paradoxical and even nonsensical. On the one hand, Müller's *The Task* obviously deals with the failure of the three revolutionary emissaries from Paris (Debuisson, Galloudec, Sasportas) to export the revolution to the Third World. Ironically, Debuisson—the intellectual leader and ideologue of the group—is a native of Jamaica who abandons the revolutionary project at the moment he begins to recognize a "natural" beauty and seductiveness in his native landscape that he had all but repressed and replaced with the enlightened rationality of revolutionary ideas. In other words Debuisson dances with political class struggle, the "angel of death."[21] The self-destruction of enlightenment,[22] already apparent in the paradigmatic politics of violence and terror that determines the aftermath of 1789, produces a paradoxical awakening: Debuisson (the revolution) returns to his FirstLove, the ancien régime. On the other hand, the allegory of the woman-body (FirstLove as home, lover, nurturer, mother, revenger, treason/Revolution or SecondLove as prostitute) stages extreme contradictions, chaotic images that paralyze and distort the dialectical relationship between oppression and liberation, sexual violence and revolutionary passion. Even before "Treason" swallows him up at the end, Debuisson experiences his own castration in the feminine body when FirstLove mocks his infatuation:

> Did you hurt yourself, little Victor. Come closer and show your wounds. Don't you know me anymore. You don't have to be afraid, little Victor. Not of me. Not of your first love. The one you have betrayed with the Revolution, your blood-smeared second love. . . .
> Did you love her so much. Ah, Debuisson. I've told you she's a whore. The serpent with the bloodthirsty vulva. . . . Do you want to be my slave, little Victor. Do you love me. These are the lips that kissed you. They remember your skin, Victor Debuisson. These are the breasts that warmed you, little Victor. They didn't forget your mouth and your hands. This is the skin that drank your sweat. This is the womb that received your sperm which scorches my heart. . . . I will take back what your whore Revolution robbed me of, my property. With the fangs of my dogs I want to tear out of your soiled flesh the traces of my tears, my sweat, my cries of lust. . . .
> YESTERDAY I BEGAN/TO KILL YOU MY HEART/NOW I LOVE/YOUR CORPSE.[23]

The tone of this scene ("Return of the Prodigal Son") oscillates between mockery, remembrance of the body's former enslavement, and vengeful violence against the memory of the body. FirstLove rebels against the love ("MY HEART") that betrays her. In a double sense, then, the woman's body represents enslavement/prostitution and betrayal. How can it, at the same time, represent revolutionary emancipation, beginning with the reappropriation of the "traces" of her desire, and the rebellion against her lover, if the betrayal of her own love for Debuisson is self-destructive and, in any case, unsuccessful?

WHEN I AM DEAD/MY DUST WILL CRY OUT FOR YOU.

One cannot simply argue that Müller inscribes his allegory of death—the death of revolution and the standstill of the historical dialectic—on the woman's body or the prostitute body. It is nonetheless remarkable how much the allegory, in the sense I have applied the term to Müller's scenographies, becomes or literally writes itself as a scene of the *feminine body* and a *Trauerspiel* of the sexual and political economy of dead labor, as if the body of the prostitute were to be the privileged, even mythic site for a transfiguration of destructive violence.

Herakles' suicidal battle with the Hydra is *productive* labor after all, since Herakles destroys himself *as* he learns to be the subject of the historical process:

> he learned to read the continually changing plans of the machine which he ceased to be and again was different with each glance grip step, and he learned that he thought changed wrote it with the signature of his labors and deaths.[24]

The body of the nameless FirstLove, however, does not write history, it does not act. If it still appears as a threatening figure of revolutionary power (a castrating Medusa)[25], it does so only as a kind of radical myth of sexually uncontrolled nature, a myth that provokes fear in the men (Debuisson, Hamlet, Jason) who would like to see their impotence and their guilt mirrored in the Other. Müller exploits this mythic fear—the men in his recent plays play no role other than that of the failure of intellectual reflection and the inability to recover a lost task (including the loss of the Brechtian *Einverständnis* with the correct revolutionary tactics depicted in *The Measures Taken* and the learning play model). It is the women figures who speak, through their victimized bodies, of an unpredictable, unrepresentable resistance to history: a pure state of anarchic potential.

In the final tableau of *Hamletmachine*, OPHELIA/ELECTRA is again such a double rhetorical figure speaking through the limits (the frozen surface of the image) of the body:

FIERCELY ENDURING
MILLENNIUMS
IN THE FEARFUL ARMOR
[*The deep sea. Ophelia in a wheelchair. Fish, debris,
dead bodies and limbs drift by*]
OPHELIA
[*While two men in white smocks wrap gauze around her
and the wheelchair, from bottom to top*]
This is Electra speaking. In the heart of darkness. Under the sun of torture. To the capitals of the world. In the name of the victims. I eject all the sperm I have received. I turn the milk of my breasts into lethal poison. I take back the world I gave birth to. I choke between my thighs the world I gave birth to. I bury it in my womb. Down with the happiness of submission. Long live hate and contempt, rebellion and death. When she walks through your bedrooms carrying butcher knives you'll know the truth.[26]

Although the terror of revenge of which Ophelia/Electra speaks cannot be enacted or scenically represented, and can therefore only be called a revolutionary myth without historical reality, it is clearly located inside the discourse of women, "in the name of the victims." As the Hamlet-actor has nothing more to say ("My drama doesn't happen anymore. . . . The set is a monument. . . . The petrification of a hope") and wishes to be a machine ("Arms for grabbing Legs to walk on, no pain no thoughts"), the immobilization of the tortured bodies grows into screaming revolt whose language extends away from a particular figure (OPHELIA speaking Electra) to all the victimized, in the name of women. "Ophelia/Electra" is not an acting "role" or a living image of women's actual violence. It is unavoidable to read the pain of wounded and oppressed bodies back into a feminist discourse that has already found the asymmetrical and sacrificial structure of dominant cultural representations to reside precisely in the "feminization" or exclusion of the Other whose representations (of herself) are denied all authority. The Other's historically and socially constructed difference, has always supported the phallocratic order of symbolic representation. The attack on representation, argues Craig Owens in reference to such feminist writers and artists as Luce Irigaray, Hélène Cixous, Julia Kristeva, Michèle Montrelay, Laurie Anderson, and Martha Rosler, has exposed a symbolic structure that excludes women only to let them return into it *as a figure* for the unrepresentable (Nature, Truth, the Sublime, etc.).[27] In his effort to find a convergence between feminism and the deconstructive impulse in postmodernism, Owens goes on to suggest that such a figure of exclusion and reappearance must make "Woman" the "ruin of representation" (Montrelay). Her exteriority to the masculine imperialism of Western representation in fact stakes out its limits.

Unself-consciously appropriating feminist theory and, presumably, the terrible truth of "woman" whose irrepresentable desire obliterates the order, the male critic here resembles the male playwright whose scenography of the feminine body's revolt appropriates and mimes an *écriture feminine* which, as in Hélène Cixous's "Sorties," for example, impassionedly incarnates a savage imagining of liberation "immediately outside all law."[28] If one thinks of Cixous and Clément's reinscription of the tropes of the sorceress and the hysteric onto the desire and body of woman in order to allow her to repossess the "dark continent" reviled and displaced by anxious patriarchal tradition, one is tempted to see the work of such women performance artists as Rachel Rosenthal, Linda Montano, Karen Finley, Lily Tomlin, Carolee Schneemann, or Laurie Anderson (the latter now bravely at home with advanced technological simulations of the body, of any body) as expressions of the extreme—and sometimes violent and obscene—validation of the fluidity and *jouissance* of the woman body.

All of these artists emphasize a desire to stage the personal body (through autobiographical stories, fantasies, travelogs, and so forth) as a receptacle of this culture's violence, as a site of woman's construction as commodity[29], and as a countermodel of pleasure (cf. Silvia Kolbowski's work on "Model Pleasure") that could disrupt the reconstruction of the same discriminating symbolic order, and of our ideologically and historically conditioned ways of perceiving and acting.

Unfortunately, the theatre has always welcomed the disruptions of witchcraft and hysteria, since they are part of the ghosts and myths of alterity exchanged and appropriated within the continuous economy of its family drama (at least since the *Oresteia*). Performance art's romanticizing emphasis on feminine sexuality as the "Other," marking the limit of transgression and challenging the coercive power structure of representation and theatre, has been trapped in the oedipalized logic of hierarchical oppositions that forecloses a body *outside* of the language, outside of history.

Brecht's theatre, claimed by some feminists[30] as a model for their own dramaturgical disruptions of ideologically embodied gender and class relations, never romanticized the opposition of the body. Nor did it escape the monologues of power either: the heavy artillery of Marxism and the *Ver-*

fremdungseffekt did not ruin the logic of authority and opposition. In the learning plays, the actors play/criticize the characters (the revolutionaries and failed revolutionaries) and await the explanations of the Chorus, which takes on the familiar role of the legitimate Father.

As Heiner Müller reverses Brechts's privileged collective authority[31], the chorus has disappeared, and the oedipal family, fully assembled in *Hamletmachine*'s parodic citations of Shakespeare, is no longer physically on stage. Their names transform into sliding signifiers.

"In defense against the anarchic-natural matriarchy, the re-construction of the rebellious son into the father-figure begins," comments Müller on Brecht's paternalism.[32] Müller's own defense *of* anarchic-natural matriarchy takes a curious turn, however, when he displaces the figure of the mad victimized daughter ("Ophelia") onto "Electra", disembodied "before the law" (Cixous). He rejects her sexuality even as she speaks in the oppositional voice that I have just discussed, which Craig Owens maps onto the "Third World nations, the 'revolt of nature,' and the women's movement."[33]

But this mapping should not be romanticized either, because it invades and thus recolonizes "non-Western" territories, reconstituting them *within* the familiar totality. If "Ophelia/Electra" speaks in the name of difference, immobilized and wrapped up into a wheelchair, she is limited to a vision of death within the horizon of Jason's territory, his dying "landscapes with Argonauts."

Wilson's Landscapes of Death

Robert Wilson's 1986 productions of *Alcestis* (at the ART in Cambridge) and *Hamletmachine* (at New York University) confront the frozen dialectical images in Müller's texts with all the potently rich splendor of First World theatre, sucking the political thought out of the images and spilling a cool, architectonic-technological brilliance over the stage. Wilson's soundscapes in *Alcestis*, with the murmur of Müller's *Bildbeschreibung* text *(Description of a Picture/Explosion of a Memory)* endlessly repeated and refracted across the electronically amplified space of the auditorium, and the designed tableaux erected to simulate (with grand operatic illusionism) an archaic mountain landscape overlooking the remnants of civilization, produced a Wagnerian total theatre desperately trying to include everything. Originally intended to adapt Euripides' drama of death and resurrection, Wilson's collaboration with Müller apparently made him take seriously the playwright's cunning allusion to the various filmic and literary images and narrative particles quoted in the text of *Description of a Picture*:

> *Bildbeschreibung* may be read as an overpainting of Euripides' *Alcestis* which quotes the Noh play *Kumasaka*, the Eleventh Canto of the *Odyssey*, and Hitchcock's *The Birds*. The text describes a landscape beyond death. The action is optional since its consequences are past, explosion of a memory in an extinct dramatic structure.[34]

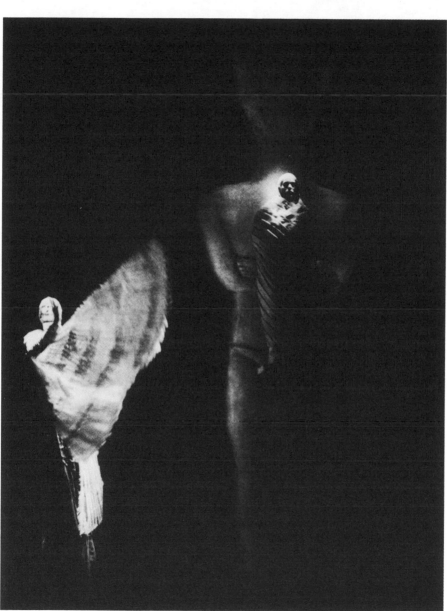

Figure 10. Robert Wilson's *Alcestis,* based on a play
by Euripides, with additional text by Heiner Müller.
American Repertory Theatre, 1986. Photo: Richard
Feldman.

Surprisingly, to many of us who have seen his painterly theatre of images of the past ten years (including the Stalin and Einstein operas and *the CIVIL warS*), Wilson here returns to the gods of the old drama. Its resurrection, which one might have deemed impossible after Beckett, turns into a bleakly parodic waiting for a *deus ex machina* that arrives in the bungling figure of Herakles and, finally, in the form of a laser beam that burns a peephole into the primordial mountain landscape. The god Apollo hangs upside-down stage right, the libations he is pouring floating upward. The mountain covers up the horizon; frozen faces seem to have oxidized into the rock, the bow of a ship (a stranded Argo?) juts through the ground. In front of the mountain, the river of death cuts its way from one side of the ART stage to the other. Alcestis and two Alcestis doubles (all three women performers wrapped into large white shrouds) disappear into the river, receding gently into the death she takes upon herself on behalf of King Admetus, who refuses to die. Equally gently, falling rocks glide down from the mountain top; a stegosaurus slowly crawls past crumbled, inorganic matter, and the entropic landscape gradually transforms itself, like a peeling fresco, into an apocalyptic vista, with its three trees upstage left exploding into fiery smokestacks that look like launched nuclear missiles.

This mythic cycle of Time is scenographically written into the strange mirroring of the nature landscape by the self-sacrificing Alcestis, who is reduced to the silence of alien matter. Its pathos results from the iconographic centrality of the landscape, lit in powerfully auratic colors: red, blue, deep purple. Within this landscape, dramatic characters and emotions are irrelevant; the proletarian Herakles, who pisses into the river and cracks vulgar jokes about Zeus, makes their triviality abundantly clear. But the actors have disappeared too, and what is left of the dispersed human voices mingles in the voice-over with the sounds of water, birds, dogs, helicopters, African chants, and electronically generated music. Laurie Anderson composed the score for the Kyogen vignette, *The Bird-catcher in Hell*, which brings a satirical Asiatic conclusion to the Western pathos of the performance. When we see human figures on stage—in the prologue they are called "Woman on platform," "Man on platform," "Woman on chair," and so forth—they are solely defined by their geometric position in the landscape and by their stylized, often Oriental movements choreographed by Suzushi Hanayagi. When performers cross the stage, they walk in slow motion, as if they had risen from the grave. We become aware of some abstract gestural language that we do not understand, foreign alphabets that are as irreducible as the weight and gravity of the objects that lie on stage. In their ritualized gestures, the bodies of the performers seem already ossified and statuesque, like the immobile "Wrapped Figure" protruding from the vulva of the huge Cycladic statue downstage right. That figure, in an androgynous voice, ejaculates Müller's picture description throughout the performance.

Wilson's production, with its stunning mythical landscape of death, manages to "overpaint" both Euripides' *Alcestis* and Müller's *Description*, even as some of his stage pictures (one could sometimes call them silent movies) seem directly linked to Müller's frightening attempt to name the possible end of all stories.

> when the growth of graveyards will have reached its limits with the small weight of the presumed murderer on the threshold. . . .
> (or) is the total picture an experimental arrangement, the crude design an expression of contempt for the guinea pigs: man, bird, woman, the blood-pump of the daily murder, man against bird and woman, woman against bird and man, bird against woman and man. . . .
> wanted: the gap in the process, the Other in the recurrence of the Same, the stutter in the speechless text, the hole in eternity, the perhaps saving ERROR.[35]

But Wilson is not interested in the construction of the Alcestis myth either. He tells the story of her self-sacrifice as if it had always been a natural part of this eternal landscape and will continue to be so. His beautiful images of mourning performed by the Chorus have really nothing at all to do with Müller's ambivalent speculation on the terror of murderous repetition, the "daily murder" in the slaughterhouse of history ("the perhaps daily—murder of the—perhaps daily—resurrected woman"), and the unknown terror of the moment when the description of that history ceases to function:

> insecurity strikes like lightning with the certainty of the ultimate horror: MURDER is an exchange of sexes, ALIEN IN YOUR OWN BODY, the knife is the wound . . . is the man doing the dance step: I, my grave his face, I: the woman with the wound at her throat . . . I: the frozen storm[36]

The moment when all the murderous signs and languages of representation become inert in a dissolution *(Entgrenzung)* of historical and subjective experience can be anticipated only with the destructive violence of an allegory that—as an image of "petrified anxiety" *(erstarrte Unruhe)*[37]—does not know what will have been (the revolt of Third World nations, of "nature", of the women's movement, or, rather, of death itself), nor does it mystify what has always been.

The deep and deeply disturbing fascination with death and its explosive force in Müller's text crystallizes the utopian element in the catastrophic "frozen storm" that could alter or end history. In response to these pressures that nearly break down the text, Wilson's grand opera is only the vain posturing of an irresponsible aesthetic self-consciousness that hides its political innocence behind the mask of ritualistic theatre magic.

That Müller's texts can be so easily coopted into Wilson's postmodern spectacles gives one pause. After seeing Wilson direct *Hamletmachine* on a much smaller scale in the studio theatre of New York University, I would argue that the pressure on the theatre to produce redundant images reveals the extent to which postmodern design and fashion have become a purely seductive surface. It is now fashionable to watch a Wilson show without bothering to ask questions about its contents, as if the viewing merely confirmed our absence from a concrete historical scene. In his staging of *Hamletmachine*, Wilson relinquishes any attempt to interpret or even illustrate Müller's scenography of the "frozen storm" that presses the feminine discourse of the "anarchic-natural" into the wheelchair of passive cultural nihilism. Completely separating the acoustic score of Müller's text (live amplified and taped voices) from the single visual stage tableau that is choreographically constructed and repeated five times in five different angles, Wilson here lets the text create its own plasticity, an "other" space that is not seen but heard.

I would have preferred a perfectly empty stage, a representation disappeared into the voice of a picture that did not own the images, a disembodied voice separated from itself (voices gliding over one another) in the washed-out topography of sound:

> I was Hamlet. I stood at the shore and talked with the surf BLA BLA BLA, the ruins of Europe in back of me.[38]

Its trajectory becomes the paralysis of language itself (the wrapped up figure of "Ophelia/Electra's" protest). Instead, Wilson shuffles the one page of his "visual book" against the language material of the "audio book,"[39] producing the abstracted and fragmented gestural lines of a cubist machine landscape that turns around its own axis. Fourteen student actors

Figure 11. Robert Wilson's *Hamletmachine*, based on the play by Heiner Müller. New York University, 1986. Photo: Bob Marshak.

("Woman at table #1," "Woman at table #2," "Woman at table #3," "Man standing upright," and so on) are moved inside the black box like marionettes, their ritualized postures following some strange unknown logic that comes full circle when we have seen the repetitions from all four sides. Perhaps we are seeing the purely mathematical logic of a machine, with all its parts functioning according to programmed movements. The movements seem different for each of the men; Why is one of them balancing on one leg? Why is another one raising his right hand, peering over a low, corrugated wall on the edge of the picture? Why do the three identical women at the table, who look like actresses from the golden age of Hollywood, turn their blank gaze and smile at the audience?

I imagine that Wilson's visual book is the emblem of a postmodern machine—the transparent, hollow faces and bodies of its serialized parts operating as perspectival simulations of a world or a reality no longer experienceable except as an "imaginary catastrophe," as Baudrillard would say. Wilson's *Hamletmachine* is an adequate visual staging of Baudrillard's implosive gesturing:

> But in the end the Revolution signifies only this: that it has already taken place. . . . All things come to an end in their redoubled simulation—a sign that a cycle is completed . . . where everything is replayed before death, at which point everything falls over far behind the horizon of truth.[40]

Nothing remains of Müller's scenography of repressed male history, of the schizophrenic production of suicidal fantasies in the fascist and misogynist discourse of the Hamlet-actor, and of the silenced scream of the disembodied "anarchic-natural" figure of woman. Beneath the evasions, Wilson's picture design captures the "truth" of the radical impoverishment of postmodern culture.

Medea

A landscape is such a natural arrangement for a battlefield or a play that one must write plays.
Gertrude Stein

This last section must necessarily be short and incomplete. I started out with a reference to Berlin and the time wall that divides East from West. I tried to think of the historical continuum in terms of the Benjaminian dialectical break between prehistory and posthistory, and in terms of the conceptual territories crossed in postmodernist discourses and art searching for their "otherness" or their constitutive post-historical moment. Heiner Müller's break with Brecht and the subsequent move toward the aesthetic avant-gardism of the West, made me wonder to what extent my own displacement to Dallas, though hardly comparable to Benjamin's passage from Berlin to Paris, might have reinforced the significance I attributed to image and body spaces as *landscapes* (or city topographies) that function as central theatrical metaphors in the texts I looked at.

I have only just begun to work with the concept of "landscape" in performance, but I now see that Müller's scenographies clearly relate to a difference between the experience of the decay and overaccumulation in the old European cities of industrial capitalism and the more unsettling experience of the amorphous and dispersed sprawl of the postindustrial metropolis. Before I came to explore Müller's metaphors of the brutalized and dispersed body, and especially the terminal images ("ALIEN IN YOUR OWN BODY") in *Description of a Picture,* I was struck by the discontinuous body of the "synthetic fragments" themselves, quite apart from the fact that they more closely resemble a "natural arrangement for a battlefield" than a play.

In 1982 Müller completed the text collage *Despoiled Shore Medeamaterial Landscape with Argonauts.* It turns out that bits and pieces of the texts were written fifteen-thirty years earlier, reconstructed into a string of associations that now seem to synthesize images of contemporary realities with images of the earliest myth of colonization (Jason/Argonauts). In an introductory note Müller says that because the texts are happening "simultaneously," any particular sequence would be arbitrary. He adds: *"Despoiled Shore* can be performed in a peep show, for example, as part of the regular presentation. *Medeamaterial* at a lake near Straussberg that is a muddy swimming pool in Beverly Hills or the baths of a psychiatric hospital. *Landscape with Argonauts* presumes the catastrophes which mankind is working toward. The theatre's contribution to their prevention can only be their representation. The landscape might be a dead star where a task force from another age or another space hears a voice and discovers a corpse. As in every landscape, the I in this segment of the text is collective."[41]

In the fall of 1986 I began working on my own adaptation of *Description of a Picture* for the stage; our Dallas project was entitled *Description of a Landscape.* I was particularly interested in the two interrelated notions of collectivity and simultaneity, and I decided to break the continuity of the *Description* text (a dense, five-page, single-sentence poem) by inserting a dialectical image constructed out of a condensed Medea monologue (from *Medeamaterial*) and the "Elevator" monologue (from *The Task*). Both insert texts, I believe, gain a new and particularly concrete legibility within the more abstract "landscape beyond death." In fact, the direct and violent conjunction of the postrevolutionary male discourse (Elevator) and the genuinely different, anarchic voice of "Medea" seemed to provide the crucial historical grounding that our performance would have. It was also important, then, that we found our own points of departure, in our bodies and their histories and in the materials they joined (texts, objects, light, sound, physical space, film and video projections, and so forth), for the performance of a landscape on an other side in an "other" network of viewpoints, discourses, images, and temporalities. But on what side, of the picture, of the description?

But what vantage point is left for human subjects who have become many-sided, no longer at home in one body, one city or land, and who are disappeared—like the disseminated capital which Paul Virilio links to the disappearance of politics (the State) and of space itself[42]—across the homogenous surface of a boundaryless world of shifting arrangements?

We felt that the most challenging aspect of Müller's scenographies is their focus on the limit of the body as a false boundary between the living and the dead, between nonreversible inscriptions that would identify and oppose the victimizer and the victimized in the daily murder. But in order to show the reversibility of history in the theatre we would have to show that we have not yet become "alien" enough in our own bodies to overcome the old divisions (masculine/feminine, strong/weak, public/private, and so on) that cut across the tissues of memories and internalized behaviors.

As our work progressed, the performance began to move toward this threshold where we can hear, but not see, the language—Müller's one, endlessly long sentence compounding the picture—itself turn into an alien property and gradually lose its order of grammar and syntax. The increasing complexity of the multitrack audio landscape, created for us by American composer Randal Davis, builds a field of sound in which the heard voices recede more and more away from "naturalistic" recitatives and dialogues (single female and female/female voice couples). The destination is a distance from which the English language can still be recognized but not really understood and imagined since the musical properties (pitch level, tonality, rhythm, cadence, and flow, of the male/female voice couple) are confounded and "denaturalized." The hearer questions the horizon of the picture, while still visually locked into the perceivable contradiction (a kind of reverse movement) between the old order (Elevator) and its preceding scene of Medea's violent renunciation of the passage she has traveled from Colchis to Corinth/Dallas.

The Elevator man presents himself as a functionary of a bureaucratic system who has become trapped in a machinery he no longer comprehends. When the elevator in which he travels goes out of order, he loses all sense of time and place:

> I step from the elevator at the next stop and I stand without any task on a village street in Peru. . . . Two gigantic natives stand in front of a billboard advertising products of a foreign civilization. A menace emanates from their back. . . .
> How will communication be possible, I don't know the language of this country, I could as well be deaf mute.[43]

The man outside the elevator finds himself in a foreign landscape, bereft of any historical task and incapable to understand why this other world (he describes it as "no-man's land") is indifferent to his fearful reasoning:

> What is my crime. The world hasn't been destroyed, provided this isn't another world. How do you accomplish an unknown task. What could my task be in this wasteland on the other side of civilization.[44]

The completely static scene of this monologue in our performance follows the very differently choreographed movements of the "Medea" scene. There we tried to intimate the return of the repressed in two ways: in a violent, anguished dance of two women performers who examine the traces of violence on their bodies, and in the cold, extremely distanced and rhythmically deformed recitation of Medea's revenge, a speech all the more powerful if the actress can indeed stand outside of the emotional images she wants to disown.

> My first and my last
> Where is my husband
> How are you living in the ruins of your body
>
> When does this end
> When did it begin
>
> Does this body mean nothing
>
> I own the images of those slain
> I own the screams of the tortured
> I left my home to follow your bloody tracks
> Treason is now my only home
>
> I want to cut you right out of my heart
> My flesh my remembrance my beloved
> Give back to me my blood out of your veins
> Back into my womb who are my entrails
> Can you laugh now Death is but a present. . . .
>
> I want to break mankind apart in two
> And live within the empty middle I
> I
> I
> No woman
> No man[45]

Words and bodies separate, but the silent expressions of the body are not optional because the consequences lie ahead of us. If the violated body disappears—

> Now it is all quiet
> The screams silenced too
> And nothing is left
> And nothing is left
> And nothing is left

—then the act of disappearance must be radical in order to create the possibility of a different return. Medea's collective "I" ("no woman no man") speaks for another history that cannot yet be seen, least of all in the old theatre. Her gesture, at this point, tries to reverse the catastrophe that just goes on creating an unfillable void.

Post-Script

Description of a Landscape was performed on the stage of the UTD University-Theatre in Dallas in February and March of 1987. The performance presented the "Description" as an audio-landscape of fields of sounds and voices, which overpainted the presence of eleven performers on stage. Their gestural movements, individually and collectively, formed a sequence of physical expressions that followed their own independent visual rhythms and accents. All the bodily gestures asked the same question: how familiar is the thought of being "alien in your own body?" In response to this question, the performers searched for their bodies and for a possible relationship to what has been lost or is being lost. Sometimes the performers increased their efforts; at other times they seemed to have abandoned the hope for an answer that would lead away from the all-too-familiar time and place that we hear about "on this side" of the "Description."

As I mentioned earlier, the performance was interrupted twice: first by the return of "Medea" and her recollections dance; and secondly by the report of the Elevator man telling of his incomprehensible arrival on the scene of a foreign civilization. On stage throughout the performance, two monitors with (single channel) video images provided a source of artificial light and occasionally showed "still lives." These "still lives" were composed of reverse images of human faces and of stills from a desert landscape (shot in West Texas) from which the human body and any sign of history and culture are absent. One very short sequence of video images, ironically juxtaposing the "still lives," presented a few broken allusions to "mythic landscapes" excerpted from a Hitchcock film and *"Roadrunner"* cartoons.

The performance onstage ended when the "Description" ran out. The final tableau froze the performers into ambivalent gestures that recapitulated the incomplete search for a new body or a new "play" that would not be the same battlefield.

The space of the stage was then invaded by a large screen lowered from the ceiling. After it had covered half the stage we began to screen the 16mm film "Daughter Courage" by Alan Sondheim. Its intense, almost unbearably fast-moving and frenzied collage of superimposed images was also interrupted twice: first by a very slow-moving interview during which the filmmaker questions the romantic pathos in Heiner Müller's writing; and secondly by a sequence of images that refer the audience to the "outside" of the theatre, i.e., to the real political and social landscapes of Dallas, as well as Central American countries (Nicaragua, El Salvador, Mexico) south of the border. The film's impression of a reality *on the other side,* in this sense, was much stronger than anything that was achievable on the theatre stage itself.

When I spoke of incompleteness, therefore, I was mainly referring to my continuing doubts, during and after the Dallas production of *Description of a Landscape:* whether a "live performance" of Müller's work can adequately perform a critical response to his vision of the Western culture's brutal contempt and masochistic guilt in its seemingly permanent state of defeated political illusions. If Müller's "Landscape" is the ice age of such defeated illusions, then probably the theatre cannot but magnify that defeat. It implies that we—the alienated spectators and performers in the Western territories where revolutionary thought and action have petrified and disappeared—have run out of political options.

Those lie elsewhere, removed from the imagination and the rhetoric of our Western intellectual and aesthetic representations. To stage a deadly landscape, to bring it *alive* on our stage, then, may not at all help us to see the relationship between the pathos of Müller's murderous vision of defeat and the theatre's own current incapacity to imagine a different reality.

After these reflections, I decided not to recreate the work when I was invited to show it in Houston during the winter of 1987/88. I decided instead to transform *Description of a Landscape* from a theatre performance into a museum exhibition in order to shift Müller's terminal vision from the present to the past. In other words, I wanted to create a space that preserves artworks and remnants of foreign cultures for our viewing and our retrospective understanding.

Installing the "Landscape" in a museum space offered the possibility of distancing both Müller's preoccupation with the Old World and its crumbling ideologies and his connection with Wilson's theatre of images that conceals this language with its grand display of beautiful and mysterious pictures.

The installation that I prepared for the Lawndale Art Center in Houston also allowed a more concrete engagement of the difference between seeing and hearing a landscape. The difference between the hearing of the seen and the seeing of the heard is a critical question that contemporary experimental theatre owes to Gertrude Stein without having acknowledged the depth of that question.

I wanted to find out what there is left to see (or to hear) once all the illusions (and their pictures) are gone. The exhibition, consequently, presented the dissolution of the visible in the dissolution of the union of sound and image. The "Description" sound installation described a landscape as if it were from another planet. The space itself was frozen into a cold blue light with nothing left in it except a few traces of familiar objects—a few chairs, a table, a pair of shoes, a coat, a plastic sack—and a few hieroglyphic traces of writing on the wall.

The banality of these objects and the emptiness of the space did not answer the questions raised by Müller's description: "Who or what is asking for this picture?" There was no picture. Rather, the space and what was left in it (the remnants of a former theatre set perhaps) referred back to

Figures 12, 13, 14. *Description of a Landscape,* performance-exhibition based on a text by Heiner Müller. Lawndale Art Center, Houston, 1988. Photos: J. Birringer.

the failed resolution immanent in the "Description," and to a different question not heard in the text: Who or what is asking for this description?

A very large audience appeared on opening night and filled the space for an hour, two hours. Eventually they thought that they may have come too late, or that the show had already been closed or abandoned, or that they were listening back to some paleolithic writing that had survived history, bringing them face to face with each other.

NOTES

1. Cf. Walter Benjamin, *Understanding Brecht*, trans. Anna Bostock (London: Verso, 1984), 8–9.

2. Cf. Karl Marx, *The 18th Brumaire of Louis Bonaparte* (New York: International Publishers, 1984), 15–20. For a highly charged if strenuous attempt to rescue Marx's and Brecht's "humor," spiced up with the now fashionable reference to Bakhtin's carnival, see Terry Eagleton, *Walter Benjamin; or Towards a Revolutionary Criticism* (London: Verso, 1985), esp. 143–72.

3. See Benjamin's theory of allegory and the baroque and romantic conceptions of the ruin in *The Origin of German Tragic Drama*, trans. John Osborne (London: NLB, 1977) and, in comparison, his later "Theses on the Philosophy of History," in *Illuminations*, ed. Hannah Arendt (New York: Harcourt, Brace & Jovanovich, 1969), 253–64. I am especially interested in the unfinished project of historical materialism as it is emblematically written into Benjamin's complex struggle to progress from his antihistoricist "Theses" on historical process to the topography of "dialectical images" with which he interprets the phantasmagoria of capitalist economy and technological modernity from which we are still trying to awaken. See his fragmentary *Passagen-Werk*, ed. Rolf Tiedemann, in *Gesammelte Schriften*, vol. V (Frankfurt: Suhrkamp, 1982).

4. After his early, Brecht-inspired production plays and learning plays of the 1950s and 1960s (*Der Lohndrücker, Die Korrektur, Die Umsiedlerin, Mauser, Zement*, and so forth), and his revisionist adaptations of Greek mythology (*Herakles 5, Philoktet, Oedipus, Prometheus*), Müller began to speak of his texts as "synthetic fragments" in the mid-seventies. We can trace the beginning of this collage technique to his play *GERMANIA TOD IN BERLIN* (1971), which also marks his departure from the model of Brecht's epic dramaturgy.

5. Text quotations, if not otherwise noted, are from *Hamletmachine and Other Texts for the Stage*, ed. and trans. Carl Weber (New York: PAJ Publications, 1984); this reference to *Landscape with Argonauts*, 134.

6. Ibid., 133

7. Ibid.

8. Ibid., 135

9. Kafka's depiction of the fascinating indifference of the "power system" to any humanist-subjectivist appeals to truth and validity, guilt or innocence, strikingly anticipates current Nietzschean speculations on abstract dead power among French poststructuralists. Abandoning political and representational theories of power, the poststructuralists now celebrate the determinism with which Adorno and Horkheimer posited the self-liquidation of the Enlightenment through its own irrational, technological fascism. The Kafkaesque writings of Jean Baudrillard are a prominent symptom of the progressive self-liquidation.

10. "Herakles 2 or the Hydra," in *Cement*, trans. Helen Fehervary, Sue-Ellen

Case, and Marc D. Silberman, New German Critique Publication, suppl. to issue no. 16 (Winter 1979): 39.

11. See, for example, Gordon Rogoff's admiring review of Wilson's production of *Hamletmachine* at New York University in May 1986, *Performing Arts Journal* 28 (1986): 54–57. See also the naive fascination in David J. Derose's review of Wilson's *Alcestis* and *Hamletmachine* in *Theatre Journal* 39, no. 1 (1987): 89–91.

12. See Jean Baudrillard, *Simulations* (New York: semiotext(e), 1983); *In the Shadow of the Silent Majorities* (New York: semiotext(e), 1983); and, especially, his critique of "referential illusions" (power, sexuality, production, capital, history) in *Forget Foucault* (New York: semiotext(e), 1987); 9–64.

13. Jean-François Lyotard theorizes postmodernism's break with history and the "dialectic of enlightenment" as the exhaustion of all "master narratives" and the dispersion of knowledge into so many dissociated and self-referential "language games." See his *The Postmodern Condition: A Report on Knowledge,* trans. Geoff Bennington and Brian Massumi (Minneapolis: Univ. of Minnesota Press, 1984).

14. "Forget Baudrillard; An Interview with Sylvère Lotringer," in *Forget Foucault,* 91:109–14.

15. "Theory has an immediate effect—a very material one as well—of being a void. It's not so easy to create a void. And besides, there's catastrophe all around it. I don't see how theory and reality can go together." *Forget Foucault,* 129.

16. This is the well-known formulation used by Jürgen Habermas in his critique of postmodernist theory and its mythic embrace of the self-destruction of Western civilization. His insistence on the continuity of rationalist thought and practice does not help to explain, however, why scientific rationality itself must *forget* its own history of destruction and nihilism. See "Modernity versus Postmodernity," *New German Critique* 22 (Winter 1981): 3–14, and *Die Neue Unübersichtlichkeit* (Frankfurt: Suhrkamp, 1985).

17. "To Use Brecht without Criticizing Him Is to Betray Him," *Theater* 17, no. 2 (1986): 31. This essay appeared originally under the title "Fatzer ± Keuner," in *Brecht Jahrbuch 1980* and in *Rotwelch* (Berlin: Merve, 1982), 140–49.

18. Quoted from *The Task* (1979), in *Hamletmachine,* 93. The play's subtitle is "Memory of a Revolution" and its treatment of the "revolutionary model" is crucial for an understanding of Müller's recent preoccupation with the death of the First World.

19. Ibid., 100–101.

20. "Schreiben aus Lust an der Katastrophe" ("writing out of lust for catastrophes") is a phrase Müller used in a conversation with Horst Laube in 1981, published under the same title in *Rotwelch,* pp. 179–85. Perhaps in reference to Deleuze and Guattari's notion of "flight lines," Müller then argued for the need of a "diffuse movement" in his writing in order to resist the almost automatic process of fetishization and insitutionalization (i.e. the successful cultural legitimation of the Marxist playwright for the art market in the West) with which its intentions would be integrated into theatrical repertoires. It is significant, in this connection, that Müller compares this resistance with intractable, uncontainable landscapes that withstand the technological and bureaucratic administration of capitalism: "like the sight of the Mississippi delta, where industrial factories are rotting in the swamps. There is something incredibly beautiful about capitalism when it has reached its limit. That limit is the landscape" (183).

21. Cf. *The Task,* 87.

22. In Adorno and Horkheimer's critical theory of the "dialectic of enlightenment," the self-destructiveness of enlightenment is understood as the return of the blind, repressed myth in modern rationality itself. That return is disguised, in the bloodbaths of inner and outer colonization, as historical progress, instrumental reason, and bureaucratic power. The close affinity of Müller's evocations of the "angel of death" to Benjamin's "Angelus Novus" has been noticed so often that we

needn't elaborate the issue. For Benjamin, the ruins of destruction have piled up: the angel's look is transfixed by the spectacle of progress. "That things just go on *is* the catastrophe" *(Central Park)*. In the Passagen-Werk, Benjamin treats modern rationality and the progress of capitalism as a passage from the dream-sleep of childhood prehistory (the mythic and archaic figures of nineteenth-century industrialization) to the posthistory of capitalist reification and commodification. There the ruins of nature (the "dead" woman's body of the prostitute is a crucial allegory of the perverse triumph of the commodity) fulfill economic and technological development. Benjamin's theatre is not written as historical drama but as a constellation of images in an urban topography (Paris) that serves to illuminate the contradictions and tensions in the dream-economy of capitalism that push toward a historical awakening, an explosion of the internalized material culture of (the) capital.

23. *The Task*, 90–91.

24. *Cement*, 40.

25. Cf. Neil Hertz's fascinating discussion of revolutionary violence and the male fear of her monstrous face in "Medusa's Head: Male Hysteria under Political Pressure," *Representations* 1, no. 4 (1983): 27–54.

26. *Hamletmachine*, 58.

27. "The Discourse of Others: Feminists and Postmodernism," in *The Anti-Aesthetic: Essays on Postmodern Culture*, ed. Hal Foster (Port Townsend: Bay Press, 1983), 59. Commenting on feminist uses of and attacks against psychoanalysis, Owens criticizes Kristeva's identification of avant-garde practices as feminine, because he sees her concern with the pre-symbolic (Nature, the Unconscious, the body) reinforce "all the discourses which exclude woman from the order of representation" (78).

28. "Sorties: Out and Out: Attacks/Ways Out Forays," in Hélène Cixous and Catherine Clément, *The Newly Born Woman*, trans. Betsy Wing (Minneapolis: Univ. of Minnesota Press, 1986), 117. For a comprehensive critique of the veiled structures of representation in Western society that hide and repress women (and reproduce their systems of gender domination) in the place of the "Other," see Clément's chapter on "The Guilty One" (pp. 1–59). It would be a challenging task to read *The Newly Born Woman* against the masculinist schizoanalysis of Deleuze and Guattari's *Mille Plateaux* (Paris: Minuit, 1980), and especially their theories of deterritorialization, nomadology, and becoming other *(le devenir femme)*.

29. This inscription of prostitution or commodity on her body is addressed in Benjamin's *Passagen-Werk* with the constellation "exhibition," "fashion," and "advertisement," which treats the transformation of erotic life into a world of fetishism and mass consumption, thus anticipating the aesthetic recommodification of all images (regardless of real bodies) under postmodern capitalism.

30. Cf. Janelle Reinelt, "Beyond Brecht: Britain's New Feminist Drama, *Theatre Journal* 38, no. 2 (1986): 154–63, and Elin Diamond, "Brechtian Theory/Feminist Theory: Toward a Gestic Feminist Criticism," *The Drama Review* 32, no. 1 (1988): 82–94.

31. For an excellent analysis of Müller's reversals of the structural and ideological composition of Brecht's learning play, see Arlene Akiko Teraoka, " '*Der Auftrag*' und '*Die Massnahme*': Models of Revolution in Heiner Müller and Bertolt Brecht," *The German Quarterly* (Winter 1986): 65–84. Her extended argument about the "poetics" of Heiner Müller has appeared in her book *The Silence of Entropy or Universal Discourse: The Postmodernist Poetics of Heiner Müller* (New York: Peter Lang, 1985).

32. "Fatzer ± Keuner," 149, here quoted from Weber's translation in *Hamletmachine*, 18.

33. "Feminists and Postmodernism," 67.

34. Cf. Müller's comments on the writing and publication of his text in "The PAJ Casebook: Alcestis," *Performing Arts Journal* 28 (1986), 95.

35. *Description of a Picture*, quoted from *Performing Arts Journal*, 28 (1986), 108–109.

36. Ibid., 110.

37. *Passagen-Werk*, 412.

38. Quoted from the opening scenario ("Family Scrapbook") of *Hamletmachine*, 53.

39. For a discussion of Wilson's attempts to build a structural equality between discrete acoustical and visual scores (audio book/visual book), see John Rouse, "Robert Wilson, Texts and History: CIVIL warS, German Part," *Theater* 16, no. 1 (1984): 68–74. See also Wilson's comments on the visual book as "mask" in "PAJ Casebook: Alcestis," p. 102. I shall return to the problematics of the mask in my last chapter.

40. *Forget Foucault*, 50.

41. *Landscape with Argonauts*, 126.

42. Cf. Paul Virilio, *Speed and Politics*, trans. Mark Polizotti (New York: semiotext(e), 1986). See especially his chapters on "Unable Bodies" and "The State of Emergency."

43. *The Task*, 95.

44. Ibid., 96.

45. Cf. *Medeamaterial*, 128–33. The version I quote was the one we used in the performance of *Description of a Landscape*.

(In front of white curtain. A path in the mountains. Snow and sun. Enter Man and Woman. He wears wintercoat and hat; she carries a camera.)

Man.   Come here, I'll show you something. Here on the mountain-top, there's a place that I often visit. I think it's a crack in the Nature of Things. . . . One has a very special view.

                            (They look through the curtain.)

Look how they act! They repeat themselves again and again. They're doing the Past, can't keep off it. And once again from the beginning, the whole thing over again. You see, the rest is theatre. The last of our magic attempts to drive away our fear. . . .

Woman. What on earth are *we* doing there? A phantasm! An echo of vision!

                            Botho Strauss, *Kalldewey Farce*

3 ◼ ARCHAEOLOGY: TRACING THE GHOSTS IN THE THEATRE

The Death of Theatre?

Sadly yet predictably enough, it has become customary to write about theatre in a mournful and apologetic style, which is one way of acknowledging the embarrassing historical condition in which theatre finds itself. It is another way of saying that there is not much to defend anymore today, at a time when it is perhaps an exclusively academic question to ask oneself why major English poets of the Renaissance, for example, felt the need to defend the moral virtues and purposes of theatre against the Puritan critics, even as the public playhouses in London played a significant and productive role as cultural institutions.

    In the Catholic country I come from, theatre practitioners will forever continue to go through annual self-flagellation and self-doubt ("Why are we here?" "What are we doing?"), which mainly serves to underscore the bad faith of those in a profession trying to be high priests of high culture, trying desperately to justify their continued existence in a heavily subsidized system. There is a peculiar irony in the fact that this system still has its scandals, such as the recent debacle over the staging of Fassbinder's *Garbage, the City and Death,* cancelled after protesters accused it of "state-sponsored anti-Semitism." The controversy soon spread across all the media, and the theatre was never given a chance to exorcize the fears and polemical charges it had unleashed. The idea that such advanced censorship of the theatre evokes the very spectre of fascism that the protesters sought to repress did not occur to anyone.

Barely repressed guilt and its vicissitudes seem not to trouble the theatre, or what is left of it, in the United States. Such a country too large and too self-absorbed and too unself-conscious fails to notice how the globalizing effects of postindustrial capitalism and its dispersive media have detheatricalized any meaningful social and political metaphors of life.

In today's mass market of overproduced images and ubiquitous information circuitries, the imaginary has trouble surviving, since reality seems already always replaced by its simulations. The suspension of disbelief is becoming irrelevant: the theatre has no share in this market. As I tried to indicate earlier, in Baudrillard we now have a theoretician of the posttheatrical age, even though I doubt very much that he has ever been inside a theatre. In his nihilistic scenario for a society beyond theatre, things and meanings are in a state of demolition. Overrepresentation of objects and affects, as well as of the accidents and scandals of history, tends to make them dissolve into the total transparency of circular commutational media effects. (Baudrillard's favorite examples are Watergate and Disneyland, scenarios that both reveal and conceal a different reality.)

> When the real is no longer what it used to be, nostalgia assumes its full meaning. There is a proliferation of myths of origin and signs of reality. . . . Of the same order as the impossibility of rediscovering an absolute level of the real is the impossibility of staging an illusion. Illusion is no longer possible, because the real is no longer possible.[1]

There is a perverse persuasiveness in Baudrillard's contention that the impossibility of staging an illusion (which implies the end of theatre as a model of interpretation) correlates to the disappearance of politics, power, knowledge, and discourse in a circular mechanism that leaves all determinate positions afloat, simultaneously unbelievable and seductive.

It is no more perverse, however, than actually watching the American secretary of state address the 1986 International PEN Congress on the issue of "The Imagination of the State" by arguing that we are all in the same boat ("Don't be surprised by the fact that Ronald Reagan and I are on your side"). A few months later, after the brutal bombing of Libya, the same secretary defended the state's imagination by describing it in terms of a successful military operation ("surgical strike"). Perhaps it was that, including a certain "collateral damage" on the civilian population. Both success and damage are accomplishments of an increasingly unreal "freedom fight" that the paranoid U.S. foreign policy is carrying out throughout the world, dueling with the ghosts of terrorism, communism, and drug lords. Reagan's definition of "freedom fight" naturally seduced his successor: the invasion and forced "democratization" of Panama under the

Bush administration echoes all the phantasms of earlier protestations of power. The only difference will be that the claims behind this operation will appear even more suspect after the reappearance of self-determined popular revolutions on the other side of the white curtain in 1989.

A link between these unreal stakes of freedom and the stakes of theatre could perhaps be found in the nostalgia that characterized Arthur Miller's lament over the pervasive "self-parody" in contemporary American theatre. In a rather helpless allegorical statement made during the 1986 PEN Congress's small theatre session (held parallel to a very large general session on "Utopia"), Miller described the current theatre condition as "a landscape of hundreds of small brooks and rivulets, stagnant ponds and marshlands . . . a kind of wet area, drying year by year in the sun."

I would like to suggest, however, that such dried-up defeatism is not the only available response. The sudden appearance in the same year of Herbert Blau's two provocative and profoundly challenging books—*Take Up the Bodies* and *Blooded Thought*—reminded us that serious reflection on contemporary theatre practices has been almost altogether absent in the American public sphere. But with Blau's writings we are invited to struggle against this absence, to find its causes, and to raise the stakes. The worst-case scenario (Baudrillard's?) would be to avoid confronting Blau's books and to behave, like the silent majority of the American theatre community, as if they could not have (or have not already had) an impact.

What I shall attempt to do, then, is to engage Blau's discourse as a significantly advanced form of critical thinking at a crucial cultural moment when such a thinking through performance could raise new issues for those institutional, discursive, and interpretive practices on whose imaginary margins it has existed all along.

Survival Strategies

As I suggested in the beginning, a defense of theatre seems improbable at this historical moment, since it is not playing any formative, mediatory, or adversarial role in late capitalist culture. After thirty years of experience as a director, teacher, and critic, Herbert Blau would be the first to admit to this erosion of the public role of theatre. It is all too obvious that recent modes of mainstream American theatre and playwriting appear thoroughly uninspired, demoralized and, to many, pretty irrelevant. In view of the fact that the place of theatre in this culture is largely undefined or, worse still, has been subsumed under the relentless commodifications of a regressive Broadway-kitsch industry, it is equally predictable that critical discourse on theatre and performance is not considered a particularly worthwhile enterprise. A persistent lack of commitment to a critical exploration of this deficit can also be noticed within the academy. The curriculum planners in our English departments and humanities programs, though forced to be innovative in other areas, generally tend to be as misinformed about the marginalization of "legitimate" theatre as they are oblivious to the conceptual shifts that have taken place in recent practices of the experimental performing arts.

Avoiding a potentially fruitful contact with theatre departments and drama schools, mainstream university education continues to treat the subject in the way in which curators conserve their museums of old masterpieces. Surely, there will always be a place in the canon for that unforgettable actor/manager/playwright from Stratford, that touchstone for canon formation and cultural authority in the academy. The infrequent visits of the Royal Shakespeare Company to this country may even serve as occasions for a field trip to New York in order to find out what a superb permanent repertory company looks like: "occasions of theatre" (to borrow one of Blau's titles) that have been illuminating for students, teachers, and theatregoers, and infuriating to native companies tired of being measured against the British.

The general public, meanwhile, remains uninformed about the fate of what is left of serious experimental theatre. The failure of drama criticism or performance reviewing, much like that of current art and music criticism, matches the relative absence of an on-going critical dialogue between the artists themselves or the artists and their audiences. This breakdown of the "function of criticism"[2] in its relation to the contemporary culture industry is reflected in the merely minimal amount of writing on theatre and drama in professional periodicals, literary journals, and book reviews.

Literary criticism's lack of attention to theatre and to the specific, sociohistorically determined relations between texts and playwriting, performances, and the conditions of reception and interpretation are difficult to fathom, but they are most likely related to the inflationary growth of activities, and their ensuing atomization and isolation, both on the stage and within the academic institutions. The fragmentation of critical disciplines resembles pluralistic contemporary performance art, which is plagued, in a schizophrenic sense that Artaud would have appreciated, by all kinds of strenuous attempts to discover a style and a name, ranging from anthropological performance and reconstruction to deconstruction and Next Wave (leaving aside all those theatre productions that have no visible concept whatever).

Blau gives us an uncompromising, self-critical, and sometimes very biting account of the diffusions, pressures, and black-outs within the "Power-Structure" of the theatre industry under the general management of the Watergate comedians (TB 29–77)[3]. For him the current uncertainty and stagnation in the theatre's search for a "revolutionary praxis" (originally projected in Blau's first articulation of his political ideas in *The Impossible Theatre: A Manifesto* [1964]) boils down to its insufficiently rigorous confrontation with what *makes* it theatre as it is trying to forget what it is not. Theatre begins to work when it can trace and retrace the desire of its language to speak, to appear, to show, and to *think through* its elusive, vanishing yet "breathtaking" appearances in that space that is never empty, as Peter Brook suggested, but already there, structured by the order of representation binding all scenic, theatrical, verbal, and bodily languages to it. The desire, as Blau cheerfully acknowledges, is deadly. It yields moments, under pressure, that may bring back to consciousness what has been repressed; the fear, pride, grief, love, and exhaustion of the immensely vulnerable human presence, the actor putting himself or herself up to be seen and heard. The meaning is in the seeing, as one might suspect, but this is where all the problems start. Blau's self-reflexive writing allows no pause in its extraordinarily dense and convoluted tracings of the interrelations between seeing and seeming.

> Seeming is seminal. Psychosexual. In theatre, as in love, the subject is disappearance. That makes, in performance, for a sort of doubled jeopardy. Performance, to begin with, is always under suspicion. The lover knows by heart that it's a matter of credibility. Or paranoia, where the delirium of appearance covers up for stage fright. (TB 94)

The condition of appearance in the space of representation is language, and at the level of "enactable thought" (TB 91) Blau takes the whole problematics of performance and textuality in theatre to that space where we, as audience, see "the mirroring of language, world and theatre in the refractions of the performing self, a subject slipping away (but getting a lot of attention from the 'human sciences')" (TB 90). It is this dangerous "slipping" which pushes theatre to an edge of disappearance implied in Blau's notion of the "vanishing point." The key principles of Blau's theoretical reflection on theatrical praxis are situated at that curious borderline between perception and language, a borderline that cuts across the disciplines of the "human sciences" that concern themselves with the subject as representing subject and as being-subject, already subjected to a system of exchange. Blau opens up new possibilities for a discourse on performance by reconsidering the very specific model of production that theatre represents in the enactment of and play with the body of language and writing.

> Nowadays, various disciplines are concerned with language as it determines the logic and limit of thought, and what's on the other side of it. While the use of language in the theatre, or its absence, has been a major problem over the last generation, and I will discuss it, the stress will be on the theatre as a language desperately struggling beyond its limits to what, possibly, may be on the other side.
> What is remarkable about the other side is that it always appears to look like theatre; that is, it can only be represented. (TB xviii)

It is a good model, and a bad one as well, as Hamlet knows when he praises the "monstrous" dissimulation of the First Player representing his "dream of passion" (II.ii. 545–46),[4] and then goes ahead to rewrite and design the performance of his mousetrap for Claudius.

The theatre has a history of histrionics and hysteria (that it continuously rewrites) as well as a history of dreams that get trapped by the actor's forgetting what there *is* to be performed:

> Do it again, we say in rehearsal, in unconscious testament to an Eternal Recurrence. The Same, but not quite. Do *what*, however? The characters don't know, and maybe shouldn't. How can the actors be sure? The director is guessing. The play's the thing, we used to say, as if we knew what the play was. (*BT* 28)

This brings me back to my epigraph and the question of the forgetting of theatre. I shall try to speak about that conceptual problematic that determines the visibility or invisibility of the actors, our peculiar "Echo des Gesichts" (as The Woman in *Kalldewey Farce* calls him or her), which informs the theoretical practice one might, tautologically, call theatre theory. In fact, the two words—*theatron, theorós*—are of the same root; the Greek *theorein* derives from the coalescing of *thea* and *horao*, *thea* meaning the outward look, the aspect, in which something shows itself, and *horao* meaning to view closely. I must confess that I find it infinitely difficult to review or explain what Blau is doing in his two books, except that one could call his performance of writing them a "vanishing act" itself, a demonstration of what it means to think through the "burrowing" rehearsals, the interminable dreamwork, of the theatre's building of appearances.

Kafka's remarkable story, "The Burrow," is one of Blau's favorite allegories of the rehearsal process during which "blooded abstractions" spill over the perceptual space and assume bodies, proportions, shapes, rhythms, and aspects of a deeper "power structure" that provides the grammar of thinking through acting about acting (*TB* 103–08).

It is equally futile, if I understand Blau correctly, to consider the books a "guide" to theatre, drama, or a clearly definable method of acting based on a theory (in the sense in which one tends to think about Stanislavski's *An Actor Prepares*, for example, or Brecht's "Short Organum for the Theatre"). On the contrary, the books are "technical" only in the sense that they playfully exhibit the various intersections of discourses that in the past few decades have freely borrowed from the theatre in order to speak about their own constructions of the order of words and things. These discourses attempt to advance their own agonistic theories of Postmodern Man/Woman, soon to disappear with the present arrangements of knowledge that made him or her emerge, if we are to trust Foucault's ironic prediction, or who will repeat himself/herself, like a terrified, choking actor, in the magic irrealities ("simulations") of an endless, "indefinite scenario of crisis,"[5] as we are told by Baudrillard who also tells us to forget Foucault.

While the enfolding metaphorics of unstable theatrical forms and perceptions in Blau's and KRAKEN's work ceaselessly deconstruct the boundaries between performer, spectator, image, and reflection, they inevitably suggest the mutation "from work to text" that Roland Barthes has described as a breakdown of "discipline" and "author-ity." Metaphorically speaking, Barthes proposes, the Text, bound to a certain pleasure, "plays" dangerously with its writing/reading; and "the reader plays twice over, playing the Text as one plays a game, looking for a practice which re-produces it, but, in order that that practice not be reduced to a passive inner *mimesis* . . . also playing the Text in the musical sense of the term."[6] In other words, writing about theatrical performance, like the "writing of the stage" itself that Patrice Pavis has taken as the object of his semiological studies,[7] puts one at a loose end. Standing in front of an imaginary curtain, one must discover one's complicity as producer—*in* the scene—of the illusion that one's life is more than just theatrical illusion. When the Man in Botho Strauss's *Kalldewey Farce*, looking down from the "mountaintop," declares that the "remainder is theatre" ("Und bleiben wir erhalten, ver-flucht in eine ewige Komödie, verbannt ins Grauen heftiger Belustigung. So überleben wir und wiederholen uns und werden's wohl für alle Zeiten"[8]), he speaks with a Derridean accent, from *inside* the growing wasteland of textuality that knows no outside to which anybody could be "sent."[9]

The theatre itself has begun to reflect on the earnest obsessions of recent poststructuralist theory with its postabsurdist farces (not quite forgetting Beckett) and its multimedia performance collages. Theatre strug-gles with the hyperrealism of our mediated reality and—Blau reminds us again and again—wants to take back the night where the "taking up" of very real bodies becomes meaningful since it can dramatize, in its process, the ontological and epistemological problem not only of "knowing where we are but where we are in the topography of illusion" (*TB* 95). The actor's *presence* is at issue, in the structure of what there is to be played, and even the reformation of structures of play (in not yet privileged or "legitimized" forms such as intermedia performance art, scientific-technological theatre, new dance/music theatre, feminist theatre, and so forth) cannot succeed in reclaiming a place and an audience as long as theatre merely indulges in pure, gratuitous playing with loose ends as if it were imitating the ex-cessive theatricality in the discursive life of critical theory after Barthes, Derrida, and Baudrillard.

The sixties rebellion against the patriarchal economy of the drama and the institutional framework of the "culinary theatre" (Brecht) spread the idea of an Open or Living theatricalization of everyday experience, quickly exhausting a distinctive thought of performance onstage in the drift of the appropriating strategies of other disciplines (literary theory, psy-choanalysis, anthropology, cultural and political theory) that eventually seemed to trivialize the theatre or, at least make it look superfluous. The complete displacement of "performance" from stage to writing and to the proliferating styles of postcriticism would not only deprive the theatre of its audience, but of any social value.

If Julia Kristeva, in an important yet rarely discussed article, can therefore claim that "modern theatre does not take (a) place," she means to say that the theatre no longer has anything to *show* to the community except, perhaps, that it has died in the prison-house of language from within which it quotes the old commandments of an "out-dated code."[10] New experiments with language and representation *in* the theatre, I take her to be saying, must therefore keep investigating the possibility of Artaud's dream of a dancing poetry in space, a wordless mise en scène of colors, intonations, gestures, and images—ending in madness and death, the only events within this semiotic limit of the representable. Some of the feverish projections of perishable desire onto the screenlike stages in current avant-garde productions go a long way toward confirming Kristeva's prediction that the fantasy reconstructions of the subjective space of our postmodernity will make theatre and cinema inseparable.

The question whether one is able to *see* the death of identity and desire, not to mention the desire to *enact* it, returns us to Blau's insistence on the separate phenomenology of the theatre and on the specific challenge, at this historical juncture, to imagine it taking a last step toward performing its own denial of theatre, before it has been completely expropriated. But putting an end to play, Hamlet's recurring nightmare (" 'tis a consummation/Devoutly to be wish'd" [III.i.63–64]), is precisely what live theatre cannot stop worrying about. It is a palpable thinking body that can speculate on its absence even as it invents new ways to act out its fear, which also makes it stubbornly human, although that may be another paradox in the late age of mechanical reproducibility and electronic information processing.

Unlike Richard Schechner's weary and bitter assessment of the failure of the American avant-garde to develop its acting techniques or to transmit its ephemeral, multiplex performance texts *(The End of Humanism)*, Blau tends to trust the persistence of what he refers to as the idea of acting, the idea of the theatre, and "the idea of the text as the initiating pretext of thought" *(TB* 174). He criticizes the nonnarrative, antirepresentational ethic of postmodern performance and its disabling preoccupation with surfaces, yet his critique of postmodern image construction (as in Bob Wilson's hypnotic visual-architectural "motion-pictures") and character deconstruction (after Grotowski, the Living Theatre, Foreman, the Mabou Mines, and so forth) is somehow contradicted by his own rigorous theory of a theatrical practice that must "turn abstractly away" from the traditional repertoire of gestures and Method in order to find out what it is still haunted by, and why it is haunted *(TB* 278).

The idea of a haunted stage, with the barely discernible murmur of its ghosts in the cellarage, strikes me as an especially appropriate way of reviewing some of theatre's inherent contradictions that provide endless occasions for the kind of performance (performance "memory" or "history") Blau has in mind. Whether or not these occasions can find an audience will depend, to a large extent, on the much-needed response from the "interpretive community" of theatre practitioners and theorists.

Hamlet's Ghost

> Finally one begins to have no further idea of
> what is meant by coming, coming before, com-
> ing after, warning, coming back—and the differ-
> ence between generations, as well as inheriting,
> writing one's will, dictating, speaking, being
> dictated to, etc.
>
> Jacques Derrida, *La carte postale*

> I'm not Hamlet. I don't play a role anymore.
> My words have nothing to tell me any longer.
> . . . My drama, if it were still to take place,
> would take place in the time of the revolution.
> The hope has not been fulfilled.
>
> Heiner Müller, *Hamletmachine*

In a sense, the revolution has already occurred. We now live in a culture of spectacle and performance anxiety, in a time of carnivalesque "polylogue" (Kristeva) moving from defeat to defeat, unable to abolish the structure of representation from within which the temporal subject has managed to analyze (Gr.: *analyein*, to dissolve) its own dislocation. Our perceptions have been shifted to writing and reading, to textual production and unending interpretation, and to the noncentered relational network of forces that fabricate and inhabit the subject, the text, the reader, the writer, and their relations to the real, to a material history that seems equally subject to writing and rewriting. Imperceptibly, of course, poststructuralist grammatology pleasurably exploits the paradoxes on which it has built its delaying tactics and deferrals, always already. The aporias of the writer's performing "self," however, reflect back on the theatre's destination, on what comes before or after the actor takes (a) part in the old drama, turning back the pages of a long history of performances. Heiner Müller entitled the opening scene of *Hamletmachine* the "family scrapbook" to which he referred, in another context (employing a complex metaphor that mixes matriarchy with Shakespeare, Brecht, and Marxist revolution), as the history of the reconstruction of the rebellious son into the father-figure.

The new theatre, Blau argues, tried to forget, not only the old drama and its old allegiances to the authority of the book (in the name of the father-playwright), but also the specific mystery that inevitably turns the space of performance into a "memory place," where the "rites of memory are passed from generation to generation" (*TB* 27). The mystery may be, simply, that there is a story to be told, although that may turn out to be more difficult than Horatio cares to admit as he reviews the bloody carnage around him:

> give order that these bodies
> High on a stage be placed to view,
> And let me speak to th'yet unknowing world

How these things came about. So shall you hear
Of carnal, bloody, and unnatural acts,
Of accidental judgments . . .

Hamlet V.ii.382–87

But is not this scene a perfect paradigm of the ancestral rites/"rights of memory" (Fortinbras) in the Western theatre of *Aufhebung*, with gestures of mourning turned into a Saturnalia where fathers and sons exchange places: "Take up the bodies" (V.ii.406)? The thematics of incorporation and expropriation are an essential part of theatre history. Horatio's image of "th'yet unknowing world" that shall be "delivered" from accidental judgments can be traced back at least to the Watchman's problem in the *Oresteia*, which revolves around the trail of "meaning in that beacon light" (signifying the fall of Troy? or the fall of Agamemnon? or Orestes' murder of Clytemnestra?) that he must announce to those who can understand bloody and unnatural acts: "But if they fail, I have forgotten everything."

In this cryptic inconclusiveness lies buried the long oedipal history of Western theatre, with its "occlusions and occasions" (*BT* xiv) of performance and its confusions of inside (the dream, the imaginary) and outside (the reality principle, the embodiment), caught up in the logic of trace, repetition, and difference.

> Now, I take you, my mother, in his, my father's invisible track. I stifle your scream with my lips. . . . Then let me eat your heart, Ophelia, which weeps my tears.
>
> *Hamletmachine*[11]

The Watchman's anxiety of performance, like Horatio's or Hamlet's, is always also a self-perversion, a self-seduction. It has to do with the regressive narcissism of the actor who must think that he is "taking up" his own body and voice, more than just a fantasy, and struggle with the desire for forgetfulness that compulsively remembers the more deadly desire for revelation, for the discovery of the scandal, in order to bind the ghost that haunts this scene of nonfulfilment. These phantasmatics of theatre, with the actor's critical anticipation of nonfulfilment, of failure, and of the perversity of the repetition-compulsion, seem to dominate the nonredemptive tone of Blau's observations on the collective work of KRAKEN out of which he reconstructs theories of performance that have accrued from the thinking techniques of the actors, their rehearsal methods, ever becoming, questioned and questionable in the process. I imagine Blau in the impossible position of a Horatio, placed on the periphery of the activities at Elsinore, inactive in order to *see* better, because without that distance from the scene one cannot speak about what is happening in it. Hamlet thinks he can. That is why his *thinking*, his acting-out, can be taken as the exemplary scenario of the performative mode.

That mode, however, is not simply comparable to poststructuralist notions of the text becoming nothing but a "performance" of itself, a horizonless "horizontality of a pure surface, which itself represents itself from detour to detour."[12] For Derrida, this "horizontality" suggests the limitlessness or plenitude of play, the pure movement toward meanings with no origin or end in sight, as if the detours of writing were unconscious and outside time. The Hamletic figure, which haunts the contemporary actor and performance artist alike, is caught up with a number of horizons: the material conditions of the performance text, the playing space, the spectrum of acting behaviors, and above all, the palpable body and its gendered memory through which the role will emerge with other bodies and other roles in the intersection of the physical and the textual, the ontological and the aesthetic, all of which becoming "an instrument of exposure and analysis" (*TB* 231).

The ACTOR PLAYING HAMLET, in the fourth scene of *Hamlet-machine*, has taken off make-up and costume before he voices his resistance to the old dramaturgical formulas for the building of the character and dramatic illusion:

> My words have nothing to tell me anymore. My thoughts suck the blood out of the images. My drama doesn't happen anymore. Behind me the set is put up. By people who aren't interested in my drama, for people whom it doesn't concern. I'm not interested in it anymore either. (56)

The self-exposure *is* the analysis, and to the extent that the structure of performance, with its spectrum of shifting behaviors and theatrical signs (body act space scale gesture color light voice intonation word mask set platform curtain auditorium music sound screen), "reflects the presence of time and labor in its passing, it acquires a dimension of history" (*TB* 225). There are always critical distinctions within this ensemble of relationships and effects, and the system of signs in the theatre, with the meanings we can attach to them, is subject to change. As Brecht pointed out insistently, there are innumerable ways of looking at the materiality of any historical event, any act of representation. We can recognize the value of a gesture or an image in relation to values belonging to another context or to an earlier historical moment—or to their "ghosts," as Blau calls them repeatedly. To *follow* the old commandments of the Ghost, as Shakespeare's Hamlet feels forced to do, creates problems for Hamlet, whose painful, self-reflexive labor of decoding and recoding the experience he undergoes opens up crucial questions about the shape of the ideological power that determines how events are signified, "authorized," invested.

Not surprisingly, Hamlet remains trapped by the commandments of the ghostly father even as he invents his own Mousetrap performance to test the limits of the ideological system of representation. Shakespeare turns Hamlet into a compulsive interpreter, a deconstructionist actor who asks too many questions, turning the closet scene inside out while remaining unable to quite understand or control the proliferation of words words words already corrupted by the court's incestuous economy. Behind/

above/between all the confusion at Elsinore is the Ghost, the "thing" that appears in "a questionable shape" (I.iv.43) but cannot be seen. Hamlet seems to see it, but we cannot be sure, although what he tells himself and us *moves* the acting process, the mise en scène.

> Nothing is there but what you make of it. The subjective process becomes a means of understanding its own nature. . . . Each actor is a ghost answering. The who which is there is the respiration of the Other. It is always a double unfolding, through the impedance of the act of fear. When Hamlet stops on the ramparts and says, "I'll go no further"—how far has he gone? When he says, "Go on, I'll follow thee"—where does he follow? and why does he stop when he does? (*TB* 214)

Didi and Gogo, in the seemingly endless repetitions of Beckett's endgame, do not remember exactly where they came from; they do not go anywhere either, but decide to wait to see exactly where they stand. They cannot stop acting in the meantime. Thinking about what is possible, however, seems utterly reduced in Beckettian drama; it revolves around eating turnips or staring into a hat. For Müller, an East German, the subjective process, as it incorporates the lines between person, identity, self, actor, role, character, gender, existence, cannot so easily elide the memory of the past ("I was Hamlet. I stood at the shore and talked with the surf BLABLA, the ruins of Europe in back of me.") and the specific socioaesthetic nexus produced by the theatre text ("PEST IN BUDA," the events in Hungary in 1956, the cold war after Stalin's death, the Berlin Wall, postmodern TV culture, Baader-Meinhof terrorism). The "ghost," for the ACTOR PLAYING HAMLET, *becomes the performance* of a horrifying dream about the revolution in which he would participate "on both sides of the front, between the frontlines, over and above them", shaking his fist at his own impotence. These violent fantasy images of failure and dissolution end with a bitterly ironic comment on a certain postmodern ideology of surface pleasure *beyond* the unconscious, *beyond* history:

> My brain is a scar. I want to be a machine. Arms for grabbing legs to walk on no pain no thoughts. (57)

The Hamlet-actor's fantasy text is crushed and dialectically reversed when we see him putting his make-up back on, stepping into the armor of the Ghost-Father, and splitting the heads of Marx, Lenin, and Mao with the bloody axe of the counterrevolution even as Ophelia, abused and crippled, whirls her fierce and brutal confession of on-going resistance into the faces of her oppressors.

The power of oppression is systemic; the structural reality of theatre practice is socially produced and usually has its unresolvable contradictions smoothed over by a "capitalist dramaturgy" (Peter Handke) of realistic or psychological acting perfected by the American Method of ideological repetition. When Dario Fo's *Accidental Death of an Anarchist* or

Müller's *Hamletmachine* appear on or off Broadway, as they recently did, they look nicely domesticated, absorbed by the prevailing system of reproduction. That *Hamletmachine*, with its dangerous impulses and radically dialectical operations, proves to be unproducible on its own terms in the United States does not surprise me. Resistance to the text's internal dissociations was strong enough to result in the cancellation of the planned premiere in Cologne in 1979 after six weeks of rehearsal. That was somewhat more surprising, since the noncommercial state theatres in West Germany do not generally feel obliged to the conventions of the marketplace. What interests me here is whether theatre practice as epistemological inquest can in fact "rehearse" confrontation,[13] i.e., demonstrate, in an Althusserian sense, the repressive conditions of the apparatus and instigate efforts towards a transformation of the structural body. And it is in respect to this question that I find Blau's writing both stimulating and frustrating. Although his work with KRAKEN resembles the hermeticism of Grotowski's former theatre laboratory insofar as it did not reach a general audience, what will persist, I hope, is the influence of his radical emphasis on *thinking through* revolutionary delusions, moving toward an understanding of the theatre's own problematic—the vicious circle of relationships between actor and material, character and self—restating its "ghosting" process in the process. It should have become clear by now that Blau is not interested in the problems of a conventional realist theatre that shows us what we have already seen. His relationship to the body-oriented or multimedia-oriented postmodern forms of theatre and performance is more conflicted. One ought to read his reaction to the "serial monotony" (*BT* 29) of recent avant-garde experiments in the light of his defensiveness towards Artaud, Grotowski, and the generation of the Living Theatre, and of his intellectual affinity with those complex theatre and literary texts (Shakespeare, Büchner, Brecht, Genet, Beckett, Yeats) that seem to inspire and justify his intense engagement with the history of drama and dramatic structure as it has disappeared and reappeared "through representation in the theatre" (*BT* 39).

Ghosting/Rethinking Theatre

I tried to add a further dimension to Blau's bloodiest dismissals of the thoughtlessness of postmodern theatre performance by grafting the collage text of *Hamletmachine* into the Hamlet character that seems to appear in KRAKEN's performance experiment with Shakespeare's material (the work was entitled *Elsinore*). I did so because the central chapters in *Take Up the Bodies* ("Origin of the Species," "Missing Persons," "Ghosting") and *Bloodied Thought* ("Look What Thy Memory Cannot Contain") indeed "follow" the Ghost in Shakespeare's most famous play in ever-widening circles of abstraction. Like the Ghost, these writings cross back and forth between theory and theatre, conceptualization and act, mind and body, form and content, past and present, as if there was no crossing, no clear boundary, and no material context except that of the theatrical "essay" itself, origin unknown. Its text: derivations. The power and fascination of Blau's search for an acting process that *is* its own theory (before that theory can be extracted and fixed by a repressive ideology of systems and categories) lies in the intensity of the whirling words and their chiasmic syntax, forever refusing speculative limits even as the specter of an endless, uncontrollable subversion of meaning begins to haunt Blau's figures of invisible writing that he derives from a particular discourse that has its own "hidden motives" and "sightlines" (*BT* 74). This fascination with theatre as thought, rewriting a privileged text *(Hamlet)* along the path traced by Barthes, Lacan, and Derrida, unwittingly reveals its own problems. Blau's drive toward holistic self-absorption—thought becomes blooded/word becomes flesh—in the process of representation cannot do the work, the critique of bourgeois theories and practices, that the activist theatre of the sixties, in Blau's view, should have done. Blau's interventionist position cannot be doubted, but the collective brainwork of KRAKEN has evaporated into very much like what was left of the radical avant-garde in the seventies. In its shadow we may read some of the maddening questions that he poses in the new contexts of the eighties and nineties, where they will be reformulated.

What I find most crucial about these questions is that they insist on using a theatrical vocabulary and a revisionist approach to the "shared language," as Bonnie Marranca has called it in *Theatrewritings*,[14] that derives from the texts of theatre and what is behind them, reflections reflecting, as if the texts of history were thinking through the actor who is revolving "it all" in the mind, trying to grasp, take up, inscribe what is not-there back upon the body and its engraved mimetic instincts, the character of the actor. In *Footfalls*, Beckett has reduced the scene pretty much to such a dialogue between a voice that asks, and a character (May) who paces the stage from left to right, right to left:

> *Voice* Will you never have done? *[Pause.]* Will you never have done . . .
> revolving it all?
> *May* *[Halting.]* It?
> *Voice* It all. *[Pause.]* In your poor mind. *[Pause.]* It all. *[Pause.]* It all.

Beckett's vision, as we have seen repeatedly, leads to a dramaturgy of the "fade out," where the stage becomes dark because "nothing is left to tell," as R (Reader) says to L (Listener) in *Ohio Impromptu*, closing the book. This kind of defeatism contrasts markedly with Blau's work. KRAKEN's primary visual metaphor, gleaned from the murky scene photographs that playfully shadow the printed text, is the circle (the *space* of an hermeneutic circle?) on the shifting ground where the actor becomes part of the boundless fabric of intertextuality from which the performance—as interpretation and remembrance of images "imagined, played, written about, or alluded to, as history has required" (*TB* 174)—can be constructed, spinning the body (everything that is left to tell) that is the book.

The form of 'it all", in the medium of theatre, is an acrobatic process of construction, always dialogic and always bound up with the psychophysical and psychosexual character of the players who act out the questions about the play. How does one enter the text? And where? What for? For whom? And to what end? Where do these things (the act, the thought of the act, its grammar of motives and rhetoric of appearance) come from? Is there something that shapes the end (the goal, the process, the ending)? Who's there? (*TB* 78).

These are, basically, Hamletic questions. More complex than the notorious "to be or not to be," all of them are inextricably linked to a phenomenology of perception (what is *being-seen*) and to our own recent history of thinking about the metaphysics of presence, psychic reality, textuality, and the status of what or who is seen, spoken, and analyzed, the politics of representation, the "subject" of semiotics, the cultural map of misreading/defining the positions of meaning, identification, desire . . .

Clearly moving beyond received models of aesthetic and dramatic theory, Blau's sceptical and informed response to the formalizations of structuralist and poststructuralist theory speaks from an already subverted theatre consciousness that takes nothing for granted. Rather, his model derives its motivating questions from poetic examples (such as *Hamlet*) bound up with the image of absolute danger, as Artaud used to describe the vengeful force of Jacobean theatre. Trying to enter the text, therefore, is like searching for a series of clues, for a source of interpretation, for a meaningful prospect, for actions "that a man might play" (I.ii.84), as Hamlet suggests admitting that they may always look false anyway, as if there were in fact no way not to be miscast. Hamlet's interpretations seem ambivalent, especially when he enacts the first gesture of the performative utopia, namely to speak to "that within which passes show," the unseen, unspoken inner self not subject to the *scene* that belongs to the order of writing and symbolic exchange. This is, Blau would argue, "if it can be imagined, the source of our idea of illusion" (*BT* 84).

The uses of illusion in the process of thought, the thought that nearly drives Hamlet mad, concern the materiality of theatre. We cannot apprehend it (the questionable shape of the Ghost) unless "it bleeds into the body of performance" (*BT* 100), into the structured language of voice, speech, body, gesture, and motion. The performance is a structured *appearance*, of course, a revolving trick, complicating matters through the constant doubling (the play-within-the-play) of representation where the very thing that is embodied or re-membered appears to invalidate the form because it will not stand still. "It" has not exhausted all speculation.

Before one loses sight of the real problem in the theatre, Blau argues, one must face the process of textualization, the invisible writing (what Derrida has called "arche-writing"), that gives birth to the performance and keeps us looking for the authorizing image of its genesis. Nobody in noncommercial theatre believes anymore in the idea of *Werktreue*, a staging faithful to the author's intentions or the authority of the text or the "spirit" of the play, although an older generation of living playwrights seems presently engaged in trying to reclaim lost sacred territory. At the same time, the more radical resistance to language in experimental theatre, which began with establishing the "public domain" status of classic texts and led to strategies of piecing in collages, action events, and the various forms of transdisciplinary performance art, has not been sufficiently theorized. Neither the confessional seizures of the actor performing his or her "authenticity" (in bad imitations of the spiritual self-penetration of the Grotowskian actor), nor the cool conceptual landscapes of Minimal Art or the *nuova spettacolarità* of technological movement composition (as the "post-avant-garde" in Italy defines itself) have as yet yielded new ways of understanding the relationship between aesthetic practices of "interruption" or "distraction" (Benjamin) on the postmodern stage and the spectator's attitude towards the apparent unreadability of structural interferences on multiperspectival visual/acoustic performance levels.

When Blau speaks about KRAKEN's *Elsinore* experiment in comparison with postmodern attempts to erase or preempt textuality in the theatre, he is obviously concerned about the bad faith among those practitioners who thought they could elide the inscription of difference in the performance present, thus avoiding any historical differentiation within the thought of performance. He is also concerned about the effects of this distrust in the *language* of theatre on the new vogue of descriptive compartmentalization ("theatre of images," "energetic theatre," and so forth) that establishes unexamined hierarchies among heterogeneous expressions (image, sound, text, music, motion, etc.) and thus practices a kind of mutilation, as Simone Benmussa has very succinctly described it in directing her play *The Singular Life of Albert Nobbs*. Benmussa's concern about the mutilation of theatre (separating the "image" from the "text," the "voice" from the "gesture," for example) may express a playwright's defense of language against performance art. It also refers us to the more fundamental and unresolved separation of theatre and language (literature) envisioned by the historical avant-garde. Blau's main challenge to contemporary conceptions of performance, therefore, lies in his claim that the material elements of the theatre always situate us in language, whether or not there are any spoken words. When Artaud demanded the creation of a new physical language of the theatre, no longer based on words, on text and linear narrative, he imagined a kind of *poetry in space* composed of gestures, incantations, gesticulations, and scenic rhythm: a "language," paradoxically, that one would not have been able to "see" or "read" outside a system of signs. To overthrow prior codification means, literally, to *begin*, to constitute the "nonrepresentable origin of representation," as Derrida defines the dream in his essay on Artaud.[15] The theatre, Blau reminds us, "is always beginning over. . . . there is always one thing to be remembered" (*BT* 112). The words and signs return to the performance like displaced persons, like ghosts, "subject to the interior 'writing,' " like the reflexes of the "old writing in the body" (*BT* 97), which is the trace-structure where the original has necessarily disappeared because it was never constituted.

This view of textuality in the theatre corrects a persistent Romantic tradition in drama scholarship and criticism that believes in the existence of an Ur-*Hamlet* or an Ur-*Faust* or, worse, in the possibility of authentically recreating the original Shakespeare, if not in a "straight" performance in the reconstructed Globe theatre on the South Bank, then at least in the "authoritative" text edition of an uncontaminated Good Quarto. But a play, perhaps more conspicuously than any other work of art, is always already a "bad quarto" in the sense that it is decomposing into the history of performances and the textuality of history, waiting to be recomposed by those who can reclaim the hidden relations and the missing persons.

Dr. Faustus, in another paradigmatic moment of textual theatre, anagrammatizes/unwrites the script(ures) that would doom him into repetition. Something else appears—first Mephostophilis, then the burning inscription on his arm—reminding him that such magical feats mean nothing, except that the desire (*Schaulust*) to see these fresh blasphemous gestures performed, congeals the blood.

The "writerly" text in the theatre, more painful than a lover's discourse, is an interpretation of the dreadful cost of thought, "the challenge *in* the Text, *to* the actor, *on behalf of the Text*, and to the apparent viewer on behalf of the total structure of appearances which constitute the performance" (*BT* 34). I imagine it is on behalf of the dreadful cost that KRAKEN's process of "ghosting" in *Elsinore* can be understood as a reconstruction of acting possibilities deliberately set against some newer forms of theatre in our culture. These newer forms assume that the crisis in the semiotic and referential relationship of the sign with the world is irreversible and a visual practice that abandons language as mediation of images can avoid the overdeterminations of the old drama. Blau describes KRAKEN's work as a group process in which each of the actors, as "a body of knowledge," carries "with him his version(s) of the story, or hers, each with its own compulsive life and course, intersecting and colliding . . . forming the one structure of *Elsinore*" (*TB* 204–06). He not only revalidates the language of poetry in *Hamlet* but also the power of narrative as it precipitates cross-reflexive fantasies among the actors who are "displacing the content of *Hamlet* with our own and being displaced in turn by images of the play which return like the Ghost, with the insurgent appeal of an originating cause" (*TB* 201).

Blau's focus on questions of origin, the trace, and the mental and physical *emotion* moving through the trace-structure forms an important element in his analysis of the group's practice of mediating between the actor and what wants to be seen as "character": the forms, moods, shapes of feeling relative to who is perceiving, with the actors improvising off each other in order to find the accurately felt equivalents for the words that count. Even if they cannot be trusted, as in *Hamlet*, or in KRAKEN's ghosting of *Hamlet*, they are the only means of imprinting meaning on a presence that cannot be counted upon. The Ghost is not; but "it" invites an acting process, "a way of thinking through the theatre" (*TB* 213).

Blau's recollections of the various physical experiments that his group made are fascinating to read. In my concluding remarks, however, I wish to turn to the more troubling aspect of his polemical gestures toward saving the subject of appearances in the drama of words, in a theatre that he can alternately describe as an incurable place of perversion and as *la grande affaire*, the scene of the flowery pathos of mimetic desire where illusion must survive so that our oppressive reality is more endurable.

Blau's fusion of meaning and method is strongest when he reminds us of the necessity of "thinking through theatre," and through its unabandonable language that still "remains the one human activity which undeniably socializes, and most cohesively in its separations" (*BT* 85). The separating and the abstracting count for Blau because theatre must think through the social structure it belongs to even though that may imply that it wishes to struggle beyond its limits. Among its limitations I would include a politics based on a theory of poetry, a rhetoric of appearances based on such time-serving theatrical metaphors as "cannibalism" or "terrorism," and a theoretical vocabulary derived from a privileged canon of texts (from Shakespeare's Sonnets, "a virtual manual of theatre craft, an ontology of theatre" (*TB* 94), to Kafka, Pound, and Yeats) and a seductively powerful psychoanalytic discourse painfully attracted to the hysterical patient, the actor.

Blau's strategic appropriation of the deconstructionist challenge to mimetic representation in conjunction with his thorough-going de-mystification of the old conventions of realism and illusionistic drama *and* the newer conventions of experimental theatre and performance art has challenged the illusion of an uninterrupted presence in the insidious "orthodoxy of non-meanings" and flat surfaces (*BT* 77). Blau's unsparing analysis of the recent history of drama in the theatre is acted out with poststructuralist assumptions about the procession of textuality and the conditionality of the subject desiring continuity and presence, and his own grammatological performances with KRAKEN reflect a demotivation and displacement of the "customary appearances of theatre—behavior, purposive action, narrative, the last semblance of roles, etc" [*TB* 219]. However, we are not sure how much his persuasive theory of the "thinking body" of the actor is grounded in the very structure of representation that it condemns as the producer of the hysteria yet sarcastically redefines as the proper humanistic sphere where the body matters because it cannot be questioned.

When Blau calls the theatre a "structure of incompleteness" (*TB* 147), he intends a familiar incompleteness that cannot disguise the persistent phallocentrism of the discourse in search for closure, truth, self-identification, and mastery. Blau's attempt to recuperate a method of thinking through theatre inevitably comes to resemble a tragic legend in which the demand for a totalization of presence (as in Artaud) is killed, and what disappears and reappears (reconstructed by the audience), with teleological consistency, looks like a certain political economy of repre-sentation/theatre that positively reshapes itself in the name of the absent Ghost-Father. As long as the inscribed structure and the cultural codes governing the symbolic order are perceived as unchallengeable, "perspec-tive" will remain "troubling," as Blau admits.

> "We thought we could expose the ideological recessions, the hidden motives of time, by developing techniques of alienation, as in Brecht, or strategies of ontological disruption, as in Foreman, to take things out of the falsifying appearance of perspective. . . . But when we looked another time, every exposure was a secretion. The form is ghosted, as we are, by the mental habits of the form, which encrust our habits of perception." (*BT* 74).

The first revision that one might want to suggest concerns the universal "we." I am not convinced that Blau is willing to consider the possibility of *seeing* the forms differently, although I notice his reference to Brecht's advice that "some exercise in complex seeing is needed" (*TB* 200). In many heterogeneous ways, recent feminist theories and practices have already traced a new path toward systematic analyses of the coercive codes of representation and narrativity, and the feminist cultural project of es-tablishing a semiotic space for the woman subject (for instance, Kaja Silverman, Teresa de Lauretis, Julia Kristeva, and others) presents a major dynamic for various other semiological, psychoanalytic, Marxist, and post-structuralist reexaminations of the dominant patriarchal institutions and symbolic structures. The political goals that combine these revisionary commitments demand a transformative relationship to language, to in-terpretational and disciplinary forces, and—significantly—to the processes of seeing and institutional voyeurism that were analysed by Foucault (*Discipline and Punish*) and recontextualized by important new movements and analytic models in recent film theory and criticism. I am thinking especially of contributions to the critique of discursive formations, visual pleasure, the gaze, narrative space, and the construction of sexual differ-ence that have been published in avant-garde journals such as *Screen*, *Camera Obscura, Ciné-Tracts, m/f*, and so forth, which followed in the wake of earlier studies of the cinematic apparatus by Stephen Heath, Jean-Louis Baudry, Laura Mulvey, Claire Johnston, and others. When Julia Kristeva suggested some time ago that feminism should only be negative, at odds with the existing culture and its reproductive relations, she seemed partic-ularly concerned about the question of complicity with the Law (which is always *affirmed* by deconstruction, as Derrida has repeatedly pointed out), of self-oppressive participation in those symbolically represented struc-tures of expectation and control that shape communication and audience/reader behavior in the bourgeois public sphere or in that space of the ghosts which Blau has invoked.

Theatre and performance as "disciplines" are part of a dominant expectation of cultural production, and their rules and mechanisms are still crucially located in our consumerist culture with its fantastic elaborations in its entertainments—its Olympic Games, its festivals and exhibitions, and its TV soap operas. The issue of complicity is raised but left behind in Blau's writing, and it seems to me that if KRAKEN's practice was aimed at producing perfect knowlege of its performance, it cannot actually play a role outside a self-reflexive theoretical discourse and praxis that, in asking the right Hamletic questions, already circumscribe the answers.

Blau's practice of deconstruction constitutes a "pessimistic" deconstruction that rediscovers the laws and logical operations in theatrical space-time, their "*time-serving* illusory processes" (*BT* 93). It does not step back to *see otherwise*, in the crucial sense in which Adrienne Rich, Christa Wolf, Monique Wittig, and Marianne Goldberg,[16] together with a growing number of contemporary writers, performance artists, dancers, choreographers, filmmakers, and composers have suggested and demonstrated the possibility of re-marking the intercourse of body and word, time and space, image and sound, look and identification, the visible and the invisible, in a kind of "maverick dance"[17] in excess of the familiar dialectical oppositions.

The metaphor of the dance is hardly innocent. Annette Kolodny's politics of "dancing through the minefield"[18] have not been greeted with enthusiasm because they minimize the crucial question, not so much of difference itself, but of differences. But the multiplicity of differences in postmodern performance, and especially in postmodern dance, has resisted interpretation and the "law of genre" (Derrida) precisely because it tends to destructure structure and perspective by making it difficult to *see*, or by marking out, with a clarity almost to painful to see, the problematics of the theatre's structure of spectatorship, thus exposing the desire for closure and identification underlying all representational acts.

> this must be the spook house
> another song with no singers
> lyrics / no voices
> & interrupted solos
> unseen performances

This is the beginning, in Ntozake Shange's choreopoem *for colored girls who have considered suicide / when the rainbow is enuf*, of a process of unearthing the "unseen performances" of a black woman dancer who cannot remember the sound of her own voice and the melody of her body. And I see this beginning in connection with, for example, the dark, violent, and frenzied expressionism of Pina Bausch's recent choreographies for the Wuppertaler Tanz-theater ("Cafe Müller," "Blaubart," "1980"), with the embodiment of contrasting metaphorical visions of historical "characters" and historical process in the collective creations of Ariane Mnouchkine's Théâtre du Soleil *(1789, 1793, L'Age d'or, Les Shakespeare)*, with the bewildering distortions of the space-time continuum and the "dancing voices" in Meredith Monk's theatre cantatas and operas *(Juice, Education of the Girl-child, Quarry)*, and with the nomadizing, disemboided voices in between the silent action onstage and the unidentifiable memories of desire narrated offstage in Marguerite Duras's *India Song*. Considering these, I would not necessarily disagree with Blau's observation that the break with the established discourse of drama and "the extension of theatre into other conceptual space led to a reconstrual *in* the theatre of every aspect of performance" (*BT* 55), but rather with his qualifying remarks about the brain-damaged "repetitiveness of ritual and the gratuitousness of play" (*BT* 91) that he associates with the theatricalization of voice, sound, dance, and destabilized space.

I welcome undisciplined and distracting performance events on the contemporary stage. Although the proscenium has not fallen yet, the scopic drive is driven wild by the constant permutations of the aural-visual-kinetic elements and part objects in the mise en scène, which demand to be reorganized perceptually by each of the spectators. The performers may serve tea in the aisles, or push you out of your seat, as happened during a recent Pina Bausch *Tanzabend*. Or they may almost literally take you captive and confront you with rituals of extreme physical danger, as I experienced in 1989 during several anarchist open-air events performed by Survival Research Laboratories, La Fura dels Baus, and Brith Gof/Test Department. Before the Welsh theatre company Brith Gof began the staging of their Celtic battle scenes in a flooded ship-factory, they issued a warning to the audience: *Gofynodd neb iddynt sut y dylai theatr edrych* ("Nobody asked us what theatre ought to look like"). What is scandalized in postmodern performance is not so much the "idea" of the thinking actor which Blau defends, but the old positions of text and stage and the spectator's theatrical competence or optical control over the "languages" of the stage.[19]

Although Artaud's and Brecht's analyses and concurrent failures still dominate today's theatre, as Jean-François Lyotard has argued in his call for a new "energetic" theatre,[20] the transgressive energies of postmodern performance have at least demonstrated that the theatre can remain a field of experimentation where the failure to revolutionize the structure of representation will be seen or where new challenges for "complex seeing" are raised continually. Robert Wilson's Wagnerian dream of a new total theatre can be placed among the failures and the challenges. In his uncompleted twelve-hour opera, *the CIVIL warS*, he collaborates not only with Philip Glass but, unthinkably, with Heiner Müller and an ensemble of performers, musicians, dancers, and technicians from theatres in Cologne, Rotterdam, Rome, Tokyo, Marseilles, and Minneapolis. The hour-long opening scene in Cologne dreams of the future, has two figures in space suits floating around in midair, and remembers "history" (a drummer boy who looks like the young Frederick the Great; a mechanical toy American Civil War soldier; Voltaire) and narrative (several fairy-tale figures appear and disappear). Along with Glass's musical score, Wilson creates a construction in time and space that simultaneously destructures our perception with at least four discrete acoustical and visual scores, live and miked

Figure 15. Robert Wilson, *the CIVIL warS,* Act I A.
Schauspiel Köln, 1984. Photo: Manfred Förster.

voices juxtaposed to various scenic images, filmic projections, sound effects, shifts in scale, quoted text fragments, and changing rhythmic patterns and colors—a dense collage of overlapping signs that provoke the semiological activity of the audience.

This opening scene, perhaps emblematic of the new trends in avant-garde theatre, opens new spaces for interpretation by asystematically combining serial repetition of music and sound, conflicting orders of "narrative" time and visual space, uncertain divisions between bodies, voices, and roles, and alogical relationships between immaterial "characters" (as in Duras's *India Song*) and quoted text-materials (from Müller's "family scrapbook"). All narrative, temporal, visual, and aural registers are dispersed, but this does not suggest a new orthodoxy of non-meanings to me, as Blau might suspect, but the production of a new way of seeing and of remembering the montage of irremediable choreographies.

It is in this sense that I would like to carry Blau's emphasis on "thinking through theatre" a little further along the way that postmodern performance and feminist theory have already traced: toward rethinking thinking itself, even if that implies that the old theatre of oedipal dramas can no longer be recognized or identified as they used to be, and that the tables of memory are overturned.

I am not arguing that the theatre can forget the limits and frames of the conditions of its theatricality. But we are beginning to see performance practices that think of themselves as "acts from under and above" (to use the title of Meredith Monk's latest performance work)—acts that need the limits of the theatre in order to be able to imagine different realities, under and above our normal ways of seeing.

NOTES

1. Jean Baudrillard, *Simulations* (New York: semiotext(e), 1983), 12, 38. See also his "The Ecstasy of Communication," in *The Anti-Aesthetic: Essays on Postmodern Culture*, ed. Hal Foster (Port Townsend, WA: Bay Press, 1983), 126–34.

2. Cf. Terry Eageton's critique of the "critical institutions" in our postindustrial, mass-mediated public sphere, *The Function of Criticism. From 'The Spectator' to Poststructuralism* (London: Verso, 1984).

3. This account, covering the years in which Blau was cofounder and codirector of the distinguished Actor's Workshop in San Francisco (1952–65), codirector of the Repertory Theatre of Lincoln Center in New York (1965–67), and one of the founders of the California Institute of the Arts (where he laid the groundwork for his own experimental theatre group KRAKEN in the late sixties), helps situate the movement of its theoretical discourse in relation to an agitated period of political dissidence, out of which KRAKEN's work and training methods became its own theory of theatre. *Take Up the Bodies*, then, is a little less than theatre but more than a "book" or, in Hamlet's words, a "table of [a] memory" (I.v.98). All references are to the abbreviated titles of *Take Up the Body: Theater at the Vanishing Point* (Urbana: Univ. of Illinois Press, 1982) [*TB*], and *Blooded Thought: Occasions of Theatre* (New York: PAJ Publications, 1982) [*BT*].

4. References to *Hamlet* come from the Arden edition, ed. Harold Jenkins (London and New York: Methuens, 1982).

5. Jean Baudrillard, *In the Shadow of the Silent Majorities* (New York: semio-text(e), 1983), 86.

6. Roland Barthes, *Image-Music-Text*, trans. Stephen Heath (New York: Hill & Wang, 1977), 162.

7. Patrice Pavis, *Languages of the Stage: Writings on Performance* (New York: PAJ Publications, 1982) 29ff.

8. "And thus we are preserved, damned to live in an eternal comedy, exiled into the horror of strenuous amusement. Thus we survive, and repeat ourselves, and do so for times to come" (my translation). From Botho Strauss, *Kalldewey Farce* (Müchen: Carl Hauser, 1981).

9. Cf. Derrida's "Sending: On Representation," *Social Research* 49, no. 2 (1982): 294–326.

10. Julia Kristeva, "Modern Theatre does not Take (a) Place," *Sub-Stance* 18/19 (1977): 131–32.

11. References are to Heiner Müller, *Hamletmachine and Other Texts for the Stage*, trans. and ed. Carl Weber (New York: PAJ Publications, 1984).

12. Jacques Derrida, *Writing and Difference*, trans. Alan Bass (Chicago: Univ. of Chicago Press, 1978), 298. The epigraph to the third section of my essay was taken from Derrida's *La Carte postale* (Paris: Flammarion, 1980), my translation.

13. In the sense that such a practice would not only confront the internal contradictions of the system but seek to collectively concretize the restructuring of the social process, it is directly related to Rustom Bharucha's provocative and inspiring study of political theatre in Bengal: *Rehearsals of Revolution* (Honolulu: Univ. of Hawaii Press, 1983).

14. Bonnie Marranca, *Theatrewritings* (New York: PAJ Publications, 1984), 136.

15. *Writing and Difference*, 234.

16. Adrienne Rich, "When We Dead Awaken: Writing as Re-Vision," in *On Lies, Secrets, and Silence* (New York: W. W. Norton, 1979); Christa Wolf, *Vorausset-zungen einer Erzählung: Kassandra* (Darmstadt: luchterhand, 1983); Monique Wittig, *Les guérillères* (Paris: Minuit, 1969); Marianne Goldberg, "Ballerinas and Ball passing," in the special issue "The Body as Discourse" of *Women & Performance: A Journal of Feminist Theory* 3., no. 2 (1987/88), 7–31.

17. The "dancing" that I have in mind would move in between the binary difference, the grammar and syntax that governs the decorum of all codes, in order to "thwart the *assignation à résidence*, escape those residences under surveillance. . . . [changing] place and above all [changing] *places*." Cf. "Interview, Jacques Derrida and Christie McDonald, 'Choreographies,' " *Diacritics* 12 (1982): 69.

18. "Dancing through the Minefield," *Feminist Studies* 6, no. 1 (1980): 1–25.

19. Cf. Timothy Murray's interesting analysis of the limits of institutional codes of spectatorship and judgment in "Patriarchal Panopticism, or the Seduction of a Bad Joke: *Getting Out* in Theory," *Theatre Journal* 35:3 (October 1983): 376–88.

20. "The Tooth, The Palm," *Sub-Stance* 15 (1976): 107.

> Theater places us right at the heart of what is
> religious-political: in the heart of absence, in
> negativity, in nihilism as Nietzsche would say,
> therefore in the question of power.
>
> Jean-François Lyotard

4 ▮ SELF-CONSUMING ARTIFACT: *HAMLET* IN WEST BERLIN

Hamlet—a play to end all plays; or, rather, a play that has pushed theatre to the limits of what is dramaturgically possible. The dying Hamlet's request that Horatio tell "his story" has been taken up, again and again, by Shakespeare's critics as well as by the theatre which, Horatio-like, must at least pretend that it can speak again "to the yet unknowing world/How these things came about."

An Italian interpretation of the story, staged in 1982 by the Compagnia del Collettivo at Parma, used a brilliant visual image to illustrate Horatio's heavy burden ("all this can I/Truly deliver"): the actor played a blind man (a blind seer?) with a crutch who, as if to reverse Polonius' tactics of eavesdropping, staggered across the stage "seen unseeing."

In West Germany, the case of *Hamlet* is paradigmatic of the endlessly continuing struggle over the *definition* of Shakespeare production, a struggle that will never be resolved since a very strong central tradition of literary and aesthetic criticism in the academy has formed its own canon of Shakespeare reception against which all theatrical interpretations are measured, judged, and found wanting. The critical controversy about

An earlier version of this essay appeared in *Theater* 16, no. 1 (1984).

what constitutes a conventional "werkgetreue Inszenierung" (production "faithful" to the text) or an adaptation is of course often reflected in the choices that are made in a production (e.g. the choice of a particular classic or contemporary translation), but it is perhaps more appropriate to say that the German theatres themselves, over the past three decades, have developed their own attitudes towards Shakespeare's dramatic texts, towards what *can* be represented ("truly delivered") in the specific historical and political context of postwar German culture.

Since the late 1950s, theatrical productions on the West German stages have had their own dynamics and, pervaded by the impact of modern drama and contemporary theory, preferred to explore the extremes of radical experimentation and rigid formalism, swinging wildly back and forth between brooding symbolism and provocative playfulness. Avant-garde directors and their ensembles in the 1960s and 1970s were concerned less with the recreation of the "original" texts than with the possibilities of their transformation, with the spectacular effects of new montage versions, and with symbolical and "relevant" political lessons that could be constructed out of practically every kind of Shakespearean drama (especially the histories and tragedies). Considered by some as intellectually challenging and inspired, productions by Peter Zadek, Hansgünther Heyme, Hans Hollmann, Peter Palitzsch, Claus Peymann, Luc Bondy and others more often evoked violent criticism of the kind that sees any deliberate departure from *the* text—and this, for Germany, used to be the institutionalized, early nineteenth-century Schlegel-Tieck translation—as a reduction or, to repeat the terms most frequently used, a rape and deconsecration of the "wahre Geist" of Shakespeare's drama. It is to be expected that the invisible "Geist" in Shakespeare's drama will continue to haunt and to incite theatrical experimentation on the German stages, and although it has been said that the heyday of the reductionist director seems to be over, it would be a mistake to underestimate the distinct qualities of the tightly knit, state-subsidized theatrical scene in the country, where everybody knows everybody else too well, and where the pressure on reinterpretation and innovation creates an extraordinary pattern of performance intertextuality. The irrepressible willingness to confront Shakespeare's scripts with new approaches is in fact part of the general developments in postmodern performance that have brought about such events as the fifty minute *Hamletmachine* (Heiner Müller), first staged by Jean Jourdheuil at the Théâtre Gérard Philipe in Saint Denise (1979), or the nine-hour marathon called *Shakespeare's Memory*, directed by Peter Stein at the Schaubühne am Halleschen Ufer in 1976.

The Schaubühne, West Germany's most renowned company, reformulated the question of the "rights of memory" (cf. Fortinbras in *Hamlet* V.ii.394) and of its cultural heritage in a more radical way when Klaus Michael Grüber's production gave the uncut, slightly expanded text running close to seven hours—a performance that quite deliberately set out to establish huge dimensions for its daring and (pre)sumptuous enterprise.

The 1982/83 *Hamlet* also marks the climax in Grüber's own, relatively young career as one of the leading Schaubühne directors whose recent work includes the *Bacchae* project (1974), Hölderlin's *Empedocles* (1975/76, with Bruno Ganz), the *Winterreise* production in the Berlin Olympic Stadium (1977), and the highly controversial *Faust* Fragment at the Berlin Freie Volksbühne (1982). The hugest dimension in which Grüber's *Hamlet* situates itself is the space of memory or history—a space for many ghosts. In its particular context this is the space of an aesthetic tradition in German cultural life reaching back to Goethe's time, to the Romantic Schlegel translations and Eschenburg's somewhat earlier prose translations. The production uses Schlegel, with additions from Eschenburg. The connection to Grüber's *Faust* cannot be overlooked, either, although in that production he reduces Goethe's monumental text to a monodramatic work centered entirely on the nightmarish "endgame" quality of Faust's stream-of-consciousness. In the *Hamlet* production, the aura of the hallowed classical text is fully exhibited, even exaggerated, but the visual images go beyond the refined, beautiful, aestheticized Schlegel poetry and evoke a second aura—the painterly traditions of medieval, Renaissance, and Baroque art. Gesture and movement, extremely carefully choreographed, frequently allude to portraits and paintings which also served as models for the historical costumes. The physical space itself functions as a complex metaphor; although the stage remains empty throughout, the floor, a marble mosaic, is an elliptical allusion to the richly patterned ornamental pavement in Holbein's famous Tudor portrait of "The Ambassadors" (1533).

Architecturally, the playing space is embedded in the immense, semicircular concrete hulk of the Mendelsohn apse whose sheer size dwarfs the players. The naked walls have a height of 58 feet reaching up to a canopy of tiny blue lamps under the roof; the playing space is 74 feet wide and 61 feet deep. There are various openings at three levels of the bare walls through which the actors enter and through which the light creates its own effects and designs.

The performance is double-edged from the very beginning. A monumental text, Shakespeare's most frequently performed play in West Germany, is presented in its almost mythical grandeur; almost always slightly distanced from the action to which they refer, Schlegel's verse lines are spoken with deliberate emphasis, almost recited, every speech a poem remembered, called back from the deeper recesses of German Romanticism. The words, at the same time, are spoken within/against the colossal emptiness of the vast architectural space, a cathedral distancing itself and yet menacing the audience through its sheer magnitude. Almost inevitably, the calculated aestheticism of the verbal presentation and of the actorly tableaux begins to disembody the actors; they do not come to life, they do not act together. All these *Verfremdungseffekte* are achieved entirely through art, self-conscious artificiality, and explicit mannerism. At the center of the performance, then, there is an absence, a strange lifelessness, which one can also read as the shadow play of a power that is either invisible, as

Figure 16. *Hamlet,* directed by Klaus Michael Grüber. Schaubühne am Lehniner Platz, Berlin, 1983. Photo: Ruth Walz.

represented in the ghostly appearance of Old Hamlet, or hidden behind the artificiality and hypocrisy of the splendid gowns, heavy jewels, and statuesque postures of the court figures.

> **Hor.** What, has this thing appear'd again tonight.
> **Bar.** I have seen nothing.
> **Mar.** Horatio says, 'tis but our fantasy.

When the silent Ghost (Jochen Tovote) appears, we can see nothing but what is in our fantasy; when the Ghost walks downstage in front of a huge iron curtain that is slowly lowered from above, the only light of the house glares off his shining armor, blinding the audience.

The interplay between visibility and invisibility is repeated throughout the performance; the dark stage often becomes a scenario for the most extraordinary lighting effects—striking visual images that set up and defer their own meanings. Thrown onto the geometries of the ornamental floor, the constantly shifting patterns of light can define, cancel, and redefine playing spaces almost as if the light itself were part of the intrigues at Elsinore. At times, the light would enter the stage from small doors left ajar on either side, and the actors would be half in the corridors of light and half in complete darkness.

There were three moments in this choreography of lighting that worked particularly well. First, in I.v, Hamlet is downstage after his

Figure 17. The Ghost in *Hamlet*. Schaubühne am
Lehniner Platz, Berlin, 1983. Photo: Ruth Walz.

encounter with the Ghost, scribbling the words of the father on a small
tablet; when he throws himself on the floor in his vow of vengeance,
nothing but his hand raised for the oath is visible on the totally dark stage.
In the first eavesdropping scene we see Ophelia and Hamlet walk toward
each other from opposite sides of the stage, each of them confined in a
separate, narrow beam of light. They do not see each other, and Ophelia
keeps reading her books as Hamlet suddenly turns and steps forward into
complete darkness to recite the "To be or not to be" soliloquy during which
he remains invisible to the audience. Then he turns round to step into
Ophelia's beam of light. This uncertain play of light and dark reaches a
climax in Ophelia's last scene, when the entire theater goes black except for
three tiny spots of light in center stage that the confused, tumbling girl
(played by Jutta Lampe) wanders into and out of, playing her lute and
softly humming her mad songs.

  These shifting spatial arrangements and the constantly changing light
effects did not so much hold the performance together as rather counterpoint the verbal text and the shifting styles in which that text was put on.
The elaborate geometrical placing of the actors in the space, the formality
of Rosencrantz and Guildenstern's synchronized movements created a

sense of unreality which heightened the spatial, physical, and emotional disconnectedness of the characters. The darkness and emptiness of the nonexisting center in the performance was supplemented by the shifting ground (brightly lit triangles, rectangles, and circles cut out from the darkness) on which Claudius, Gertrude, Polonius, Ophelia, or Hamlet tried to make their identities appear more than just shadows of shadows, voices in an absence. The problem with our perception of their identities or roles is that we can never be sure how to read the signs, the self-effacing duplicity of all the faithless words and symbols that are led back upon themselves, or are doubled over, by the plays-within-the-play in *Hamlet*. Perhaps the question of *role* or *identity* cannot be posed at all, since Grü-ber's production clearly suggests that Hamlet's search for an act(ion) that could "denote" him "truly" is meaningless. The more Hamlet thinks and talks about his predicament, the more is he drawn into the circuitousness of the illusions that sustain the theatrical life at the court.

> Seems, madam? Nay it is, I know not 'seems.'
> 'Tis not alone my inky cloak, good mother,
> Nor customary suits of solemn black . . .
>
> Together with all forms, moods, shapes of grief,
> That can denote me truly. These indeed seem,
> For they are actions that a man might play!

Ironically, Bruno Ganz performs his mourning in a beautiful, theatrical manner, putting on the deeply melancholic air of the nineteenth-century Hamlet, the isolated, solipsistic poet grown "desperate with imagination," as Horatio describes it. But as his trappings of grief are exchanged for his even more theatrical "antic disposition," it becomes increasingly less clear, to the actors at the court as well as the audience, what to make of Hamlet's maddening word-plays, riddles, and rhetorical tricks.

Hamlet himself quickly loses control over the parts he plays, and when he takes on the role of the acting instructor (III.ii), it is highly ironic to see the discrepancy between what he says ("suit the action to the word, the word to the action") and his own stage behavior. And yet, there is something inconclusive about the breaks and gaps that open up the different levels of theatrical discourse and action. The wandering "tragedians of the city" who suddenly burst into the scene appear as lost in the senseless plotting and counterplotting at the court as Gertrude (Edith Clever) or the abused Ophelia, for example, or as Horatio (Gunter Berger) who always stands apart, not-present, at the far edge of stage.

When the tragedians begin their ambiguous Mousetrap performance, the previous effect of the real grief so successfully mimed by the First Player (Bernhard Minetti) in his account of Priam's slaughter is deconstructed again as the light of real torchfire flickers across the highly wrought, deliberately contrived pantomime of the "Murder of Gonzago." The shifting figurations and refigurations of the images of death and murder cannot be reconciled in the text or in the playing; nor can Hamlet's doubling of so many supplemental roles—son, lover, father, clown, madman, revenger—escape getting caught up with the violent mechanism of "accidental slaughters" and mistaken purposes that cuts across the apparent difference between fictive Mousetraps and the actual scapegoating Hamlet performs on Ophelia and Gertrude.

Grüber's production is very much aware of this potentially infinite chain of substitutions and transformations and shows us how Hamlet's melancholy of the early scenes gives way to the barely repressed physical violence that is part of his "antic disposition." After the apparent success of the Mousetrap, Hamlet's performance in fact becomes quite literally "blasted with ecstasy" (III.i.162). His whirling words fluctuate between frantic self-congratulation and the virtually incomprehensible mock-ballad

> Why, let the strucken deer go weep,
> The hart ungalled play,
> For some must watch while some must sleep,
> Thus runs the world away

that he sings while dancing hysterically on the chairs left on the deserted platform. After having demolished the chairs, he bursts into a self-defeating parody of the strutting and fretting of the would-be avenger ("Now could I drink hot blood . . ."). This piece of mad fantasy is repeated, although with a difference, in the immediately following scene where Hamlet acts out his confusion in a violent sexual assault on his mother, which takes place on one of the vertically rising floor segments. Both Gertrude and Hamlet fail to achieve their purposes, and the literally fallen Gertrude, like the audience, cannot perceive the absent Ghost to whom Hamlet pretends he is talking.

> **Queen.** To whom do you speak this?
> **Ham.** Do you see nothing there?
> **Queen.** Nothing at all. Yet all that is I see.

This paradoxical confusion between what is and what is not is extended into the finale of the Schaubühne production, where it becomes the unstable ground on which practically all the visual, aural, kinetic, and aesthetic dimensions of the high style which Grüber's theatrical representation had established overturn themselves, and where the high seriousness of the tragic ending *and* the tradition of serious endings in the history of *Hamlet* performances are ironically collapsing within themselves.

Gertrude rushes onstage to report her barely repressed delight over Ophelia's romantic suicide. Likewise, Hamlet and the Clown (Wolf Redl) in the gravedigger's scene do not philosophize about the meaning of death but instead play football with Yorick's skull, only to be interrupted by a grief-stricken Laertes (Willem Menne) who does not know the rules of the game. The grand formalities of the duel preparations quickly dissolve into the bloody farce of consecutive, grotesquely staged murders, with Ger-

Figure 18. Edith Clever as the Queen, Peter Fitz as the King in *Hamlet*. Berlin, 1983. Photo: Ruth Walz.

Figure 19. Jutte Lampe as Ophelia, Bruno Ganz as Hamlet. Berlin, 1983. Photo: Ruth Walz.

trude and Laertes somersaulting to death at exactly the same moment with exactly the same stylized movements.

The language of Schlegel's classic translation has broken down and is displaced by the colloquialized prose in which Hamlet's dying voice—in three consecutive death scenes—tells and retells the story that cannot be coherently told. To stage the catastrophe of the ending as a grand travesty of a "self-consuming artifact" (Stanley Fish) might be considered a daring provocation to the tradition of *Hamlet* performances in Germany; in the context of the Berlin production's self-conscious exhibition of the myth of a cultural monument, however, such a confrontation, with the high artificiality of the interpretive convention which that myth subtends, must quite logically throw us out of our *normal* perspective and thus allow us to reexperience the underlying structural paradoxes and indeterminacies inscribed into Shakespeare's text itself.

The deromanticization of the Romantic Hamlet in Grüber's production therefore achieves a remarkable insight into the problematics of representation dramatized in Shakespeare's art and foregrounded in the recent theoretical practices on and off stage that I discussed in my previous chapter on Blau's "ghosting."

The structural instability of the performance text, and the ambivalence of light/visibility in this production, invite us to look again at the beautiful, ordered mosaic design painted on the Mendelsohn stage. Since the allusion to the Holbein painting cannot be accidental, it is tempting to speculate on its implications. Holbein paints the two splendid figures standing in front of a rich collection of objects and emblems, all of which reflect the power and control of Renaissance man over his world. Yet slashing across the mosaic pavement (in the center of the painting) is the extraordinary anamorphic representation of the death's-head, which invades the complex harmonies and symbolic forms created in/by the painting. Viewed frontally, the skull is invisible. Only from a displaced position at the side of the painting is it suddenly recognizable. The skull, not seen from our normal perspective, throws a shadow on the elegant floor, a shadow that seems to deny *and* affirm the presence of death's centrality.

In Grüber's *Hamlet*, all the figures on the stage throw large shadows on the floor as they move around the empty center, which is filled blindingly, for a short moment, by the invisible Ghost-Father. In relation to the unreadable presence of death, all other questions, Grüber seems to be saying, become necessarily artificial and playful. It is our relation to death that we are looking at through the theatre, and through the play in this theatre. Even as its ghost disappears from sight, it holds power over us. The questions addressed to this theatre of death are clothed in the pathos of the architecture, the set, the costumes, the acting styles, the interpretive and editorial traditions. In addressing its own pathos, the shining artifice of the theatre only survives as abject travesty. But the paradox posed by the *memento mori* continues to give the theatre a particularly powerful edge as it acts out the anamorphosis, turns on its own pretenses, and allegorizes the work of mourning in the collapse of the monument.

As we have seen in Beckett's increasingly minimalist variations on the abject travesty, in the doomed figures of his doomed drama, the theatre is conscious of its economy of death precisely when it stages its own ending and repeats it over and over. In Beckett's late plays, the narrated and dramatized progression toward death and toward the silence of "closed eyes, closing eyes" (*Rockaby*) is a compulsive reviewing and recovering of time: "that time you went back that last time to look was the ruin still there?" (Voice A in *That Time*).

That time in Berlin, the Wall still standing, the self-deconstruction of Grüber's *Hamlet* production seemed to echo the sarcastic comments of the actor in Heiner Müller's *Hamletmachine*. I repeat them,

> I'm not Hamlet. I don't take part any more.
> My words have nothing to tell me anymore.
> Behind me the set is put up. . . .
> I'm not interested in it anymore either.
> The set is a monument

because they throw into relief what must have occured to Grüber when staging the other *Hamlet* in the Mendelsohn building, perhaps one of Europe's most gigantic and technologically sophisticated playhouses. The building became the set for a performance that perhaps indicated the end of an era for the Schaubühne ensemble that had started out in the early 1970s with the radical politics of a Marxist theatre collective and had now reached the celebrity status of an institution. The 1983 *Hamlet* was the last production of a classic I saw in Berlin. Shortly afterward, Peter Stein announced his resignation as artistic director of the Schaubühne, and when Grüber later that year began to work on his Chekhov adaptation, *An der grossen Strasse*, he moved the production out of the Mendelsohn building to an abandoned house in the Kreuzberg district. It would be futile to argue that this removal had any effect on the institution of theatre or on the proclivity of the Schaubühne to design monumental productions for its bourgeois subscribers. This proclivity toward spectacle seemed to grow exponentially with the progressive sense of exhaustion and stagnation that became pervasive as the 1980s wore on and the political denials ("I don't take part any more") subsided. When Robert Wilson staged *Death, Destruction & Detroit 2* at the Schaubühne in 1987, the "denials" of the rites/rights of memory through the collapsing exhibition of a cultural myth had been effectively replaced by the postmodern architectonics of a purely technocratic spectacle whose ubiquitous images circulated around the audience on all four sides (and from above) and imposed the aura of a new panvisual culture of simultaneity that erased memory and history.

The distance between the *Zusammenbruch* of the Romantic pathos in the German *Hamlet* and the colossal projection of Wilson's sublime American pastiche of ruins seems small, and the influence Wilson has had through his work as a director in German and European theatre is perhaps hardly surprising. But in the collapsing distance between the European classical and modernist traditions and global American postmodernism lie some of the ironies that I want to confront as I continue to trace the contradictions and pretensions of the postmodern.

Figure 20. Mother-board of a computer. Photo: J. Birringer.

5 ■ OVEREXPOSURE: SITES OF POSTMODERN MEDIA

Les Immatériaux

Nightmare of a traveler: slowly driving across Southern California on identical freeways, from San Diego to Santa Barbara, feeling increasingly disoriented from the images of mountains, beaches, deserts, barren suburbs, and glossy shopping malls that flash by the window. The map offers no help; the inanimate, blind landscape on the other side of the window conspires to collapse the driver's point of view. Los Angeles has disappeared into hundreds of miles of deterritorialized zones. It is neither city nor country nor desert. The opposition between center and periphery has disappeared too. Sheer contiguity replaces the spatial logic of oppositions, the syntax and grammar of representation that normally order the grid structure of an industrial city. Los Angeles is invisibly seductive because it can no longer be comprehended geographically; the vision it produces has to do with the speed and energy spent in movement across obliterated boundaries. The apparent infinity of routes and the equivalence of all directions only heighten the sense of circular drift. The car radio may be

An earlier version of this essay first appeared in *Performing Arts Journal* 29 (1986).

the last indicator of a change in territory, yet there is no guarantee that weather reports or hit parades will differ from one wavelength to another.

This scenario of the "overexposed city," as the French urban sociologist Paul Virilio calls it, captures the postindustrial ambience that we begin to experience in the changing relationships of our bodies and our consciousness to the sprawling ubiquity and instantaneousness of information in our electronic culture. Virilio explains this sprawl in terms of a telecommunicational world of absolute speed that will ultimately obliterate cities and their inhabitants. But there is another fiercely debated French theory. Jean Baudrillard's concept of "simulation" seems even more pertinent to American perceptions of the technological "revolution" and the new "automobility" of audiovisual information.

For Baudrillard, the idea of orbiting around L.A. is directly correlated to a postmodern mentality conditioned by several decades of American mass culture. No more subject, focal point, exteriority, no more distance between subject and object, no more scene, no illusion, no secret. What is lost cannot be found because it has been simulated in advance.

It now seems a long time ago that Artaud, in *The Theatre and Its Double,* attacked the theatre for *representing* life instead of being life. In Baudrillard's nihilistic scenario of contemporary mass media culture, the whole idea of "theatre," or any representational art, is completely inverted: the distinction between representation and reality has become irrelevant because the real itself has been eclipsed by a self-regulating, global technology of "programs," "models," or "genetic codes." Baudrillard's favorite example for such a model is Disneyland: the miniature operation of phantasms set up to conceal that all of "real" America is Disneyland.

We may not be inclined to suspend our disbelief in such French speculation on American models, but what are we to do when French theory travels into the Beaubourg museum to *dramatize* the questions raised by the postmodern culture of simulacra? When I visited "Les Immatériaux" (March 28–July 15, 1985) at the Centre Georges Pompidou in Paris, I felt as if I have walked into a theatre. Upon entering a long, airportlike tunnel, I was given a set of headphones, and to complete the *Verfremdungseffekt,* I first heard a low electronic hum in my ears, followed by a dramatically recited fragment from Beckett's *The Unnamable,* a convoluted monologue of an "I" who can neither speak nor remain silent. But when I looked, I found myself in a dark, mirrored vestibule entitled "Theatre of the Non-body." Apart from my headphoned reflection in the mirror, there were five dioramas of stage sets empty except for imperceptible shifts in the lighting. As if I had met the last riddle of the old subject/ object dualisms at the crossroads, this disembodied remainder of a theatre opened onto five meandering paths that provided passages—interrupted by music and spoken texts—through the gigantic metallic labyrinth into which the Beaubourg exhibition in the fifth floor gallery had been arranged.

It was a labyrinth of sounds and sights, indistinctly divided by silver gauze screens and lighting effects into sixty sites interpenetrated by the broadcast zones and their invisible infrared signals. A viewer is immediately aware of the unsettling audiovisual juxtapositions: the sound in one's ear (e.g. literary and theoretical texts by Borges, Artaud, Baudrillard, Barthes, Blanchot, Virilio, etc.) did not refer to the technological displays and objects in the sites. During the walk, one could refer to a computerized index of the exhibition's concepts. But both the index and the catalogue of the show were illegible; they referred to new scientific theories of circuits, cells, energy states, genetic manipulation, and so forth. I heard several visitors complain that the catalogue offered no help at all—which was precisely the point.

Organized by the French philosopher Jean-François Lyotard and a large team of collaborators from the Centre de Création Industrielle, "Les Immatériaux" was indeed meant to create an interactive environment for conceptual explorations of our world, a "reality" no longer securely representable in human or artistic terms but increasingly dependent on technoscientific operations. "Les Immatériaux", in other words, was not an exhibition that exhibited anything (least of all paintings). It was a provocation to the practice of viewing art in a museum as well as to any aesthetic or art-historical narrative based on anthropocentric and historicist notions of continuity and tradition. The references to Artaud and Beckett were hardly accidental. We were confronted with the postmodern fulfillment of an older avant-garde battle cry: no more masterworks.

"Les Immatériaux" radically broke with the idea of domination and control over perceptual space as such. In another sense it also abandoned the Foucaldian concept of the "panoptic" museum of human nature, the relationship between power and the gaze, and its subjection of the body.

It is quite impossible, then, to describe the exhibition without distorting it, since it primarily sought to evoke a temporal, multisensory experience of an authorless, discontinuous, world of invisible interfaces between heterogeneous objects, artifacts, industrial products, and complex theoretical constructs. The *effects* of these theoretical constructs, the new "immaterials" of postmodern culture, inform our experience: computer-generated signals, electronic processing, biogenetic manipulation, telecommunications, filmic, holographic and video simulation. Disneyland, Hollywood, and Silicon Valley all at once.

Walking past the sixty sites turned out to be a nightmare of a different sort, namely the familiar experience of total information overload. It was a significant effect, however, because the five paths that started in the "disembodied theatre" also turned out to follow a certain logic that made them eventually converge in a concluding site entitled "The Labyrinth of Language." This site, with its profusion of computer consoles and text processors, repeated what was implied by the dispersed jumble of projectors, photocopiers, microscopes, spectrographs, VCRs, sound synthesizers, microwave ovens, and designer robots (including a set of Japanese "sleeping cells" equipped with radio, TV, telephone, and climate control!) in the preceding sites. First, we live surrounded by machines that facilitate a flow of plural messages with which we as individuals can no longer keep up. Second, if everything is the immaterial function or effect of messages, then "Les Immatériaux" would seem to suggest that the labyrinth of reproduction and technoscientific reinvention is organized, after all, according to general interactions within a communicational system.

And here we come to the most problematic aspect of Lyotard's conception of "Les Immatériaux". While dramatizing the experience of *over-exposure* and *dispersion* in postmodern culture, he held on to a structuralist model of the communication process (sender, receiver, code, referent, and so on), which lay behind even the most disparate high-tech special effects. Human creators and material objects (the mirror of the subject) have disappeared from the center; "messages" (and their control) determine the horizon of this technological labyrinth.

In various interviews, Lyotard refered to this posttheatrical stage setting as an "operational structure," a kind of "scenography" of our postmodern condition that can be understood as a nervous system of instabilities and mutations within the parameters of the communicational circuit. According to Lyotard, "the model of language replaces the model of matter. The scale on which the structure is operational in contemporary technoscience and artistic experimentation is no longer a human one. Humans are overwhelmed by the very small (microchip), which is also the only means of information about the very large (astrophysics)."[1] Lyotard is able to equate "contemporary technoscience and artistic experimentation" because they are on the same order of dispersed "language games" and synthetic processes that have displaced all the older unifying theories of knowledge claiming control over physical reality. The "material", he suggests, "disappears as an independent entity."[2] Both mind and matter, in other words, have become part of a general code of rational abstraction (a new metaphysics of the perpetual absence of reality in the code?) that replaces subjective or objective "reality" with a cybernetic pattern of circulation.

This is not a comfortable vision since it implies that the coded system *is*

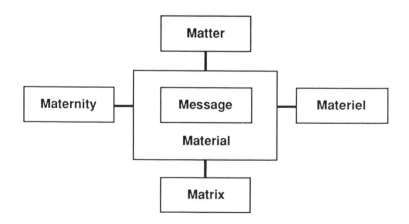

the instrumentation by which everything (any message) is available and interrelatable. But "Les Immatériaux" made a great effort toward showing—even as I heard the voice of Artaud in my headphones protesting the "presence of my corporal pain"—the consequences of Virilio's and Baudrillard's scenarios of an overexposed culture: the disappearance of consciousness into the space of technology means the disappearance of bodies. Far from being human extensions, as popular mythology describes our machines, "Les Immatériaux" displayed countless examples of how humans might be duplicated: everything could become subject to simulation at any time. In all five paths of the exposition, the most diverse "messages," from holograms to fast food, from music video or computer music to synthetic skin or olfactory simulacra, were shown to be artificial replacements of/for the human body and its material activities.

I shall conclude my report on the self-enclosed structure of Lyotard's postmodern exposition by briefly pointing to the concerns that performance research might share with scientific thought. If we look at current multimedia experiments that incorporate media culture and the technical apparatus of electronic production and reproduction into the hybrid forms of conceptual and theatrical performance, we see that the ancient theatrical conundrum—What is the nature of reality/appearance?—has been fully subsumed by mutated, mediated "realities." These intermedia performances dissolve the subject, and the subsequent loss of identity creates the condition of a vertiginous mimicry that permanently destabilizes the perception of difference—between original and copy or between live presence and its prerecorded and projected versions. As *mimicry*, in the sense in which Roger Caillois described the mimetic assimilation of the animate to the inanimate as an *assimilation to space*, multimedia performances tend not so much toward erasing all differences but toward flattening and reducing them. Difference becomes indistinguishable from its disappearance yet functions indeterminately through this disappearance.

In the sense of Virilio's perception of this volatility, which I paraphrased at the beginning of this chapter, we could describe multimediated performances as *overexposures* in which the topologies of images are distributed and controlled by time movement. Virilio's "aesthetics of disappearance" address technology and technological culture in terms of the effects of this distribution or manipulation of time movement and duration. One way of charting the effects of acceleration (cinematic, videomatic, audiovisual speed) is to look at what is left behind, what is liquidated or forgotten. Perhaps the late Andy Warhol's endless series of silkscreens of recycled mass-cultural images will be remembered only through the commodity icons—the soup cans and Marilyn Monroes—which refer neither to Campbell or Monroe nor to Warhol but to the commodity system itself. Warhol's assimilation to the totalizing commodity system was so complete that it exemplified the disappearance of art's separate status and of all traditional aesthetic values of distinction. In its convergence with fashion, advertising, and the production of commercial culture as such, Pop Art's method of reproducing mass-reproduced reality—in the surfaces of soup cans or the faces of stars—made it an art of disappearance that paradoxically both exposed the commodity character of all contemporary art production and exaggerated its visual synthesizing of all mass-cultural forms. It did so to the extent that its parasitical appropriations gained a critical edge, a menacing edge perhaps. I'm not sure whether such a menace was implied in Warhol's famous statement, made in 1963, that "everybody should be a machine." But Pop Art's double exposure of commodity culture and commodity art was undoubtedly a final act when it appeared in the 1960s. The survival of art can be understood, in retrospect, as a logical extension of the parody of transparency and indifference posited in Warhol's factory image: the relation of art to the world is characterized by its own endless reproducibility.

In the accelerated rhythms of transatlantic postmodernism over the past twenty-five years, survival has become recognizable in the disappearances that are continuously replayed on the edge of parody and within the logic of fetishism, including those parodies of pop culture that are less ironically Warholesque but more violent, such as punk rock, or more pathetically melancholy, such as the German and Italian neoexpressionist painters and their more cynical American imitators. In the theatre and in performance art, the question of overexposure and disappearance is less directly related to the fetishized surface of the image as such. Rather, it is the ephemeral nature of performance, its physical and kinetic materiality, that is resuscitated and tested against its assimilation into the electronic and audiovisual recording machines. This resuscitation, however, is already an effect of the technological dominance in recent multimedia performance. The work of Squat Theatre uses such dominance to exaggerate the perceptual ambiguities that had already been built into their earlier indoor/outdoor performances. In the period after their emigration to New York from Hungary in the late 1970s, Squat worked out of their storefront space on 23rd Street, consistently blurring the lines of theatrical perception by opening the "interior" space onto the real life on the sidewalk and by "mixing" the staged, fictional events inside with staged, fictional and accidental events outside. These earlier performances (*Andy Warhol's Last Love, Pig! Child! Fire!* and *Mr. Dead and Mrs. Free*) were relentlessly aimed at the audience's perceptual processes and their physical and psychic relationship to their own position *inside* the splitting stage. After the loss of their home on 23rd Street and with *Dreamland Burns*, performed at the Kitchen in 1986, Squat seems to have retreated behind the proscenium.

When the performance of *Dreamland Burns* opens we look at a screen in front of the stage and watch a film starring Eszter Balint (recognized for her leading role in Jim Jarmusch's *Stranger Than Paradise*). A disjointed narrative, the film depicts Alexandra (Balint) in several scenes of departure and urban travel, ending with her falling asleep in her new apartment. The film in fact ends with the screen burning up (a trompe l'oeil effect on the screen, with real fire on the stage behind), and several actors from the film reappear in the ensuing live action onstage. The ironic allusions to film, dream, and the magic of special effects multiply over the course of the performance, whose subject matter remains exceedingly banal in spite of Alexandra/Balint's self-reflexive play on her real and fictionalized status as immigrant and outsider. It is perhaps precisely the banality of the conversation onstage, and of the physical objects/props that keep falling down from the fly space, that heightens the tension director Stephen Balint achieves by further confusing the relationship between "live" and mediated and superimposed action. Near the beginning of the live performance we see a tableau of four dummies that resemble the actual actors or the film actors. Occasionally these dummies become animated when films of the actual actors' faces are projected onto the inanimate dummies' faces. In one of the pivotal scenes, perhaps reminiscent of King Lear's savage fantasy of cutting up the body of his daughter to discover the concealed evil, the dummy body of Alexandra/Balint's departed lover (in the film) is cut open by two men with an electric saw. They discover contraband. The idea that there is something to be found behind the facades and screens and copies that is not already fake or perverted or merely fantasized is followed through up to its melodramatic false ending which could be straight from a grade-B-Hollywood movie. It is also a depressingly ironic ending, stranger than dreamland, which could have been filmed by Jarmusch, and its ambiguity reinforces the bleak vision through which the Hungarian company views their unassimilated double life in the foreign country that is their home.

Their formal retreat into the proscenium stage, away from actual interventions on the street level to very complex conceptual forays into the melodramatic imaginary of American film, TV, and theatre, raises the question whether their reliance on clichés and cartoon characters foregrounds the severe reduction of our audiovisual lives produced by this imaginary. In the physical performance onstage, this reduction is presented as a kind of *overmediation* that has edited out any self-expression. In 'L' Train to Eldorado, a production Squat showed at the Brooklyn Academy of Music in 1987, a soap-opera plot opens with a married couple embroiled in a domestic argument leading to their breakup. However, we don't see the actual, physical argument between the two actors (Eszter Balint, Mark Boone), but a film projected onto the empty faces of painted cut-out sculptures. The following live action parodies the soap-opera's never-ending, fragmentary narrative of excessive emotions, romance, and suffering, by forcing the stereotypically feminized male protagonist (Boone) into the increasingly tearful and passive role of the abandoned husband, closely monitored by an onstage camera crew of half-naked, devilish-looking men claiming to film a documentary about his plight. There are several poignant scenes during which the camera crew directs the stage actor playing the feminized husband how to express true and convincing emotions for their documentary which turns out to be a fictional melodrama. The performance ends with an even more fantastic, Ovidian metamorphosis: in front

of the spectacular photographic projection of an abandoned urban wasteland (the burnt-out shells of the South Bronx), the husband is transformed
into a tree. The imaginary 'L' train has brought the abandoned lover to a
perversely happy and disembodied ending.

The actor's disappearance in Squat's performance is echoed, though in
a considerably more violent way, in another important work in the mid-
1980s, *Deep Sleep*. Written, filmed, and directed by John Jesurun for New
York's La Mama Theatre in 1986, *Deep Sleep* fully adopts cinematic techniques (jump cuts, flash backs, wide angle/close-up/reverse angle shots,
and so forth) for the writing as well as the staging. In its powerful dialectical setting, the film/play dramatizes the apparent contradiction between screen life and real (stage) life with four actors trapped between two
huge movie screens suspended at opposite ends of the performance space.
Their frantic dialogue is conducted with two actors on screen, and when
they gradually get sucked into the film and onto the celluloid, they dematerialize. In spite of their efforts, they find it impossible to break out of
the frame again, with the exception of one actor who refuses to be "projected." Forced to maintain and operate the projectors, this remaining actor
becomes schizophrenic.

In various ways, these performances employ a strategy of cultural
realism that does not conceal the extent to which our audiovisual lives are
possessed and managed by cinematic and televisual conventions of melodrama that manipulate ideological and social conflicts in emotional terms.
At the same time, their spatial, narrative, and technological design ex-
aggerates the cyborgian dimension of postmodern reality (hyperreality)
by suggesting that realities, identities, subjectivities, and bodies are merely
doubles—projected ghost images—already diffracted into the media and
no longer distinguishable from their simulation by the media. The diffrac-
tion onto multiple surfaces and screens is staged as a disembodiment of
identity that in the specific tension of physical acting (stage) and projection
(screen) appears unresolvable except through a heightened and fantastic
style parodying the whole idea of a resolution to the question of identity.
In *Dreamland Burns,* the parody includes the notion of a given, "naturalized" or adopted national identity. The animation of the dummies in
Squat's work is particularly fascinating because its surrealist effect (the
postmodern Max Headroom effect) plays not merely upon the distinctions
between "animate" and "inanimate," or "actor" and "model," but also
upon the more complex issue of the *technical regulation* of fantasy, of
fantasized identity, through the surface/medium of the body.

I shall return to the technological inscriptions of the body in my last
chapter, but in the context of Squat's work and of *Deep Sleep* it is worth
noting that the use of screens and film/video projections in the theatrical
"live" performances superimposes the synchronic temporalities of
electronic media into real-time theatre. The exchange of images between
screen and stage inevitably shifts attention to the variable boundaries of

the body and to the question of what constitutes the body-in-performance once it is permeable or replaceable, dematerialized into its blown-up or minituarized electronic doubles.

With the inconclusive ending of *Deep Sleep* in mind, it might be tempting to reconsider "Les Immatériaux" as a schizophrenic vision of our postmodern culture. On the other hand, that exposition clearly suggested a "natural" loss of reality because of the excess of information, which from now on might simply transcend the human mind and bodily materiality through electronic processes that can be read and decoded like the consciousness or "neurovegetative system" (Lyotard) they simulate. If my language has turned circular, it is only because my reflection is already caught in the logical and calculable operation of the cybernetic model dramatized by "Les Immatériaux." Assuming the compatibility of mind and system-operated language (artificial intelligence), cybernetics has developed a theory of messages and their control which would *define*—for users of simulation technology—what can be expressed, invented, and exchanged within the frame. We could find countless examples of such frames (video games, MTV, TV serials are the most obvious media formats), but we would not yet have answered Lyotard's question: what happens if knowledge (emotional knowledge, sensitivities, personal and cultural memory, sexual experience, and so forth) is reduced to computed information? What happens when artistic experimentation is indistinguishable from technoscientific operation? At the heart of such questions lies the modern history of scientific thought, and perhaps one could see "Les Immatériaux" as an ironic confirmation of Heidegger's prediction (in his 1954 lecture "The Question Concerning Technology") that modern science was becoming a tool of technological modes of "enframing" our condition in the world.

The history in question has advanced in quantum leaps from older cognitive models that projected the logicomechanical operations of the mind onto a natural cosmos viewed as nonprobabilistic, causal, and mechanistic to the explosive rethinking of reality, the nature of matter, and our representations of it, after the physics of Einstein, Heisenberg, Gödel, Monod, Morin, and Thom. If concepts of uncertainty and relativity are now being discussed in terms of the exchangeability of signs, maximum entropy, noise, and redundancy, we have reached a stage in the dialectic between modern physics and cybernetics where the postmodern paradigm of "mind," *information processing,* is based on the deterministic, calculable operations through which computer technology can transform the world and supersede human creativity.

It is not surprising, therefore, that the Beaubourg exposition, sponsored by the Centre de Création Industrielle, no longer envisions a realm in which the systematized operation of "embodied mathematics," as computer engineers lovingly call their machines, could be contested. That realm, Heidegger once recalled, used to be art.

Image World/Flat World

For the last part of this essay, I propose to reposition the realm of con-tention—postmodern art—by making a transatlantic jump cut from Paris to New York and Houston and to two American art exhibitions which are different from "Les Immatériaux" and yet similar in their enframing of our condition in the world. The American exhibitions, which opened in the winter of 1989, did not share the philosophical sophistication and scientific bias of the French concept. "Image World: Art and Media Culture," a massive survey curated for the Whitney Museum in New York, and the smaller-scale video installation "When the World Was Flat" by Terry Berk-owitz, curated for Houston's Contemporary Arts Museum, both re-sponded to the challenge posed by "Les Immatériaux" with a retreat into a narrow arthistorical/museological frame of presentation while thematically addressing the most crucial and repressed subtext of the art-and-media based "World" they represented: namely the alignment of cultural produc-tion with advanced consumer capitalism. Both exhibitions took the current media-saturated society of the spectacle for granted. Lacking a critical theory of the image-making apparatus that has collapsed aesthetic and commodity production onto each other, both exhibitions tended to show the trajectory of media culture as a progression and accumulation of image technologies in the visual arts, from early photography to the latest multi-video sculpture. And it was rather ironic that the postmodern world of mass media representation, from their All-American perspective, was re-ferred back to art and not to the economic, social, and political relations of power that have been affected by the mediation. I want to explore the contradictions in their representation of media culture by focusing on the political side of postmodernism's relation to late capitalism, the side most obviously repressed in the instrumental view of technology at "Les Im-matériaux."

The Whitney exhibition was sponsored by the Polaroid Corporation. In the Foreword to the exhibition catalog, the sponsor is "very pleased to be associated with 'Image World.' Throughout our history, a basic enjoy-ment of images and a natural curiosity about them—in everyday life, in the sciences, in industry, in education, and in art—has helped to define our corporate culture."[3] Inspired by so much corporate pleasure expressed in an all-inclusive definition of "our culture," both the catalog and the mise-en-scène of the exhibition sought to trace a comprehensive outline of the parallel progression of modern art (seamlessly linked here with the history of photography and motion pictures) and commodity capitalism. In its simplifying and unifying narrative, the exhibition first claimed that mass culture has become an overwhelmingly visual culture in which the media's images define visual thinking and communication, and then assembled a vast array of media works from the last three decades, including works of the most affirmative or playfully affirmative as well as the critical and subversive kind. Even though an attempt was made to engage critical practices that exercise public and situationist modes of address outside of the art institutions, the commission of several posters and large billboards by Barbara Kruger, Lorna Simpson, Jeff Koons, Chuck Close, and Gran Fury, as well as a public projection ("GLASNOST IN U.S.A.") against the wall of the museum by Krzysztof Wodiczko, did not push any specific questions about the urban outside, or about the city dwellers' "visual thinking" (i.e., their interpretation of the public messages) in relationship to the artworld inside. Neither did Gran Fury's activist détournement of "United Colors of Benetton" advertising slogans into a less romantic public-service announcement ("KISSING DOESN'T KILL: GREED AND INDIFFERENCE DO. CORPORATE GREED, GOVERNMENT INACTION, AND PUBLIC INDIFFERENCE MAKE AIDS A POLITICAL CRISIS") compensate for the inside exhibition's failure to grasp politically the history of technology. Technology is not neutral and has never been. The collusion of media images and media-based art is the very model of reproduction that needs to be dissected if we want to shift attention to the intersections between image technology and institutional power.

We could draw certain conclusions from the model represented by "Image World." The rise of photography as a new medium coincided with the rise of the industrialized nations and the relentless expansion of capitalist economy into available world markets. The history of photography is also entangled with the modernization of warfare and military technology, and advanced consumer capitalism is unimaginable without the integration of the visual languages and technical means of the media with the production and consumption of consumer goods, information, and entertainment. At this stage in the postindustrial economics of flexible accumulation and multinational capital, we watch the dominant media rapidly encompass every aspect of social experience. In other words, the international flow of images links the industrial apparatus with mass cultural consumption to such an extent that we no longer even recognize the corporate control over information in the ongoing spectacle. From the daily talk show to the Super Bowl, from the last presidential election to the next stock market crash, events take place as media events. They are no longer interrupted by commercials because commercial images are an intrinsic part of the program flow. The overpowering presence of the media constructs and describes the surfaces and surface values of the world we watch. We ourselves become the screens of a dispersed audience on which consumable images of identity, consensus, fashionable difference, conflict, fear, and desire can be tested.

The serial production of cultural commodities in TV and advertising doesn't mediate any real human needs or experiences but refers back to its own model of symbolic economy. The news is now part of this economy too, purely designed for consumption. "60 Minutes," for example, earns $35–40 million a year for its network. The privately owned networks support a government that supports and represents the interests of capital.

SEEING IS NOT BELIEVING
DON'T FIND YOUR WORLD IN OURS
WE NEED HEALTH CARE AND HOUSING
    Barbara Kruger (poster design)

Television's instantaneous capacity to present "live" images of real catas-trophes or real revolutions elsewhere reinforces the naturalness and trans-parency coded into the medium's ordered and orderly coverage. The order is insci ibed in advance because it results from the repetition of the same in the regular programming.

THE REVOLUTION WILL NOT BE TELEVISED
WHEN THERE IS CHAOS THERE ARE NO COMMERCIALS
    Lorna Simpson (billboard design)

Our corporate culture reflects corporate interests and regulations of the dream of accessibility and pluralism. Corporate power determines what gets produced and exhibited culturally and what is excluded or restricted. The meanings and standards of "public acceptability" can be shifted around just like capital. And the Energizer-battery rabbit runs across the TV screen images, energizing nothing in particular. We laugh at the mes-sage we may not understand.

In a slightly exaggerated form, this is the premise I deduce from the Whitney Museum's display of the "Image World". At the same time, the museum must have assumed a critical role of the arts in this American model of the world. It was not clear at all, therefore, why the exhibition did not choose to explore the impact of critical theory (in Marxism, feminism, psychoanalysis and poststructuralism) on critical postmodern art but, in-stead, shuffled its cards and adopted the view that art and mass culture have achieved a complete interpenetration. From examples of early Con-ceptual Art and Pop Art to the most recent photo or computer collages and multimedia installations, the show reveled in the spectacular transforma-tion of art through which an older dialectical struggle between high mod-ernism and mass culture had been superseded by a postmodern reproduc-tion of existing images. This mode of reproduction, whether playful, ironic or critical, was identified—and thus unavoidably compromised—with the existing "American media landscape of teletransmissions, channels, feed-back, playback and interface."[4]

Walking through the exhibition turned into a strange experience of déjà vu. Everything that was piled up in the cramped space of the Whitney (over 100 works apart from a separate program of 250 films and videos) seemed almost instantly recognizable: an endless series of secondhand images, borrowed from the media, related to the media, satirical of the media. After looking at Warhol's *Double Elvis* and the early Rosenquists, Liechtensteins, and Rauschenbergs, among the dozens of magazine ads, altered movie posters and large Cibachromes depicting film stars and celebrities, one was hardly surprised to see how more recent art by Frank

Majore, Glegg and Guttman, Richard Prince, or Jeff Koons continue to be attracted to the myths of Hollywood and commercial fame. Art as self-advertisement is no longer a contradiction. However, when it appropriates the language and forms of the mass media to expose or critique the "image world," then it can't pretend to be innocent of its own status in the mainstream market. Its success as a critique, ironically, guarantees that it will be reappropriated by the market and the institutions. Most of the important feminist media interventions and critiques of the institutions (by Barbara Kruger, Cindy Sherman, Sherrie Levine, Dara Birnbaum, Silvia Kolbowski) now hang peacefully on the walls of the institutional forces they tried to resist or deconstruct. The museum, like other public spaces, corporate architectures, and channels of information occupied by media images, represents the aestheticized culture of late capitalism, the world as we know it.

Hans Haacke's phototextual critiques of corporate culture represent that very culture with all the contradictions it entails. Intended as a political protest and a challenge to capitalism's indifference to its own contradictions, Haacke's critical evidence provides a categorical moral position that opposes capitalism's presumed amorality. But such moral opposition depends on what it seeks to oppose, and since it cannot effectively replace or alter it, its own assumption or position becomes merely complementary to what it represents. In the Whitney show, Haacke's 1979 piece, entitled "The Right to Life," reproduced a "Breck girl" picture from the shampoo ad of the American Cyanamid Corporation. He had then recontextualized the ad with a simulated copy-text that exposes the company's false concern for employees of child-bearing age who are exposed to toxic substances. These employees, we read, were given the choice to be reassigned to a lower-paying job, to leave the company, or to have themselves sterilized in order to stay in their old jobs. Haacke's text mentions that several women chose sterilization and then ends with the company slogan: "American Cyanamid. Where Women Have a Choice." The disruptions between text and image determine the ironic play set in motion against the "facts" of institutional power, while the dis-play of corporate power and its relation to the disparity of choices at Cyanamid in fact remains wholly indeterminate. Since Haacke's disruptive collage cannot control its moral imperative, it remains unclear to whom and for whom this collage is speaking, or whether a cynical corporate capitalism could not speak it too.

On the other side of the corridor the Whitney displayed three photo-text posters by Barbara Kruger, whose work has been concerned most directly with the politics of address ("YOU ARE NOT YOURSELF") and the radical contingencies of the choices of interpretation and identification. Paradoxically, the anitcapitalist assaults in her shifting references and verbal addresses derive their visual and verbal power from the rhetoric of advertising and televisual address. Her disintegrating address at the Whitney, "YOU ARE NOT YOURSELF," splattered over the fragmented photo of a woman's face reflected in a shattered mirror, would have offered a stronger challenge to the surrounding masculine-encoded "Image World" if gender relations or sexual politics had been diacritically examined in the exhibition. Similarly, after we have grown used to seeing video installations in museums and discotheques all over the country, the disruptive effect of reframed, repositioned and altered images/TV-sets is completely minimized.

Earlier feminist disruptions of the commodification logic sought to unmask the powerful mechanisms through which the dominant media constantly construct models of identity, gender role behavior, sexual difference, patriotism, hero worship, values and attitudes of public consent. Today's politicized styles of resistance, fully indebted to the wide-ranging impact of feminist theory yet guilty of contributing to the growing commodification of its practice, tend to be cynically resigned into a minimalist form of appropriation that plays with found materials and the inconsequential effects of montage. In Gretchen Bender's "TV Text and Image" installation, for example, we saw three rows of three TV sets, each tuned to a different network or cable channel. We were made to watch the beautiful flow of their synchronized images through tiny phrases superimposed on the surface of the screens: MILITARY RESEARCH, SELF-CENSORSHIP, GENDER TECHNOLOGY, PEOPLE WITH AIDS, and so forth. The arbitrary conjunction of image and supertitle was disorienting and upsetting for a few moments. Viewing habits seem to adjust almost immediately, however, and the people next to me stayed for a while to follow the New York Giants game or a scene with James Stewart in *It's a Wonderfule Life*. Bender's critique aims both at the content and the *mere presence* of the media. And their mere presence (Marshall McLuhan's "The medium is the message") guarantees the uselessness of Bender's critique, since their power does not depend on the content at all. Since they do speak about military research and people with AIDS, the problem of "self-censorship" or disinformation, for example, arises face-to-face with their power to construct selectively mediated realities without reciprocity. The viewer has no access to media responding only to themselves or simulating public involvement through engineered effects of ratings systems and talk shows in which the viewer watches other "live" viewers watching. At the same time, Bender's attempt to force us to read her supertitles as a form of reinformation against the surface of the media pointed to the crucial question of our positions as viewers within a structure of social relations.

In this sense, Nam June Paik's colossal monitor wall, "Fin de Siècle II," pushed the problem to the other extreme by suggesting, in the most absolute terms, that we are reduced to zombielike customers of a grand discotheque. Paik's Korean sense of humor is here completely overwhelmed by the spectacle of Korean high technology zooming at us with a flood of fragmented, recomposed, multiplied, and computer-controlled image quotations. These quotations are culled from disparate sources—a Joseph Beuys live performance in Tokyo, a David Bowie music video, a

Figure 21. Nam June Paik, "Fin de Siècle II," video installation, 1989. Photo: David Allison. Courtesy of Whitney Museum of American Art.

dance by the Canadian company LaLaLa Human Steps, naked female bodies from a porno film, abstract color designs,—and they appear as a perfectly homogenous montage on the 280-monitor mosaic. This multichannel videotape actually has a short running time but is looped to flow endlessly, or at least to create the televisual impression of a ceaseless image continuum that refers to itself in its successive, droning repetition. It is a small world of utterly diminished significance with no end or apocalypse in sight.

If Paik's robotic computer-video wall were a triumphant embodiment of the consumer culture as "Image World," the quantitative logic and fetishizing effect of its weightless signs may refer to nothing but a law of equivalence in which everything can be exchanged in this spectacle of social relations. Undoubtedly, it will be viewed in many different and conflicting ways, and its apparent weightlessness is precisely a function of the mass cultural fetishization of redundant images, of visual excess, and of monstrous proliferation. Paik's wall even has a mythical dimension in its rhetorical sublimity. With its deliberate and relentless repetition it may evoke a sense of fatality that is phantasmagoric. It is not the end of history (there is no history and no memory), but the fatality that derives from an anxiety of emptiness.

In Terry Berkowitz's media installation for the Houston Contemporary

Arts Museum, "When the World Was Flat," the same sense of fatality was invoked for different reasons. Although her work is closely related to the appropriations and collages of found materials from the "Image World" I just discussed, her interest in the politics of representation aligns her with the feminist-influenced practices of Barbara Kruger, Dara Birnbaum, and Gretchen Bender. Postmodern art's political pretensions are nowhere more apparent, however, than in a critique of media domination acted out *within* and *through* the pervasive scenario of the capitalist "Image World" itself. I want to examine the problems of complicity by focusing on the critical propositions behind Berkowitz's video sculpture and on her mise-en-scène. It is possible to speak of a "staging" of video in this case, since "When The World Was Flat" sought to break the overloaded visuality and flatness of the installation form (as in Paik's work) by expanding images and sound into a physical environment.

The underground space of the Perspectives Gallery at the Houston Contemporary Arts Museum was used in an intriguing cavelike manner. After passing through the threshold hearing birdsong, one entered the dark interior, which turned out to be the familiar womb of cinematic spectacle (wall projection) and daily television. In order to estrange us from this

Figure 22. Terry Berkowitz, "When the World Was Flat," multimedia installation, 1990. Photo: Rick Gardner. Courtesy of Contemporary Arts Museum, Houston.

familiarity, the ten monitors were thrown into "abnormal" positions, as if discarded on a junk heap, some of them stacked onto a large pile of generic face masks made of silver papier-mâché. The heap of faces surrounding and supporting the images and their containers was the most interesting conceptual aspect of the work's dialectic between physical material and disembodied, electronic information. The so-called neutral mask (as opposed to the ritual masks in non-Western sacred and theatrical performances) is modeled directly upon the human face.

The orchestration of the disembodied information was simple. After a few glances one could easily identify the two video channels (six monitors) from the four TV monitors tuned into local TV stations. During my visit I watched a symphony of two daytime soap operas, a talk show, MTV clips, a video tape of a still frame showing birds flocking to a TV antenna, and a heavily edited video tape showing close-ups of consumer goods, shopping malls, and suburban track homes interspersed with black-and-white mug shots of human faces. The larger video projection on the wall repeated a six-minute sequence of stunning slow-motion images, with distorting close-ups and freeze-frames, extracted from newscasts from all over the world: Soviet military parades, Pope John Paul II celebrating mass, Islamic fundamentalist rallies, British soccer hooligans, Chinese soldiers dancing on Tiananmen Square, a marching band of North Korean school children, Salvadoran rebels or soldiers engaged in battle. While these images unfolded, I heard voices and noise that progressed from low density to extreme high density. From the overwhelming cacophony I can only remember the rattling sound of chains and, early on, the soothing voice of a commercial ("How does it feel to have saved more than $1000?"), the harsh voice of a demagogue ("We must penetrate every area of our society"), and the rallying cry of the Nazis: "Sieg Heil." The primary objective of Berkowitz's audiovisual sculpture, I assume, was to make people think through the sensory overload and consider how they are programmed by the media. Like birds flocking to the antenna, we watch, eat, shop, consume, listen, watch. Exceedingly banal, the message remained in a closed circle, and the images of birds, shopping aisles, praying Christians, and dancing Communists converge in the space and the technical-aesthetic design form of the music-video clip. As images, these reframed media images didn't have the power to criticize anything; nor did they function indirectly as strategic devices, historicizing and distancing the overexposed continuity of an administered culture. Berkowitz is obviously concerned with the mediated economy of American capitalism; the convergence she wants to expose raises very serious issues. While her audiovisual sculpture acknowledges the construction of consent through media bombardment and the pressures of commercial mass production, it simultaneously wants to expose the repressive channels that allow their homogenizing effects. Berkowitz questions neither the presence of the media nor the democratic value of consensus; the choice of political content in her large image projections, however, locates the dangers of homogeneity not only in consumption but in militarism, nationalism, and fundamentalism. If the American "Image World" produces homogeneity, then it must project military, moral, and nationalist integration on a very large scale indeed. And if the American "Image World" is presumed to be the model for a universal, global mediascape of images, how does integration operate outside of the museum, the home-entertainment systems, and the shopping malls, in those arenas within the societies of the spectacle riddled with oppression and exploitation, cultural differences, and an economics of inequality?

The pile of generic faces (handcrafted by artisans in Barcelona) strewn over the floor of the museum weakens as a metaphor. To whom can such a sculpture be addressed? The assumption of a homogeneous culture in the face of a socially and racially divided America (not to speak of other countries) is plainly absurd. The images of the pope, the Shiite Moslems, the British soccer fans, the Chinese soldiers, and the Korean school children can *only* be understood as metaphors, since their political and ideological contexts are so different from each other that their collage can only produce nonsense. As a political critique of violence and repression, Berkowitz's slow-motion clips merely skim the surface and actually make it seductive instead of breaking the mask of official, authoritarian *information.* These images, for example, say nothing about the fundamental conflicts, economic crises, and ethnic struggles that have provoked revolution or resistance in China, Eastern Europe, Russia, or South Africa. With its randomly (dis)connected metaphors, the wall projection doesn't provide an interpretive or historical framework that would allow an analysis of the presumed hegemonic authority of American media culture. Although Berkowitz synchronizes advanced American capitalism with "dominant culture," the realities outside of mainstream media harbor many different languages and reflect radical economic and social disparities under the mask of the world market. The question whether there is an outside, or whether and how the fractured realities of our multicultural societies can be represented, can only be raised once the projected loop in Berkowitz's media world breaks down. (In the world according to Paik, that won't happen.) Instead of inserting multiple narratives of differentiated historical positions (of the oppressed, of minorities, of women and men struggling for self-determination within capitalist and socialist economies), and instead of reinforming the viewer about the asymmetrical relations between cultures and peoples, between rich and poor, between participation and consumption, the uniform loop merely heightens its aesthetics of interchangeability.[5] The pope raises his hands; Chinese soldiers dance on Tiananmen Square. The conspicuous avoidance of American issues (Panama invasion, interracial relations, the AIDS crisis, homelessness, urban violence, and so forth) is only surprising if one forgets the equally abstract relationship between the video images and the Spanish masks on the floor. These eyeless faces have no recognizable frame of reference; their and our history has been edited out. As masks of appropriated and imported labor, they merely duplicate the blind loop in the video sculpture.

Perhaps the blindness of the loop as a work of art perfectly fits art's own hyperreality in the institutional framework of museums pretending to be neutral. Locked into this traditional, aesthetic space and into the presumption that its abstract, metaphorical "image world" could perform a critical separation from the larger junk heap of the real "Image World," the video sculpture can produce political meanings only in spite of itself. The viewer must situate the images of politics and see them differently, exposed to the historical processes that will overtake them, when the dancing stops on Tiananmen Square, after the massacre, and on the Berlin Wall, after its fall.

NOTES

1. Jean-François Lyotard, *Immaterialität und Postmoderne* (Berlin: Merve Verlag, 1986), 11–12 (my translation).
2. See Lyotard, *The Postmodern Condition: A Report on Knowledge* (Minneapolis: Univ. Of Minnesota Press, 1984). For his specific commentaries on the exhibition see *Epreùves d'écriture,* exhibition catalog, ed. Jean-François Lyotard and Thierry Chaput, Centre Georges Pompidou, 1985, 259–63. Lyotard's design of the structuralist-linguistic model of communication is quoted from "Les Immatériaux," Petit Journal, Editions du Centre Georges Pompidou, 1985.
3. MacAllister Booth, "Sponsor's Foreword," exhibition catalog, *Image World: Art and Media Culture* (New York: Whitney Museum of American Art, 1989), 11.
4. Cf. Lisa Phillips, "Art and Media Culture," exhibition catalog, 57.
5. At the 1989 film and video festival "In Visible Colors" at Vancouver I encountered a fascinating example of such differentiation. Vietnamese filmmaker Trinh T. Minh-ha presented her *Surname Viet Given Name Nam* (1989), a disturbing and difficult interrogation of the country she comes from, since the film questions both the neutrality and truth value of ethnographic documentary as well as her own mode of constructing a self-defining history against media stereotypes. Her film is a performance in the sense that it completely undermines a monologic or authoritative narrative and instead choreographs a polyphonic discontinuous collage of voices, images, sounds and rhythms with which she reconstructs a historical and a changing Vietnam. Asking actors to reenact scripted monologues transcribed from recorded conversations with a number of Vietnamese women, Trinh interweaves these scenes with archival footage of women interacting in the resistance movement and in folk cultural activities. At the same time, the film's recording of these oral histories is interactive in another sense. It reconstructs the process of the transcriptions (subtitles, translations) and Trinh's open reflections on the process (voice track). Her comments intimate that she respects the separate identities of the sources and subjects of her film. The work provokes the viewer's recognition of the movement between media, of the gap between then and now, between the stages of history. For further reference see her newly published book *Woman, Native, Other* (Bloomington: Indiana Univ. Press, 1989).

6 ▬▬ PINA BAUSCH: DANCING ACROSS BORDERS

It is not too long ago that the 1984 Olympic Arts Festival in Los Angeles, with its marathon program of more than four hundred performances and exhibitions from eighteen countries, went out of its way to demonstrate the seductiveness of spectacular consumption in the name of the arts. Or, rather, in the name of major foreign artists who were brought together so that corporate sponsors and multinational culture producers could speak of their art as a "universal language, a bridge of illumination that connects all of us"[1].

Whatever the hidden motives of such advertising, it is a gesture toward a kind of innocent and immediate consumption. But when Pina Bausch's Wuppertaler Tanztheater, still unknown in this country outside of New York, opened the Olympic Festival with such emotionally devastating pieces as *Café Müller* (1978) and *Bluebeard* (1977), the festival had its first unpredicted scandal.

With the hype surrounding Bausch's return to the Brooklyn Academy of Music's (BAM) 1985 Next Wave Festival (she was there first in 1984), we entered a second stage in the reception of her "language" and in the critics' predictable entrenchment. Whereas BAM can afford to be ironic by an-

This essay first appeared in *The Drama Review* 30, no. 2 (1986).

nouncing that the West German tanztheater will help "deprovincialize New York City"[2], it is somewhat more preplexing to notice how the critical writing on performance in New York City mimics the new provincialism by launching its defensive missiles against the challenge of Bausch's ineradicable Germanness.

Anna Kisselgoff of the *New York Times*, for example, falls back into unwarranted clichés. She argues that audiences accustomed to the formalist aesthetic of the United States' "pure dance" are necessarily startled when they see the innovative interaction between theater and dance in foreign works (such as those by Bausch, the French Groupe Emile Dubois, and butoh performers) that have pushed the borders of their disciplines by adding expression, feeling, and angst to the form[3]. When Kisselgoff asked Bausch whether she would be interested in working only with "pure form" and without the need to express feeling, the choreographer probably didn't even understand the question.

I'm glad however, that it was asked, because its striking disingenuousness and incoherence intimate the more general breakdown of critical faculties and languages vis-à-vis a pluralistic and diversified culture in which there are no pure, autonomous forms but constant transformations, mutations, and recapitulations inevitably producing indifference to the specific borders (and ideological limits) of a work of art, of a performance. And occasionally, they also produce fashionable, self-stimulating controversies about equivocal meanings, as if the conditions for an unequivocal, adversarial avant-garde still existed.

The borderline in Bausch's tanztheater is the concrete human body, a body that has specific qualities and a personal history—but also a body that is written about, and written into social representations of gender, race, and class. We tend to take representations of the body for granted, whether we see them in advertisements, films, photographs, pornography, or in the beautiful, ethereal poses of ballet dancers. Every pose, every still, and every movement of the body partakes in the particular representational economy with which a culture directs and dominates what is perceived as reality.

Our physical conventions, like the "official" images of the sexual body, are part of that reality and that perception. In Bausch's works we are confronted directly with the gestus of conventions and internalized norms we no longer see. In *Don't Be Afraid* (1976), the seducer repeatedly sings "Look at me—don't be afraid" in a soft voice before he throws the woman to the ground and rapes her. The woman (Helena Pikon), who resisted the seduction for a long time, then gets up and joins a whorish company of men and women in colorful slips and corsets. They dance the hilarious, cross-dressed dance of victims who have grown tough and professional. "We are the objects of your suave entrapment" (Barbara Kruger)[4]: bodies are continuously dressed up and down, fashioned and cosmeticized for *our* pleasure, but the make-up spills all over. Kruger's ambiguous statement could serve as a leitmotif here; it captures the thrust of Bausch's staging of

Figure 23. Pina Bausch and Wuppertaler Tanz-theater. *Bluebeard* (1977). Photo: Ulli Weiss.

the Kurt Weill songs and Bertolt Brecht text in *The Seven Deadly Sins/Don't Be Afraid* (1976). The slipping of the subject positions—who is the "we" and the "your"?—is a crucial dramaturgical strategy in her work that should not be overlooked by us, the audience. We are members of the economy of onlookers.

That women pose and are posed as victims in our society is part of the problem, and Bausch confronts it head-on in her bitterly ironic treatment of Brechtian didacticism. Brecht was a powerful parable-maker and theorist of his own political theater. In *The Seven Deadly Sins,* he tried to raise critical consciousness by demonstrating, through the double image of Anna I/Anna II, how women teach themselves to be sexual commodities under capitalism's obscene reversal of the "deadly sins" now proclaimed virtues if only they turn a profit and produce middle-class comfort. Larger social processes of contradictory self-education under capitalism are exposed, in other words, by reimposing and rehearsing the image of woman-as-victim.

In Josephine Ann Endicott's performance of Anna II we see that process of Brechtian image-making exposed, too. In all Bausch's works, from the early *Rite of Spring* (1975) to *1980* (1980) and *On the Mountain a Cry Was Heard* (1984), the authoritative male voice-over is replaced by an

Figure 24. *Don't Be Afraid* (1976). Photo: Ulli Weiss.

Figure 25. *Kontakthof* (1978). Photo: Ulli Weiss.

estrangement effect that makes itself felt through the skin. Often we see silent dances and strangely familiar rituals performed with such emotional intensity that the process of watching the scene makes us painfully aware of the conventions of watching. At the same time, Bausch's dancers acknowledge and investigate the presence of an audience. Frequently, the house lights come on, and the dancers stroll along the aisles or come downstage looking curiously at the on-lookers. Occasionally they serve a cup of tea, or, as in *Kontakthof* (1978), they may need to borrow a quarter from a spectator to operate the automatic hobbyhorse on stage.

In *Kontakthof* the "setting" in the theater is put under intense scrutiny. The actual constraints of public exposure/theatrical production are thematized and shown to overlap with the individually experienced complexes and fears of inadequacy. The dancers parade up and down the stage, accompanied by bouncy popular songs and ballroom music, sending up the concrete working situation of public performers. They display themselves in profile, show their backs, their teeth, their hands and feet. Embarrassed attempts to hide physical inadequacies—the breasts are too small, the nose too big, the dress never quite fits—intermingle with outbursts of compulsive exhibitionism, which the company members automatically applaud. Bausch's principle of montage, inherited from the Brechtian theater, is used to interweave an extraordinary series of self-revealing mechanisms: the whole repetitive catalog of gestures and behaviors with which we sell the best aspects of our personalities.

Figure 26. *1980* (1980). Photo: Arici and Smith.

Bausch reveals how individuals feel physically compelled to participate in the games people play—seeking recognition, affection, and social acceptance. Deeply felt, unadmitted human truths are glimpsed through the fragile veneer of mandatory conventions that negate sensual freedom in the face of simulated happiness. Popular romantic songs and Hollywood clichés are played off against tragicomic effects produced by the dancers' "fulfillment" of our expectations. They show us how beautiful they are, how affectionate and aggressively successful they can be, and how desperately they need contact. Running toward the front rows, they threaten to fall over the edge that separates audience and stage. Such explicit references to the social reality of the theater merely highlight the process through which Bausch's choreography of the social physique translates emotional needs—experienced as a generally oppressive compulsion that assumes specific male and female forms—into a wider constellation of cultural attitudes toward the genres that inform such attitudes. Without effort, a Bausch evening crosses and recrosses the boundaries between love song, film, ballet, revue, circus, and social dance. Each crossing, however, reflects a high awareness of the content and the potential inhibitions of a chosen form. The audience's automatic expectations of or responses to the forms are incorporated into the parodic action on stage.

Sometimes, the dancers (Jan Minarik and Dominique Mercy in particular) grotesquely exaggerate this doubling of theater reality; more often, they plan these shifts from one emotional atmosphere to another with perfectly deadpan seriousness. There are certain limits to the crossings, of course. I have seen the company perform in Germany, Italy, France, and the U.S., and each time they make considerable efforts to approach particular audiences. The spoken bits of dialog are usually rendered in the language of the host country. Nevertheless, "automatic" audience reactions differ from country to country, from evening to evening.

BAM audiences in 1985 sat perplexed and unmoved through an episode in *Kontakthof* in which the dancers seated themselves with their backs to the audience to watch a German documentary film on the breeding behavior of small water animals. The joke was lost on the American audience. Similar problems arise when audiences can't feel any of the connotations of the German love songs of the fifties or in the sentimental tango that the German middle class danced to during its post-World War II reconstruction.

In the works of Bausch and other postwar German choreographers such as Mechthild Grossman's *Where My Sun Shines For Me* (1984), the parody of conventions and the truth of parody, are always linked with a sense of personally experienced history. Repressed memory of childhood traumas can be retrieved if only one listens carefully enough to the repetitions of the socialized body. "We must look again and again," Bausch once said in defense of her excessive repetitions, "and maybe the saddest thing about our obsessions is that they often look so cheerful." I counted perhaps forty or fifty different childhood games in 1980 and *Arien* (1979). When the

Wuppertal dancers recall the youthful joy with which they used to drive away the fear built into all children's games, the hide-and-seek exercises always look ambiguously sad and cheerful at the same time. Bausch's dramaturgical method becomes more accessible over time; these adult remembrances of things past are made to evolve slowly and unobtrusively. They take time, and sometimes we cannot see them all at once because they run parallel, commenting on and overlapping with each other. Sometimes they return in a different context and assume a different emotional quality, like the many stories that emerge and disappear again, accentuating the subjective reality of experiences that are both pleasurable and painful.

Silvia Kesselheim, in *1980,* repeatedly tells us how, as a child left alone in the dark, she would cry out, and how her nanny would come in and "turn on the light—and she would hit me, she would hit me, she would hit me." After we have heard the story five times, it becomes poignantly clear that the pleasure of pain can become almost mechanical, automatic. We must listen again and again.

Even with the overtly brutal treatment of the theme in *Bluebeard*—a piece about an obsessive male sadist who kills the women he loves—I am tempted to emphasize the redemptive effect of repetition. While "Bluebeard" is caught up with his machine, "listening to a tape recording" of his murderous desire (the voices that sing about love and death in Béla Bartók's opera), the women dancers gather their strength with their backs to the walls, laughing at the monster in their midst. Since most American audiences were outraged by the violence portrayed in the performance, one might ask why they responded to the violence and not to the sharply focussed process of recognition that leads from the pathos of self-absorbed sexual obsession to the much larger patterns of mechanical evasion that a guilt-ridden society resorts to when it prefers to deny the consequences of its continuing aggression.

In her earlier pieces, Bausch seemed less interested in the grotesque aspects of male violence. In her choreographic treatment of Stravinsky's *Rite of Spring*, the ritual dance was constantly repeated—to the point of total exhaustion—as a central metaphor for the well-rehearsed behavior of men following the rules of society and selecting women as sacrificial victims, even as the women themselves envision and anticipate the selection. In *Arien*, the stage is not covered with brown earth, as in *Rite of Spring*, but with ankle-deep water. It is surrounded by reflecting mirrors that create an almost surreal combination of surfaces. The tone has changed, too. In a series of parodic images of narcissistic self-regard, *Arien* establishes a melancholy mood that seems provoked by the individual's constant effort to maintain a sense of self-expression and self-comprehension in the face of the mechanical violence that so often dominates the appearances, if not in the theater, then certainly in our lives.

In Bausch's recent theater pieces, such efforts are often comic because they literally carry out the beautiful metaphors of our operas and classical

Figure 27. *Rite of Spring* (1975). Photo: Rolf Borzik.

ballets. In *Arien,* fairy-tale queens and divas who are grotesquely decorated and dressed up by their partners plunge into movement phrases and word litanies. They look and sound nonsensical in comparison with the old Italian belcanto arias (recordings by Beniamino Gigli) and Beethoven's *Moonlight Sonata.* Is it the music that makes no sense or the words and movements? We cannot be sure; certainty seems lost as the dancers show us how forms, or formal atmospheres, can come together momentarily, only to disintegrate.

The naked reality of the performers' bodies in *Arien* begins to shine through the wet costumes as they slosh through the water, tumbling forward with the desperate determination to act out normal routines under abnormal circumstances. They do so with high operatic pathos, worthy of Wagner's *Götterdämmerung,* as when Lutz Förster solemnly carries the lifeless Beatrice Libonati across the pool, their lips glued in a kiss. But that pathos is a dead language, like the reified media gossip that the dancers shout at each other and at the audience. When a huge hippopotamus rises out of the water, nobody seems to notice the incongruity. Bausch's

tanztheater lives through such incongruities; the stage is awash with consumer objects that seem out of place or useless, but the actors cling to them
for dear life. How life is deformed by such clinging is shown during the
grand dinner party in *Arien,* surely the most chaotic scene ever staged on
the BAM Opera House stage. The solemnly disintegrating party drowns in
an all-out, deliberately self-indulgent schizophrenia that is frightening—if
we care to see our culture reflected in it.

Arien has many such dark undertones that undercut our laughter. Jan
Minarik's antics as the party photographer or Josephine Ann Endicott's
Titania-like love affair with the sad-looking hippo offer comic relief that is
coupled with a sense of danger. It is as if we were taking pictures of a
society doomed to drown its catastrophic desires in a continuous masquerade of optimism, an on-going party. "What do you think of arias?" one
of the dancers asks as she puts thick make-up on her face. "I associate them
with blood-red fingernails and torture," is one of the answers.

It is pointless to ask Pina Bausch what her pieces are about. "It is never
something you can describe exactly," she told me. "Basically one wants to
say something which cannot be said, so we make a poem where one can
feel what is meant. You see it, and you know it without being able to
formulate it." The East German playwright Heiner Müller once said that in
Bausch's theater "the image is a thorn in our eye"[5]. Her works are too
uncompromising to let themselves be easily domesticated, and there are
perhaps no answers to the reality of experience depicted in them. If
anything, the Wuppertal dancers show us what it means to keep questioning beyond the point where repetitions appear merely exhausting and
deadly, or perhaps just normal.

It is also possible, of course, that Bausch's continuing performances of
human self-degradation and self-oppression will reach a point of no return, where the tenderness and the hope for love are no longer recognizable. Bausch's darkest piece, *On the Mountain a Cry Was Heard,* provoked
deep distress among BAM audiences, since even those who admire her
work felt numbed by the bleak, destructive images of the group scenes.
The piece refers us back to the menacing atmosphere of *Rite of Spring,*
whose stage is also covered by a deep layer of earth; the dancers seem lost
in this vast and empty landscape. There are quiet moments when individuals or couples cry out for help and affection and when their vulnerability becomes a positive force. But these moments of longing are
overwhelmed by unconditional violence. In one scene, repeated several
times to the blaring sound of the triumphal march from Mendelssohn's
Athalie, two groups of men chase Helena Pikon and Francis Viet across the
dark stage, capture them, and brutally force them to kiss each other.
Undoubtedly, there is something deeply disconcerting about these images
of fatal enclosure and social pressure. The unloving couple, forced to love
each other, cannot escape. But they continue to struggle and to resist.

I am interested in the astounding ironies of this image, not only
because they reveal an implicit alternative to the radical historical pessi-

mism and the collapse of individualism depicted in Heiner Müller's plays but also because they must be seen with the German sensitivity toward historical determinations in mind. If some American critics prefer to miss the ironies and find themselves appalled at the vision of painfully distorted bodies and victimized individuals, it may be that the general optimism (the "official" image) in this body-building and aerobics culture has locked up any perception of irony in a heightened state of repression that feeds a mindless consumerism and an automatic dream of endless survival. Images of pain or fear of death disturb the American landscape; they don't accommodate the rhetoric of beauty, power, and speed in a technological Disneyland. Images of violence are acceptable in films and MTV, where they can be made to look beautiful. As for the dance: why should anyone want to see distorted and victimized bodies that don't even dance most of the time?

Although it may not have been consciously planned, the Fall 1985 program of the BAM Next Wave festival turned out to be the site of a vociferous encounter between proponents of German tanztheater and American postmodern dance. Both traditions share common roots but have gone in different directions. Halfway through the festival it was already clear that New York audiences had the unique chance to see the leading choreographers of the current German tanztheater movement (Bausch, Reinhild Hoffmann, Susanne Linke) side by side with some

Figure 28. *On the Mountain a Cry Was Heard* (1984).
Photo: Arici and Smith.

post-Cunningham American choreographers (Laura Dean, Nina Wiener, Margaret Jenkins).

Cunningham's influence has been so strong in the United States that today's postmodern dance can only be understood in relation to his programmatic rejection of Graham-style modern dance with its emphasis on emotion, theatrical decor and costumes, character, dramatic phrasing, and narrative. Even those familiar with contemporary dance must have been struck, however, by the amount of frustrated anger vented upon tanztheater. At a symposium cosponsored by BAM and Goethe House New York on 8 November 1985, directly after the opening nights of Hoffmann's *Callas* (1983) and Wiener's *In Closed Time* (1985), some critics objected to what they felt was the self-indulgence of Bausch's long and repetitive performances and her wallowing in pain and angst.

Hoffmann and Wiener were present at this intercultural event, and both looked exhausted after hours of heated discussion about the respective merits of the formal, movement-oriented concerns of American postmodern dance and the concrete emotional and social content expressed in the German works. The problem of cultural perceptions of the relationship between form and content remained a stumbling block, but the symposium made it clear that our common vocabulary ("movement," "narrative," "motion," etc.) needs to be more carefully defined with regard to the specific aesthetic, including its political dimension, that makes the apparent violence in Bausch's works so objectionable to so many people in the United States.

At the same time, such a clash of perceptions may also help redirect attention to the easily forgotten roots of early modern dance shared by both traditions and mediated by the highly influential work of American dancers such as Isadora Duncan in Germany and later on by the teaching of Rudolf von Laban and Kurt Jooss. The pupils of Jooss's Folkwang School, including Bausch, Hoffmann, and Linke, are central to the revitalization of expressionist dance.

Seeing the BAM premieres of Wiener's *In Closed Time* or Laura Dean's *Sky Light* (1982), *Transformer* (1985), and *Impact* (1985), one still notices the fundamental difference between some American thinking about the validity and beauty of movement qualities or rhythmic forms and these German choreographers' deliberate insistence on questioning the conditions of social performance themselves—those gender-identified roles and behaviors that determine our relationship to each other and to our culture at large.

Those roles and behaviors, so natural in the United States, are not always beautiful. Hoffman's *Callas*, not unlike Bausch's *Kontakthof* and *Arien*, dramatizes various images of prostitution, self-oppression, anxiety, and self-humiliation that stand as realistic counterparts to the popular myths of beauty, happiness, and success. The reality of the fantasies, represented by daily routines and ever-repeated efforts to impress others, is exposed as a constricting network of internalized social conventions. In one scene, the dancers parade in front of huge mirrors, and before long,

Figure 29. Reinhild Hoff-
mann and Bremen Tanz-
theater in *Callas* (1983).
Photo: Klaus LeFebvre.

the mirrors are tied to their backs, and we see them carrying the burden of their self-images.

Likewise, Bausch's repetitive masochistic rituals and the struggle for love and recognition that her male and female dancers perform on each other with aggressive affection can only be considered offensive to the eye if one completely misunderstands the implied social critique. In order to see art as a form of cultural intervention, one must remember the specific German theater, opera, and ballet tradition whose classics have always dominated the repertories of the state-subsidized theaters. It is this cultural repertory, with its social/political implications, that the women choreographers—the true heirs of Brecht's epic theater—rebelled against with the full rage of a generation of daughters that witnessed the successful reconstruction of the old patriarchal regime, shortly after the horrors of fascism had arisen from Western civilization.

In view of this experience one can perhaps better understand the admittedly painful image in *On the Mountain a Cry Was Heard* of a woman dancer kneeling down, repeatedly and patiently, to receive the punishing blows of her male oppressor. Jan Minarik's menacing figure stands in for the many fathers and lovers who are like children playing with weapons in order to learn the competitive rules of the game.

In this sense one can read the episodic dance sequences in *Callas* that represent the various stages of a career—here embodied in the figure of the famous opera singer. Through it one may learn the belcanto of stardom and success, but only at the great personal cost of losing all dignity. The limited range of "movement" in tanztheater is perhaps an apt expression of its antiaesthetic stance. When Bausch explains that she is "not so much interested in how people move but in what moves them," she is also addressing classical ballet, which disguises its repressiveness with beautiful acrobatics and stunning spectacles.

American postmodern dance is not perceived to be struggling against an overbearing system of well-subsidized ballet and repertory theater, as is the case in Germany, where the majority of the state theaters house ballet companies. There are only about ten tanztheater troupes; half of them are unaffiliated, so-called free groups. The traditions of modern ballet and modern dance in the United States evolved independently from each other, and the emancipation of "pure dance" was achieved when Cunningham's generation freed itself, not from the constraints of any government-subsidized structure, but from the heavy emotional drama of an older choreography.

Tanztheater critics, of course, would consider the term "emancipation" paradoxical in an American context.[6] For them, the acrobatic, multimedia postmodernism of Bill T. Jones and Arnie Zane's *Freedom of Information* (1984) or *Secret Pastures* (1984), for example, can only indicate a regression into seductive spectacles and "superficial attractions".[7] Such Brechtian criticisms miss the point, however, because they do not grasp the different ways in which American reality is represented and representable.

At the same time, I do not doubt that the freedom of information in postmodern dance is yet another illusory freedom. After all, there is something very puzzling about the self-referentiality of American abstract dance, namely the apparently unperturbed self-confidence with which it pursues "solutions to its formal problems"[8] without ever acknowledging the contradictions that lie in the assumption that dance is not a social practice but an art too beautiful and self-contained to engage, for example, the issues of violence and repression.

The pure energy of the relentless spinning in Laura Dean's *Sky Light*, or the spatial juxtapositions of Wiener's dancers against the huge plastic "buildings" in *In Closed Time* (designed for the BAM stage by Miami's leading commercial architecture firm, Arquitectonica) could be interpreted as reflections on the dehumanizing speed and urban density of American life here and now, were it not that the spinning, or the muscle flexing in front of geometrically shaped design elements, appear hopelessly arbitrary, equivocal, and unconscious of its articulated social content. The refusal to deal with this content deprives these works of any emotionally and intellectually significant meaning, and this is a limitation that audiences may begin to realize once they have stopped worrying about the un-American angst in Pina Bausch's tanztheater works.

NOTES

1. Robert J. Fitzpatrick, "The Making of the Festival," 1984 *Olympic Arts Festival Catalog* (Los Angeles: Los Angeles Times Syndicate, 1984).

2. Harvey Lichtenstein, "Introduction," *1985 Next Wave Festival Catalog* (New York: Brooklyn Academy of Music, 1985).

3. Anna Kisselgoff, "Dance that Startles and Challenges Is Coming from Abroad," *New York Times*, 13 October: H1, 14.

4. Barbara Kruger, *We Are the Objects of Your Suave Entrapments*, black and white photograph, 1983.

5. Heiner Müller, "Blut ist im Schuh, oder Das Rätsel der Freiheit," in *Rotwelsch* (Berlin: Merve Verlag, 1982).

6. Jochen Schmidt, "Erfahren, was Menschen bewegt: Pina Bausch und das neue Tanztheater," in *Tanzlegenden*, ed. Ulrike Hanraths and Herbert Winkels (Frankfurt: Tende Verlag, 1984).

7. Norbert Servos and Gert Weigelt, *Pina Bausch Wuppertal Dance Theater or The Art of Training a Goldfish* (Cologne: Ballet-Bühnen-Verlag, 1984).

8. Nina Wiener, "German and American Modern Dance: Yesterday and Today" symposium (New York: Goethe House, 8 November 1985).

> Theatre is action. Maybe theatre itself is not re-
> volutionary; but it rehearses the revolution.
>
> Augusto Boal

7 ◼ REPETITION AND REVOLUTION: THEATRE ANTHROPOLOGY AFTER BRECHT

Rehearsals of Revolution?

Augusto Boal worked in conditions and within class relations where the popular theatre of Brazil that he helped to create was defined as a theatre *of* and *for* the oppressed. It defined itself in opposition to the bourgeoisie, the professionals, the military, the ruling apparatuses and their texts. This theatre's practices and techniques have been understood primarily as a *liberation of the spectators* who could learn to experiment with the social mechanisms of their oppression and the possibilities of freedom in a performance situation where they can choose the subject matter and confront their own reality.

Such a confrontation, Boal explains, can demonstrate confrontation, resistance; theatre is not only an intellectual process, in the Brechtian sense of *Bewusstmachung*, it is a "répétition de la réalité," a "Wirklichkeitsprobe" that can test particular acts of social change and transformation.[1] Or, perhaps, particular utopias of social transformation.

A segment of this essay was first published in *Gestus* 1, no. 3/4 (1986).

When Allan Bolt, who has helped to create a network of more than three hundred small theatre groups in Nicaragua after the Sandinista Revolution, speaks of their training methods or theatre events, he speaks of "social action diagnosis" and "communal research"; in other words, of a popular culture movement that *is* part of an actual revolution and involves the communities and villages in a learning process for which there are no models. There are plenty of questions (political, economic, existential), and the traditional Nicaraguan performance modes—dance, music, storytelling, rituals, ceremonies—can be used to explore a disturbed collective memory, and to educate themselves for another social reality after so many years of colonization.

For many of us in the Western world living in advanced technocratic societies under the spectacular signs of multinational capitalism, to speak of resistance or social change through theatre seems to be an unrealistic or unintelligible proposition, even if we remembered the models we have and how they may still influence theatre practices in the West and elsewhere. What particular utopia of another social reality or what images and discourses of our own cultural struggle would our theatre have to project in order to be taken seriously as a social practice? Or how to remind the patrons of our institutionalized theatres that they, too, are among the oppressed?

Perhaps in our postmodern condition we have trouble remembering our most recent history, the rebellious energies of the 1960s or the political defeats. We have more trouble remembering the revolutionary projects of earlier artistic movements that defined our Western notion of the avant-garde and its struggle against political repression before it became necessary, much later, to acknowledge the avant-garde's obsolescence. New theories of theatre, whether we think of Artaud's or Brecht's and the influence they have had, seem to have arrived too late.

Today, as we listen to the European debates on the end of History and the end of the "dialectic of enlightenment," European theory advises us to study the social and technological changes in the American "model" of mass cultural production and consumption, or what I have earlier described as Baudrillard's vision of a universal "operation of simulation models," in order to understand how communication technologies are replacing historical process. Such a replacement implies the loss of a humanist consciousness of a historical frame and of active critical reflection on lived experience inside or outside the theatre. Outside the theatre, in the continuous present of the twenty-four-hour flow of commercial television and MTV, the loss seems programmed. More and more consistently, music videos become advertising paradigms that already display the confusion of boundary between human and nonhuman of an advanced technological culture. What would our "social action diagnosis" consist of, if we were indeed losing our awareness of representable real differences? What if we were inscribed into a simulated world where social relations are converted into electronic signs and where "the real," as Baudrillard suggests, is always already reproduced as image? How could we still believe in a public sphere, or in a natural, ecological and human environment, or in a community of people whose actions might produce actual changes in the dominant culture? What would be *our* simplest "natural" street scene model for a theatre "whose origin, means, and ends are practical and earthly"?[2]

When Brecht wrote down his *Versuche*, his essays about basic models for an epic theatre, he had been in exile for several years. Their practicality was questionable in view of the changed reality in Germany. And when I said earlier that Brecht's and Artaud's theories for a new theatre came too late, I also meant to imply that our attempts to receive them are bound to be motivated by very different concerns. Let me quickly mention an example of such a remotivation that I found in a book of "new interpretations" of Brecht's drama, published in 1984.[3] In it Rainer Nägele's article, "Brechts Theater der Grausamkeit," proposes to read Brecht through Artaud, and Artaud through Brecht, and to go beyond the apparent opposition between a Brechtian theatre of enlightened rationality and Artaud's vision of a nonverbal, physical theatre poetry or what he once called "unperverted pantomime,"[4] when he thought he had glimpsed its living embodiment in the performances of Cambodian and Balinese dance.

> Through the labyrinth of their gestures, attitudes, and sudden cries, through the gyrations and turns which leave no portion of the stage unutilized, the sense of a new physical language, based upon signs and no longer upon words, is liberated. These actors . . . seem to be animated hieroglyphs. . . . Their sense of the plastic requirements of the stage is equalled only by their knowledge of physical fear and the means of unleashing it.[5]

Artaud's fascination with Balinese dance, similar to Brecht's reaction to Chinese acting after seeing Mei Lanfang in Moscow, can be historicized and reinterpreted today in light of the Eurocentrism that colored their perceptions of the Asian performance troupes that toured Europe in the 1930s. Intercultural performance study has reached a stage at which a long-standing interest in alternative models of theatre will have a profoundly different meaning for those in the West influenced by the Brecht/Artaud couple and their search for a revolutionary and participatory theatre with the "knowledge of physical fear." While this knowledge played a greater role for Artaud than for Brecht, both shared the same frustration that made them want to break through the illusions of the petrified bourgeois aesthetics of naturalism and realism. And although Brecht did not conceive the physical language and the body of the actor as the source and medium of performance, his experimentation with the *Verfremdungseffekt* became a technique to expose illusions and to study social phenomena through the historical conditions that produce contradictory demands on social behavior. His polemic was directed against the audience's passive emotional identification with the central character of conventional realist or expressionist drama. His own theoretical and practical efforts toward creating a new "dialectical" or "didactic" theatre were based on the revolutionary objective of a social learning process. Brecht's theatre was above all a sociopolitical theory of what theatre could be if it were no longer just theatre but a conscious, critical method/rehearsal for changing social behavior and actions. His practice was not concerned with a physical or psychological condition onstage but with the progressive understanding and demonstration of how it could be changed for a revolutionary process. With a revolutionized audience in mind, Brecht argued that only the dialectical praxis would correspond to the new historical context for a *theatre of the scientific age;* there was no "sociological space" for drama anymore. "In the end the new plays only served the old theatre and helped to postpone the collapse on which their own future depended."[6]

At the other end of Brecht's political vision of the new age but equally dependent for its antithetical stance on the old theatre, which wasn't collapsing, lay Artaud's spirited search for a lost unity (community), for a positive athleticism that would yield a new, nonalienated locus of identity beyond the representations and repetitions of the old codes, beyond the exhausted parodies of the demotivated "central characters." Those parodies came to occupy the stage in the classical phase of existentialist drama, postponing the collapse of theatre in Beckettian endgames of a heightened consciousness trapped in a decaying and immobilized body. We could consider Nägele's reinterpretation of Brecht/Artaud a productive proposal if we read it through Beckett and in relationship with the compulsive reduction and trivialization of the body in mainstream theatre, musical, or opera, as well as in our fashion and body-building industry. We could also read through the petrification of what is left of body and consciousness in Beckett's late drama toward the brutal self-estrangement of the body in performance art, in connection with the visual technology and the dissolution and fragmentation of the human figure—a new practice "more cruel than Artaud's Theatre of Cruelty which was still an attempt at a dramaturgy of life."[7]

In other words, in the new age of the technological engineering of culture, what "sociological space" would be left for the theatre if it did not concern itself with what is most human and most fragile about it: the human actor? One answer has been given by the new emphasis in the research and pedagogy of theatre anthropology and cross-cultural performance study. Similarly, intercultural performance practices, by multiethnic theatre and dance companies that perform internationally, have complicated the whole question of how we understand other performance models, languages, codes of acting, and techniques of the body, and how we distinguish different cultural traditions and their intrinsic qualities from the "perverted pantomimes" of these qualities. These appear intermittently in Peter Brook's adaptation of *The Mahabharata,* the Théâtre du Soleil's *The Terrible but Unfinished History of Norodom Sihanouk, King of Cambodia,* Tadashi Suzuki's interpretation of Euripides' *The Trojan Women* or Kazuo Ohno's butoh tribute to *La Argentina,* to name a few recent examples.[8] This emphasis on the reinterpretation of cultures, practices and bodily performance techniques coincides with larger political and cultural reorientations in Western societies toward recognizing the built-in ethnocentrism of the Euro-American educational systems and ideological values, and toward acknowledging the Asian, African, and Latin-American traditions as independent sources of knowledge and techniques in their own terms. We are obviously only at the beginning of a long process. The current reexamination (in anthropology and performance ethnology) of the Western intellectual tradition of representations of the cultural other will influence contemporary and future conceptions of subject, body, gender, and identity in social institutions and cultural performances. It is no coincidence that the *political dimensions* of epistemology are most directly articulated by postcolonial writers who have searched— perhaps under the influence of Edward Said's powerful critique of "Orientalism"—for their own understanding of the formation of identity and ethnicity.[9]

I find this critique missing in Andrzej Wirth's understandably optimistic evaluation of the international pluralism and syncretism of new theatre practices. No longer locally bounded, Wirth argues, theatre has begun to circulate interculturally. He succinctly observes the stagnation of literary theatre in Europe and the considerable impact that new performance theatre and performance art experiments have had on cultural exchanges in performance techniques. When he speaks of expansion, however, he tends to think of the incorporation of "other" traditions (from Japan and India) into Western theatre. And in his conclusion, he predicts that "the technocratization of highly developed countries created a new basis for cultural exchanges. As a result we observe the development of a global postmodernist language of art which replaces traditional national idiolects."[10]

This conclusion echoes the rhetoric of appropriation and incorporation that I sought to contest in my opening chapter on global American postmodernism. I want to interpret "cultural exchange" differently, leaving room for a cultural pluralism that supports open dialogue and collaboration across cultural borders, refusing the concept of a "dominant" language that commodifies and homogenizes ethnicity. Guillermo Gómez-Peña's forceful critique warns us of a new interculturalism that would cover up the actual asymmetries between the North and the South and between the mainstream and so-called marginal communities: we must remember that the "contemporary art world needs and desires the spiritual and aesthetic models of Latino culture without having to experience our political outrage and cultural contradictions." He then recalls a graffito he has noticed on the Mexican border: "SIMULACRA STOPS HERE."[11]

In the context of these challenging redefinitions of cultural performance, the question of "social action diagnosis" in the theatre and in theatre anthropology gains a significant new meaning. The "boundedness" of highly developed visual codes and performance techniques (gesture, movement, dance, chant, declamation, song, rhythmic and emo-

tional tonalities, focalization, narrative gestus, make up, masking, costum-
ing, etc.) in Asian theatre, for example, offers a particularly interesting
point of departure from which formalism and realism, and the contextual
reception of "the real" through codified abstractions, can be studied beyond the conventional Western perceptions of psychological realism in
acting and the interpretive separation or opposition between text/narrative
and its theatrical representation. Likewise, some Western performance art
has foregrounded the body of the performer in order to dismantle all
narrative and representational codes, and this notion of the performer's
pure presence and energy could be addressed in terms of the rigid cultural
and formal coding in Japanese, Chinese, and Indian acting which always
precedes the particular performance event without overdetermining it. The
integration of form and content in the total physical form, observes James
Brandon in reference to Kabuki, is centered in the actor as the source and
geidō for the performance.

> The overriding emphasis upon the person of the actor in Kabuki is usually
> attributed—by Japanese commentators—to the desire to show off the actor's
> 'physical attractiveness' *(nikutai miryoku)*. . . . Yet, there is, it seems, more to it
> than this. Kabuki acting style is legitimately based on using the physical
> possibilities of the human body. Its aesthetic of performance is centered on
> projecting human character and feeling through the total physical form.[12]

When such cultural practices and perceptions of the actor are brought
under crosscultural examination, as it has been done by Eugenio Barba's
international pedagogical workshops throughout the 1980s, the contrasts
between and within Western and non-Western practices can be elaborated
as a "study of human behavior on a biological and socio-cultural level in a
performance situation."[13] For several years Barba seemed to focus most
directly on the "biological" or preexpressive level of the performer's
physical-technical training and body work. In his initial definition of how
he understands "theatre anthropology," Barba utilized the distinctions
between "daily" and "extra-daily" body behavior in order to explore the
changes (across cultures) between mimetic performance and the invented
or constructed body/self in performance.[14]

In this research Barba more or less tried to avoid psychological and
narrative aspects of representation assuming, I believe, that transcultural
categories could be located on a preexpressive level of physiological technique historically and contextually unbounded. More recently, the political
dimensions of historical and cultural difference have returned to Barba's
workshops in a way that some of his critics[15] might as well have anticipated, since his work as I know it has always been fully informed by an
awareness of the sociocultural determinations of knowledge. The elaborations and reelaborations of relationships on the physical-technical and
gestural level are the *modus vivendi* of Barba's return to the materials of
concrete action, or "restored behavior" (Schechner's term for the
reconstruction of a living action), that would then bring different cultural

codifications (theatrical, choreographic, narrative) into exchange with each other.

In a stunningly complex analysis of Barba's 1987 workshop in Bari, Italy, Patrice Pavis describes how such an exchange took place when Barba invited Japanese buyo and Indian odissi dancers, coming from highly codified national choreographic traditions, to confront the Faust myth of individualism, freedom, and knowledge and to let this cultural myth be seen through other cultures in a process of mutual dislocation. Disregarding the weighty philosophical and literary traditions surrounding the Faust myth, the two female dancers assimilated concrete action scenarios and materials derived from Goethe's *Faust* directly into the dancing body through gestural improvisations based on a physical or emotional gestus (temptation, seduction, drunkenness, carrying an object, throwing a book, and so forth). Asked by Barba to disrupt their traditional odissi and buyo codifications, the two dancers adapted "foreign" gestures suggested to them, and Pavis describes this process as a "voluntary deformation" that distances the Western participant-observer and forces him or her to confront the gender reversals and the "foreign" movement and hand gestures (mudras).

Katsuko Azuma (Faust) and Sanjukta Panigrahi (Mephisto) incorporated those "foreign bodies," gestures, and rhythms that they would normally reject into their performance and traditional codifications.

> This appropriation is achieved by way of a sort of "gestural graft," which [they] must tolerate without rejection. . . . The performers not only analyze a conflict, are guided by the objectivity of the *logos*, telling a story, but also dance *with* and *within* it according to the *bios*, their lived traditions. The two dancers' appropriation/incorporation of the *Faust* story is the first stage in the process of acculturation, the movement from Eastern encoding to Western decoding. . . . The dancers' improvisation constitutes the first shaping of the corporal materials, on the basis of which the mise-en-scène will effect a semiotic, ideological, narratological, and cultural reelaboration.[16]

Pavis's painstaking examination of Barba's role as "director" in this process of cultural reelaboration opens up as many productive questions as his final evaluation of the project. It is encouraging to see his sincere effort to recognize the contradictions involved in a mise-en-scène that reinvents a Western myth with the help of Oriental intermediaries speaking a foreign epic with their dancing bodies. As a social practice, their gendered bodies encounter and parody a "central myth" in a way that deconstructs conventional Western sex-role representations. At the same time, the roles are repositioned in the split between the homosexual couple, represented in the differentiated gestus of the more masculine, aggressive Indian performance (Panigrahi) versus the more feminized interiority of the Japanese performance (Azuma). These are not stable positions, however, since the cultural difference between the Indian and Japanese performances in turn produce a second inversion of the Faustian myth: Azuma enacts her "central character" (Faust) as a consenting victim, not striving for transcendence but cowering on the ground.[17]

The politics of representation in Barba's intercultural project will deserve considerable attention if we want to continue our defense of the theatre as a major force in the on-going struggle against the postmodern neutralization of cultural difference and historical positions. The relationship between Barba and Brecht has opened a space of intervention in which we may no longer see the revolution expected by Brecht, but realize the necessity to historicize the postmodern myths that postpone it. In my view of the theatre and of theatre anthropology as a "social learning process," such a realization suggests that we need to remember and understand our histories and traditions as we exchange the places and cultures through which we rehearse the changing realities we want to invent. As a practice of thought and physical action, the theatre's living relationship to its diverse histories will remain at odds with reproductive technologies of the disembodied image that cannot speak. "Theatre is a relationship, which neither establishes a union, nor creates a communion, but ritualizes the reciprocal strangeness and the laceration of the social body hidden beneath the uniform skin of dead myth and values.[18] I don't share Barba's skeptical assumption that this uncovering practice can only be carried out on a very small level, in "villages" of trained specialists. I want to extend the pedagogical practice of theatre anthropology and look at a few specific forms of contemporary theatre practice (including Barba's Odin Teatret) whose elaborations on the "social body" I can recontextualize from my own perspective. My urban perspective is European and completely untrained by the standards of Barba's transcultural village. But before I continue, I wish to backtrack for a moment and recreate the scene of my first encounter with Jerzy Grotowski and Eugenio Barba in 1984, an encounter that was the point of departure for this essay.

Theatre of Relations

Saturday, April 28, 1984. With a very soft voice, and interrupting his speech with long pauses of absolute concentration, Jerzy Grotowski begins to talk about himself, his work, his current plans. A large group of acting students and teachers sit in a densely packed room of the Yale Theatre Studies Department and listen for two hours to the man who has been one of the leading avant-garde theatre practitioners for the past twenty years, who has published a highly influential collection of essays, *Towards a Poor Theatre* (1968, with Eugenio Barba as editor), and who is now creating a new laboratory for theatre research at the not-so-poor University of California, Irvine.

It is one of those rare occasions where one can actually meet an artist whose reputation and fame have grown to nearly mythical proportions but who rarely makes public statements and whose work has never been seen in this country (except for the short visit of the Laboratory Theatre to New

York in 1970). *Apocalypsis cum figuris*, first performed in 1968 after more than four hundred rehearsals, is likely to remain the last of Grotowski's productions and, certainly, marks the conclusion of a phase of performance work and thought that evolved through the period of the "poor theatre" activities in Opole and Wroclaw.

Since then, Grotowski tells his audience at Yale somewhat reluctantly, he has been less and less concerned with forms of production, theories of dramatic performance, literary texts, acting styles, interpretations, and all those issues that seem to matter most in our discourse on theatre and drama. Grotowski himself in fact never even uses these terms, and at the end of his long talk he begs the audience, with an enigmatic smile on his face, not to ask him the "usual questions."

What is so unusual about Grotowski is the quiet and yet immensely charismatic manner in which he speaks, in a language that is not his own, about very basic, elementary aspects of the structure of play. "What is the beginning and the end of an action?", he asks us; "is it possible to stop the play, what happens if I stop, and what are the conditions under which I stop and begin again?" Halfway through his lecture the audience slowly begins to realize that Grotowski is not talking about the construction of a new theory of performance or about the new directions his current research may take. Rather, his questions continue to address, with ever increasing *precision*, those organic processes or body techniques that are the material bases of his art. These questions have not changed, although the perspectives have expanded during the years in which his Polish "laboratory" turned into a transcultural search for what he now tentatively calls "objective drama elements." When Eugenio Barba, Grotowski's former collaborator, founded the *International School of Theatre Anthropology* in the late 1970s, American academics and theatre practitioners were still discussing their ideas of the "poor theatre," Artaud's "double," and Peter Brook's "empty space," at a time when the American avant-garde had already begun to collapse under its own ephemeral weight. But while the performance of the seemingly inexhaustible pleasures of improvisation and the theatricalization of language and everyday life became the focus of much recent poststructuralist theory in this country, Grotowski had been traveling to China, Japan, South America, and Africa to reexamine fundamental questions. The objective of that research phase, which he now describes as "theatre of participation," was to reconstruct in varying contexts the frames or structures that would allow one to recognize the improvisations *within* the prepared structure of a performance situation, a ritual, a dance, a carnival, a church procession. Such recognition requires the distinction between "doer" and "seer," between the perception of performance and of daily life behavior. Going back to the origins of such distinctions, however, was a challenge that Grotowski confronted through his "theatre of sources"—a further stage of his research into forms of play behavior that can work for people of different cultures. Grotowski and a group of international actors, directors, and scientists tried to explore the levels of connection between different techniques of performance, ranging from the Peking Opera, Indian Kathakali, Japanese Nōh and Kabuki to Balinese dance, Haitian voodoo rituals, and Peruvian folklore festivals.

As Grotowski refers to these "sources" during his Yale lecture, he is not simply comparing non-Occidental acting and body techniques to those we are familiar with. Rather, he tries to show us how the relations between different cultural traditions can be studied, as we would study different ways of walking or dancing, in order to define more precisely the smallest signifying elements of theatrical practice—the elements that manipulate reality dominant in all acting and all processes. "If we are able to recognize the processual energy of such manipulations in different cultural performances," Grotowski argues, "we can also see the precise function of composition in the actor's work as a recurrent principle of all performances." We need no Brechtian *Verfremdungseffekt*, Grotowski seems to be saying, in order to recognize that the actor's work is always already a demonstration, a carefully elaborated series of performative elements that can be understood separately. At the end of his lecture, Grotowski modestly refers to Eugenio Barba and Peter Brook, two explorers of intercultural performance who have helped to develop some of the questions about the actor's "language" that Grotowski will continue to pose himself.

One of the most difficult problems, of course, lies in the assumption that the basic elements of acting are indeed "translatable" and are structurally recognizable in changing historical, social, and cultural contexts. If Barba's anthropological theatre research is designed to trace the recurrent elements of human physiological *and* sociocultural behavior in a performance situation, it will have to perform the difficult task of explaining how "rules of action" can remain fixed or formally closed intercontextually. How could audiences have a monological understanding of the process of a movement or a speech act even though no such process, to follow Bakhtin's theory of communication, can ever be totally present within one structure alone, whether physiological, linguistic, historical, or cultural? If there is, however, no metalanguage of acting that could resolve the conflictual grounds of representation, then it is all the more important to locate the precise *relations* between the actor and the acting, and between the spectator and the acting he or she sees performed by the actor in varying performance contexts.

Wednesday, May 2, 1984. As the doors to New York's La Mama Theatre Annex open, several friendly looking actors of Eugenio Barba's Odin Teatret greet the waiting ticket holders and see them to their seats in the large, arenalike auditorium. One of the actors with a slight Danish accent asks me to sit down on a chair which has the sign "Eugenio" on it. There is a small table in front of me, with an ashtray and a bottle of American beer. There are four such tables facing each other from the two sides of the rectangular playing space. Musicians play brass and strings in the cabaret style of Berlin in the golden twenties; a cook is preparing dinner on a hot stove. I chat with my neighbors on the left, a German emigrant couple and their Swiss niece. On my right sits Gerry Rabkin, one of the few people I know who saw Grotowski's *Apocalypse* when it came to New York in 1970.

While the music continues, Torgeir Wethal announces that he will play the role of Bertolt Brecht, and he then introduces us to dramatis personae taken from Brecht's life (Hanns Eisler on the piano, Walter Benjamin, Helene Weigel, and so forth) as well as from Brecht's plays (Arturo Ui, Macky Messer, Polly Peachum, Puntila, Galileo, Kattrin, the mute daughter of Mother Courage, and others). This mode of establishing relationships between the actors and the roles they will play, as well as between the actors and their local audience, reminds me of the concepts of "barter," voyage, travel, and emigration that have been fundamental to the work of Barba's Danish-based Odin Teatret. The troupe itself consists of nine actors from different European countries, and it is not without a certain irony that Odin Teatret, after twenty years of extensive touring through the world, arrives for the first time in the East Village to meet the dispersed scene of American avant-garde theatre.

Such meetings of traditions and experiences began for the Odin in 1974 in the Italian village of Carpignano, where Barba's idea of theatrical "barter" took shape as an experiment in intercultural exchange where actors from different backgrounds spend extended periods of time with a local population or working peoples' neighborhoods. Odin's usual procedure meant travel to Asia, South America, and Amazonia and a return to Europe with myriad impressions from foreign cultures and their structures of play and ritual, but their arrival at La Mama with *Brecht's Ashes 2* (first performed in Denmark in January 1982) marks a project in reverse order. The group's collaborative performance work brings to their New York audience a body of visual images, historical references, myths, texts, songs, and physical vocabularies that reflect their own European, Brechtian traditions of theatre mixed, refracted, and laid experientially side-by-side with the on-going reception of Brecht's place within the history of European drama and politics. The most vital aspect of this reception is expressed in Barba's comment on his adaptations from Brecht's plays, poems, and journals: "we reacted against the way in which Brecht is today petrified in his texts accused of being dogmatic or reticent, commented upon as if he was the last word on theatre and revolution."[19]

"Revolution is a tiring business," Heiner Müller wrote in his play *The Task* (1979), "and our theatrical masterpieces are the accomplices of power." Müller's pessimism is played out in scenarios close to the limit of hopeless contradictions between historical positions. But his political engagement resembles Barba's insofar as both artists consistently refuse to acknowledge the notion of integrity and closure in a text or in a tradition. The false consciousness that would treat Brecht as the father of sacred texts or as the inventor of epic dramaturgy is bound to block our recognition that the violation of boundaries, the continuing engagement with these textual bodies, is a historical inevitability that forces us to confront, at the same time, the very strategies of containment and appropriation which are part of the dominant culture industry. It is even more ironic, in this respect, to discover that Barba had to rework the production and use other sources after Brecht's estate had refused Odin Teatret the use of the playwright's poems and journals for *Ashes* 1.

In a sense, therefore, *Ashes* 2 already presents itself as a dialectical response to the possibilities of repression. It dramatizes the interpenetration of texts and narratives (by Brecht, about Brecht) as a means of analyzing *how* one can *act* by countering and answering particular representations of a historical moment and by occupying different places within various conflicting political, historical, biographical, and dramatic narratives.

The tale that Odin Teatret tells and shows their audience is complex, dynamic, and sometimes confusing and elliptical. Moreover, it is a collage of many tales that never allows us to rest confident with one image, one voice, one perspective. Odin's nine actors turn the playing space into an environment, a field of tension in which events happen separately and simultaneously at various places, accompanied or interrupted by musical sketches and extraordinary visual stimuli (the tattered red flag of the Revolution; Brecht's books incinerated in the cook's frying pan). Nothing seems accidental; one quickly becomes aware of the actor's precise use of space and their bodies in space, and how they create and juxtapose themselves and the historical and fictional characters they play in an ever-widening circle of allusions, kinesthetic rhythms, and sound and body images. Most of the allusions to Brecht's life in Berlin in the 1930s, his subsequent exile, and eventual return are deliberately ambivalent. There is no fixed point of departure or arrival; what we see is a *process* by which Torgeir Wethal as Brecht constructs his self-representations as well as his works and survives the political, social, and historical conflicts and pressures Brecht dramatizes in his plays. At the same time, we see how the characters of his plays actually comment on Brecht's survival and challenge his cunning, his political didacticism, the ambiguity of his life and actions.

At one point we see Brecht as Galileo, dissecting a trout on a dinner table that turns into an operating table—the scientist cutting and digging for objective proof. At the opposite end of the arena we see Walter Benjamin ("the friend who knew so much") unsuccessfully trying to cross the Spanish border in 1940. By the time Galileo looks up from his fish, Benjamin has hanged himself (or, perhaps, is hanged by Arturo Ui who acts the part of the seductive storm trooper). Barba's direction of such paralleled tales is superb; many of the small visual details and textual allusions gradually begin to point to relations and connections, not only between Brecht and history, but also between prewar and postwar Germany and the ways we now relate to our fascist "tradition" ("Germany Pale Mother"). The actors' physical work is clearly indebted to Grotowskian techniques and ideas about bodily rigor. At one point, Roberta Carreri and Francis Pardeilhan circle the space in a kind of mad, grotesque procession carrying a skeleton between them and an oversize edition of Goethe's

Faust (a parodic allusion to Grotowski, Brecht, or *The German Ideology?*). The trauma of the Nazi terror regime is evoked in startling, horrifying scenic images, while the actors speak almost simultaneously Brechtian verse in German as well as in English: "Beware of the dead! Beware of the future! Beware of the state! Beware of the voluntary victims! Beware of the involuntary executioners!"

I do not know, however, how many members of the audience realized that the "translations" of the text fragments often shift the first-person German voice to a third-person English *commentary* on what was said before. These distancing effects enforce the ice-cold irony of the physical gestures and juxtaposed scenic images, as in the scene where we see two bricks spotlit at opposite ends of the room: water trickles down on one of them, and Arturo Ui tries to shatter the other one with a hammer. "Water wears down the stone," we hear Barba's Brecht comment on this. Then he corrects himself: "Knowledge wears down stones." We remember this when we later hear Brecht's "real" voice on tape as he tricks himself out of the cross-examination of the House of Un-American Activities Committee, desperate for a visa and passport.

The conflict between involuntary victims and involuntary victimizers is shown to be unresolvable as the pressures of history increase in the last half of the performance. The highly visceral experience of the chaos of war is created almost entirely through mime and body movement; the most haunting performance is Iben Nagel Rasmussen's Kattrin, Mother Courage's daughter, who whirls around the room for an unbearably long time, always intensely present and yet cut off from us in her mute world of screams and the unspeakable pain of her bodily contortions. As she stands on the roof of her hut and warns the community of the approaching enemy, all the other actors are preoccupied with their individual performances, and cannot hear her. At this point Brecht interrupts the action to quote from his own text: "Theatre is the representation of relations between the actors." As the action continues, Kattrin is hauled down from the roof and brutally raped in the center of the arena. The rape is collective, watched by all of us; a Christian crucifix is rammed into her mouth. Her raped body can be read like a text. The figure of the broken, humiliated, mute victim is almost certainly another reference to Grotowski's Simpleton in *Apocalypsis cum figuris*.

The sadism of the tormentors and the masochism of the victims reflect off each other in an unending dialectical process. The Odin's performance work offers no solutions but demonstrates a critical attitude to the very proposed solutions. The "task," to use Müller's play-title, has not ended with Brecht's return to Berlin at the end of a long exile. On the contrary, we are unlikely to awaken from the nightmare of history as long as we dream of "final solutions" (*Endlösung*), such as Brecht's mocking suggestion that one day "all the cooks will get the leading role." Odin Teatret's performance will remain a work-in-process, and as that it has been the most fascinating and thought-provoking theatre work I have seen in a very long time.

If the Odin's dialogue with Brecht allows for a meeting between theatre group and audience, it is only by way of provocation. Barba's unsolution at the end of the performance, therefore, is deliberately shocking and disquieting. We sit caught in a long, ten-minute blackout, but while everything is pitch black around us we can still hear the tak tak tak tak tak tak tak of Brecht's typewriter, and slowly we understand the words that live on: "Don't let them seduce you! Don't let them seduce you! Don't let them seduce you!" Tiny little lights flicker suddenly, sometimes so close to our faces that someone next to me shrieks in fear. When the house lights come on we face the audience on the other side of the empty playing space.

Grotowski has argued that a song in an untranslated language or a precise physical gesture will always stimulate a particular response, since one need not know the script of a play in order to see that the structure of the acting *is* the script. In the Odin's performance there is a considerable number of untranslated words and elliptical textual and visual quotations, yet there is also an elaborated structure of precise emphases on physical action and on the relationship between the bodily gestures. I am not so sure, however, whether the performance worked as an intercultural theatre event. When I talked to Barba afterwards, he was honest enough to express doubt about the effectiveness of Odin's critical provocation. "I have seen a lot of puzzled faces," he admitted, "almost as if the New York audience didn't know out of what cultural tradition we are coming." In his program notes Barba writes: "Our production reveals our nostalgia for an impossible dialogue."

Cultures of the Body

I don't think I realized at the time how deeply I related to Barba's work and yet resisted the idea that the dialogue between present and past and between cultures has anything to do with nostalgia. On the contrary, even if revolutionary transformation is no longer imaginable in Marxist terms of class struggle and relations of production, we still obviously need a permanent revolution as *human emancipation* (as Marx spoke of it in 1844) in light of contemporary forms of domination and repression in the West and the East. The current deep crisis of the Communist world, and the radical popular mobilization against the "actually existing socialism" in Eastern Europe, are the concrete effects of a past that needs to be recaptured through a revolutionary memory. History in the sense in which Benjamin speaks of the double exposure of dialectical images through which the significant past comes back to us and flashes up at a moment of extreme danger, needs to be recognized. This recognition is the precondition for theatre.

To think about "social learning process" in light of the dangerous unpredictability of the 1989 November Revolution in East Germany, for example, it is impossible for me not to reflect on Heiner Müller's changing attitude toward a divided German history, his own suspension between East and West, and his reception of a cultural heritage that includes the Brechtian father-figure alongside other father-figures, revolutionary and fascist. Müller was initially committed to the construction of socialism in the new, imposed political order of the German Democratic Republic, and committed to the Brechtian conception of a critical theatre. But he turned away from Brecht's *Lehrstücke* (learning plays) during the early 1970s when he felt it was no longer possible to express societal and personal experiences on the "macrostructural" level of an established Brechtian model that has already substituted its enlightened epic voice for those contradictions and resistances that it seeks to make known, to judge, to resolve within the dialectic that produces them. Müller referred to the significance of Brecht's "Fatzer-Material"—the only "experiment," Müller argued, in which Brecht never reached a rational or ideological articulation of the historical subject, in which he did not accomplish a lesson for a revolutionary model at the level of consciousness.[20]

Fatzer's asocial individualism escapes the reference system and the formal theatrical devices of Brecht's Marxist thought and dramaturgical practices. The material, unpublished and probably hardly known in the U.S., presents a crucial turning point for Müller's polemic against Brecht. The "Fatzer-Fragment" reveals an authentic crisis, what Müller called an incomplete "thinking process," which in Brecht's later work, under the real existing socialism of postwar East Germany, was no longer affordable. The "Fatzer-Material" was excluded from Brecht's collected works.

Müller's turn toward the "microstructural" level is a turn toward the subjective, to the pain and desire of bodies crowded with the phantasmagorias of anxiety produced by the collective unconscious. In *Hamletmachine, Quartet, Landscape with Argonauts, Description of a Picture,* and the productions of *The Task* in East Berlin and Bochum that he directed himself in the mid-1980s, Müller refuses to show anything but painful, obscure, grotesque subjective fantasies, the contorted language of fear and the repetitive gestus of (self-) destructiveness excavated from a repressed past that has accumulated its ruins in the mythical condition of Western society—the condition for enlightened modern rationality to turn totalitarian and violent against inner and outer nature.[21]

When I say language and gestus, I am thinking of the dense poetic quality of Müller's synthetic fragments. They are difficult, perhaps impossible, to play because they suggest that the body of the actor anatomize itself as the place or the corpse where the violence of history is inscribed, where each gesture cannot but speak of the battle that is to happen tomorrow and that has never ended. As a reinvention of theatre, against the postmodern anamnesis, these fragments deal with the body of collective memory through the disintegrating force, the repetition compulsion, that brings it back into the unredeemed present. The failed revolutions in Germany and Europe are recapitulated. The failures are the material and the ground for the collective future. *Volokolamsk Highway* (1984–87),

Müller's last project to date, is a stream-of-memory in five monologues that chart the German-Russian history since the last war as a cumulative crisis, tearing apart the subject that tries to think a way out of the vicious circle whose model, in classical theatre, was called tragedy. For Müller, there is no way out of a culture permanently suspended between East and West. In this state of unresolution, the model becomes a ghostly code, the central actor a double. In the fourth act he is called "centaur," and in the last act he is a foundling adopted by a Communist father once tortured and castrated by the fascists. Disowning his father who betrayed him in 1968, the son repeats Nietzsche's ironic stage direction: "FORGOTTEN AND FORGOTTEN AND FORGOTTEN." The son imagines that he can forget by exchanging his identity. He flees to the West, forgetting Nietzsche's warning that the past cannot be reinvented.

As he was completing "The Foundling," Müller suggested that it was time to return to the learning play model again and to eliminate the distance between actors and spectators. "All of them are responsible." *Volokolamsk Highway* was first performed in Paris in early 1988; its first German production took place in November 1988, exactly one year before the fall of the Berlin Wall. In a footnote to his play Müller argues that it is a renewed "effort at Proletarian tragedy in the age of counter-revolution that will end with the fusion of Man and Machine, the next step of evolution." As an image for this next step he suggests: "Wounded Man who in slow-motion rips off his bandages, who in quick-motion is swathed again with bandages, etc., in perpetuum. Timespace: THE MOMENT OF TRUTH WHEN THE MIRROR/REVEALS THE ENEMY. . . . The alternative is the black mirror that doesn't give back anything anymore."[22]

I shall have more to say about the fusion of Man and Machine in the essays that follow. In the present context, Müller's theatrical/political image of the mirror, and his proposition that all of us, actors and spectators, are responsible, can be used as a commentary on Barba's theatre anthropology. The crucial difference between Barba's *Faust* project and Müller's learning play lies in the latter's direct and culture-specific address. Both on the microstructural level of the voice and on the macrostructural level of narrative gestus and historical content, Müller's theatrical poem mirrors the contradictory and self-alienating movement of the German actor/spectator through the final stages of a history that ends in the defeated parody of a "proletarian tragedy." The physical performance, which suggests splitting of the voice into several different positions for the actor/spectator to take up in dialectical relationship to his or her history, cannot be modeled on or transposed onto a foreign body, since the social imaginary of the body is here inextricably embedded in ideological and cultural models (the mirror of East-West Germany). Unlike Barba's effort to find transcultural or transhistorical expressions through the elaborations of difference within the same myth (Faust) that he may assume to be universal, Müller's learning model is openly and explicitly codified by ideological contradictions that need to be analyzed by pushing them to their extreme limit where they can't be sublated anymore. A unification cannot take place in Müller's theatre.

Influenced by his collaboration with Grotowski, Barba traveled to the East and later founded the International School of Theatre Anthropology (ISTA) which—like the Danish-based Odin Teatret—seeks to explore the relations between codified acting (in Oriental theatre, but also in the Western tradition of classical ballet, the mime of Decroux, and so forth) and the daily behavior of a body that behaves according to biological laws that constitute a kind of substance without substance, "eine Haltung," as Brecht called it (Keuner-Geschichten). Only after recognizing the repetitions of the cultural body at the preexpressive, presymbolic, pretextual level can one invent or experiment with specific techniques that can "build another culture of the body,"[23] which Barba considers to be a problem of inventing strategies against automatism and, in a larger and more complex sense, against the semantic logic of causal relations between physical signs at work in Western perceptions of psychological or movement narratives.

Such a logic of perception necessarily obscures or overlooks the charges, the tensions, contractions and dilations, the "music of muscular tones and rhythms" that can flow through a new fictive body. Whatever seems illogical and contradictory in the performance of the Odin actors in fact results from a very precise and personal technique, and the actors' strong presence provokes a special kind of perceptivity that must respond to the sometimes imperceptible physical dialectic between bodies and voices, between movement and weight, rhythm and space, time and sound, energy and balance. When Barba describes this theatre as an art that enables us to see, he also formulates a utopian project; the Odin believes that a cross-cultural encounter, a dialogue between physiological and social organisms can be lived, not staged, through a body that has learned how to shape, control, and release its mental and physical energies, and how to be free to choose a different dialectical process, with a different transformation of energies, so that the body no longer resembles itself. Such a body can emigrate from itself, so to speak.

If I think of the Odin's Ashes 2 again, I would now describe it as a multilingual and polyphonic collage of images, sounds, and physical and musical actions. Barba uses an organic metaphor: "a tissue of sonorous actions in silent conflict, in counterpoint with each other"[24] that was obviously not a play but a living paradigm of their practice, their search for a discontinuous theatrical form that embodies the ruptures, the displacements, and the continuity of the paradoxical strength they experience during their migrations and their homecomings. For the Odin, theatre is a form of survival, and the encounter with Brecht must have been a necessary step in their plan to change places between and within different cultural matrices. The Odin's confrontation with the contradictory sources of their own European theatre tradition, with the historical and political past, violated the authority of traditions, theories, and myths that have shaped the cultural unconscious. In this sense, the Odin stands fully within the tradition of Western avant-garde performance (Artaud, Grotowski, Brook, Living Theatre, Mabou Mines, Wooster Group). Their unfinished dialogue, a highly visceral experience created almost entirely through mime, body movement, and rhythmicized acoustic space, nevertheless points into both directions: back to the idealist search for an "unperverted pantomime" (Artaud) and forward against the technological simulacra of the postmodern.

I shall use a key image from the Odin's "knowledge of physical fear," that of the tormentors' sadism and the victims' masochism reflecting off each other in an unending dialectic, as a transition to my concluding remarks about dance. In light of Pina Bausch's work with the Wuppertaler Tanztheater, again one could speak of a postdramatic, anthropological approach to the daily social experiences of the body. Male and female perceptions of the subjective, private and public role of the physical betray the barely veiled psychic and emotional constrictions and anxieties that become alienating as soon as we become aware of the sensual immediacy, the painful presence of the colonized body speaking about its own history. Bausch's dance theatre relates to the *physical consciousness* of the spectator; it almost always divides and scandalizes audiences that feel shocked into recognizing the banal logic of conventions, the reproduction of power, of class, race, and sexual relations tied to the logic of body language. We need no narrative dramaturgy or fable to see this logic as a mechanism of social intercourse through which men and women become colonizers and tormentors of each other, locked into specific class-related social and economic configurations and power relations that structure their behavior, their "habitus" (Bourdieu), their cultural style.

One could say, with Benjamin, that Bausch's dancers let the conditions (and the conditioning) speak for themselves, but they make "gestures quotable."[25] They work from the inside out, from an affect, a feeling of love, fear, or tenderness, a desire to hit somebody or be touched, to the repetition of an image, a moment of sadness or unbearable violence, a silent embrace or a painful fall, until everyday gestures and the often-deformed vocabulary of social routines and "techniques" are clearly recognizable and appear, at the same time, very, very strange.

As the Bausch dancers show something of their actual life stories, their pregnancies, their injuries, their insecurities, their unfulfilled needs, the collage pieces themselves—rarely ever finished and often without a title—have broken with all traditional aesthetics of classical ballet and modern dance, as well as of dramatic and music theatre. One could almost say that Bausch's Wuppertaler Tanztheater is a foreign body within the German theatre apparatus. With its emphasis on the living experience of real human beings onstage who want to say something that cannot be said, or dance something that cannot be danced, who sing to their goldfish or show the audience that the costume doesn't fit, the normal condition of spectatorship is stood on its head. The "experts" in the audience, still not allowed to smoke as Brecht wanted, feel uncomfortable, as in the piece entitled *Bandoneon,* where the set is slowly dismantled and the lights switched off during the performance, until one of the dancers addresses the audience: "Do something!"

The discomfort largely results from Bausch's relentless exploration of sex roles and the dehumanizing masquerade of gender identities derived from clichés of masculinity or femininity. The intense emotional expressivity said to characterize her work, as well as the brutality and violence, the cruel humor and repetitiveness for which she has been attacked, may derive from mimetic perceptions that misunderstand the deliberate and ironic insistence on an endless number of concrete physical tasks carried out by the dancers. It is in these tasks—dressing, undressing, pushing something, carrying somebody, spitting, breathing, shoveling dirt, feeding ducks—that gender-identified social behaviors become transparent in their constructedness, as the dancers *go through the motions* until those motions, remembered and automatic reflexes or defenses of everyday techniques of the body, have doubly inverted the truth of the cliché. What is so discomforting are the caricatures of human emotion that evolve from the endless repetition in the structure of relations between women and men, men and men, women and women. This repetition, especially when Bausch slows it down or accelerates it at various points in the performance, strips away layers and layers of acculturation with almost microscopic precision. At the same time, Bausch's dance theatre is profoundly humanist and compassionate. The self-degradations acted out, and the disintegration of identity we are made to see, are not endpoints but recurring points of departure for a stubborn re-search into the most fragile human desires—to be at home, not to be alone, to be in love, being loved, to be free, to be whole—that we don't dare to speak about because they seem to have become perverted beyond the point of recognition.

When the Bausch company performs *Carnations* (shown in New York in 1988 in conjunction with *Victor*), the stage is filled with the fragile beauty of a field of flowers guarded by watchdogs. The magnificent field of carnations gradually gets trampled down as the dancers, all dressed alike in women's dresses, romp through the happily remembered experiences of their first loves and their first fantasies. These memories soon begin to look absurdly comic in their innocence, unrecoverable, already distorted through the memory of the motions that expose them. We hear Schubert's string quartet and, later, Gershwin's "The Man I Love." Lutz Förster just stands there, tall, alone and dispassionate, translating the words of "The Man I Love" into the sign language of the deaf, hieroglyphs of a "foreign" alphabet. At the opening of *Victor,* staged in a huge tomblike pit surrounded by walls of earth, an apparently armless Anne Martin enters backstage and walks all the way to the front, smiling brightly at the audience in her vivid red dress. As the armless woman grins at the audience, we hear a male voice-over: "My name is Victor, I'm back again. May I stay here?" A few moments later we see a marriage ceremony of a lifeless couple lying on an oriental carpet. They are pronounced man and wife by another dancer who pushes the corpses together into a kiss. Their wedding music is a melancholy yet passionate Argentinian tango. The identity of "Victor" is not at issue; rather, all the dancers in *Victor* question their relationship to the world and what it is that always comes back to haunt. We may not exactly know what it is that returns, but we know it exists. Perhaps Müller's indictment is true for all cultures: We are all responsible. (Kafka said it in a slightly different way: We are all guilty.) And the theatre, unlike any other medium, makes us physically aware of the ghosts that return, even if we only imagine it because we can think it.[26] In this physical-mental relationship to the return, which I shall call performing-returning-to-life, lies the most powerful challenge that dance, as a theatre anthropology in practice, can pose to a postmodern culture obsessed with death, simulacra, and the consumption of history and memory in a self-referential televisual space that has no outside. Theatre and dance must have an outside in order to exist. How else, for example, could we understand the extraordinary archaeology of the deformed, distorted, and grotesque body in Japanese butoh dance? *Anakokuh butoh* means "dance of darkness," although its practitioners speak of it as a "joyous despair" (Min Tanaka) or a "celebration of life" (Kazuo Ohno). When butoh became known in the West in the early 1980s, the shocked reaction to its convulsive body metamorphoses very gradually gave way to the recognition, not that there may have been a historical influence of early expressionist dance (Mary Wigman) on the founders of postwar butoh (Tatsumi Hijikata, Ohno), but that one could see these dancers were trying to uncover something that was hidden and tabooed by the strict social codes of Japanese society and the performance codes of its Noh and Kabuki traditions. They were turning their bodies inside out. In a commentary reprinted in the program for Natsu Nakajima's performance of *Niwa* (shown at New York's Asia Society in 1985), Hijikata writes:

> We shake hands with the dead, who send us encouragement from beyond the body. This is the unlimited power of butoh. . . . In our body, history is hidden . . . and will appear in each detail of our expressions. In butoh we can find, touch, our hidden reality—something can be born, can appear, living and dying at the same moment. The character and basis of butoh is a hidden violence.[27]

When I saw Nakajima again at the Montreal Festival International de Nouvelle Danse in 1989, she performed together with Yukio Waguri in *Sleep and Reincarnation/From an Empty Land*, which seemed to be a tribute to the late Hijikata. Waguri invoked Hijikata's aggressive and violent interactions with live animals (in *Nikutai no Hanran*, first performed in Tokyo in 1968) in a series of extraordinary transformations of the body into animal shapes. In counterpoint to these animal ghosts, Nakajima's sustained performance of small, nearly imperceptible changes in her physical features was carved from the physiognomy and the movement of the old

farmers and women in rural areas left behind by the modern industrialization of Japan. What is striking about this reappearance of indigenous
history *as movement* is not only the permeability of the dancer's *Niku-tai* (the
"flesh-body" that is not fixed or constant but always in movement), but her
ability to dance time itself, living and dying from one moment to the next.

I don't know why so many Western observers refer to this experience
as "dreamlike." Their perception of the slow-motion movement seems to
respond to the surface inscriptions on the body and what is now "identifiable" as butoh-style (slow motion, gaping mouths, clawed hands, silent
screams, shaven head, white body paint). The quotation and incorporation
of these surface inscriptions into Western performance (such as Robert
Wilson's operas) will only add to the perceptual confusion. However, in a
recent meeting with Deborah Hay, one of the founding members of the
Judson Dance Theatre in New York in the 1960s who later on left the
Merce Cunningham Dance Company to pursue her own research in Aus-
tin, I noticed that my sense of the dance of time in butoh was confirmed by
Hay's remarkable insight into what she calls "practicing dying." Her focus
over the last few years, she explained in a workshop, had been on the
constantly changing corporeal reality of the body in its relationship to the
constantly changing world.[28] Practicing the "death of separateness" by
developing a physical and mental consciousness of the body's whole
relationship to the world-in-flux has no spiritual or mystical dimension for
Hay. Rather, her understanding of what I initially introduced as "social
action diagnosis" would explore the dispossession of the human body
precisely in those states of nonrelationship to the world when it perceives
itself most concrete, most present and centered, most technically accomplished. In order to change the dream of presence, changing perceptions
themselves must become the dance. "Perception *is* the dance."[29]

Perhaps it is true, as Heiner Müller claims (in a letter to Robert
Wilson), that we must learn—before it is too late—to adopt a new
sensuous, physical way of *seeing* (with our ears and bodies) how Brecht's
epic theatre can be made to dance. And to those who might ask whether
political revolutions can be rehearsed in the theatre, I would answer that it
depends on the conditions under which one works toward changing the
perception of the conditions. After listening to "Azothe 'amalanga," a
dance-song performed by Selaelo Maredi, Seth Sibanda, Themba Ntinga,
and Fana Kekana at the end of *Survival,* a South African protest dance they
have performed in exile for thirteen years since the Soweto uprising, I
don't doubt the tenacious memory that the theatre can have of the history
of dispossession.

NOTES

    1. Augusto Boal, *Theater der Unterdrückten,* trans. Marina Spinu and Henry
Thorau (Stuttgart: Suhrkamp, 1979), 68–69.
    2. *Brecht on Theatre,* ed. John Willett (London: Methuen, 1964), 126.

3. *Brechts Dramen*, ed. Walter Hinderer (Stuttgart: Reclam, 1984).

4. Antonin Artaud, *The Theatre and its Double* (New York: Grove Press, 1958), 39.

5. Ibid., 54–56.

6. "Shouldn't We Abolish Aesthetics?" in *Brecht on Theatre*, 20–22. The question has certainly been reformulated by the dance theatre and performance art practices of the last three decades. But it needs to be readdressed to semiotics, comunications theory, and media theory, as they were exhibited in "Les Immatériaux" or "Image World," which are tools of a technical rationality that neutralizes the human agent and reduces him or her to obligatory sign and image functions.

7. Jean Baudrillard, *Simulations* (New York: Semiotext(e), 1983), 72.

8. The controversy surrounding Brook's eleven-hour stage adaptation of the sacred Indian Hindu epic and his assimilation of Indian Kathakali performance techniques reverberated through all the theatre journals in 1987–88 and represented the first major discursive moment of postmodern theatre in which the collision of cultures-in-performance was recognized and debated. See *Theater* 19, no. 2 (1988); *The Drama Review* 30, no. 1 (1986) and 32, no. 2 (1988), *Performing Arts Journal* 30 (1987), and also Eileen Blumenthal's "West Meets East Meets West," *American Theater* 3, no. 10 (1987): 10–16.

9. As I write this, I'm preparing to participate in an African Conference on African-based systems of knowledge, with a focus on V. Y. Mudimbe's ethnophilosophical study, *The Invention of Africa* (Bloomington: Indiana Univ. Press, 1988). For the context of the current debate on the reinvention of cultures, see *The Invention of Ethnicity*, ed. Werner Sollors (Oxford: Oxford Univ. Press, 1988). For the historical development of postmodern ethnography, see George E. Marcus and Michael J. Fischer, *Anthropology as Cultural Critique* (Chicago: Univ. of Chicago Press, 1986). The growing body of work in interdisciplinary performance studies and theatre anthropology has found its most effective forum in the provocative output of *The Drama Review*, now subtitled *A Journal of Performance Studies*, under Richard Schechner's editorship since 1986. Schechner's philosophy of the "broad spectrum approach" has given *TDR* a decidedly multicultural thrust, and it has sought to decenter the study of theatre, dance, music and performance art through a more inclusive exploration of "cultural performances" in healing, sports, popular entertainment and everyday life. For a critique of this postmodernization of the concept of performance, see Bonnie Marranca and Gautam Dasgupta's editorial in *Performing Arts Journal* 32 (1988): 4–6. Schechner's own pathbreaking book, *Between Theatre and Anthropology* (Philadelphia: Univ. of Pennsylvania Press, 1985), will undoubtedly become a model for the theoretical and practical "invention" of performance processes under cross-cultural examination. See also *Rite, Drama, Festival, Spectacle: Rehearsals Toward a Theory of Cultural Performance*, ed. John J. MacAloon (Philadelphia: Institute for the Study of Human Issues, 1984), and Philip B. Zarrilli, "Toward a Definition of Performance Studies, Pt. 1 and 2," *Theatre Journal* 38, no. 3 (1986): 372–76; 38, no. 4 (1986): 493–96.

10. Andrzej Wirth, "Artistic Interaction and Cultural Influence in the Performance Arts: The USA and Europe," *American Studies* 32 (1987): 19.

11. Guillermo Gómez-Peña, "The Multicultural Paradigm," *High Performance* 47 (1989): 18–27.

12. James Brandon, "A New World: Asian Theatre in the West Today," *The Drama Review* 33, no. 2 (1989): 39. Brandon is the founding editor of *Asian Theatre Journal* and a long-time student of Kabuki. He translates *geidō* as "a way of art" that a performer achieves after having completely absorbed the knowledge of the forms.

13. Eugenio Barba, *Beyond the Floating Islands* (New York: PAJ Publications, 1986), 115.

14. Eugenio Barba, "Theatre Anthropology," *The Drama Review* 16, no. 1 (1982): 47–54.

15. For the criticisms directed at Barba's 1986 Congress on "The Female Role as Represented on the Stage in Various Cultures," held in Holstebro, Denmark, see especially Erika Munk, "The Rites of Women," *Performing Arts Journal* 29 (1986): 35–42; and Peggy Phelan, "Feminism, Poststructuralism, and Performance," *The Drama Review* 32, no. 1 (1988): 107–27.

16. Patrice Pavis, "Dancing with *Faust:* A Semiotician's Reflections on Barba's Intercultural Mise-en-scène," *The Drama Review* 33, no. 3 (1989): 41.

17. Cf. Pavis's unusually vivid and plastic description in "Dancing with *Faust,*" 45–46.

18. Barba, "Eurasian Theatre," *The Drama Review* 32, no. 3 (1988): 130.

19. Eugenio Barba, from a theatre program written on the occasion of the performance of *Brecht's Ashes* 2, January 1982.

20. References are to "Fatzer±Keuner," a speech Müller gave at the Fifth Congress of the International Brecht Society in 1979. An English version, translated by Marc Silberman, has appeared in *Theater* 17, no. 2 (1986): 31–33.

21. Cf. Max Horkheimer and Theodor W. Adorno, *Dialectic of Enlightenment,* trans. John Cumming (New York: The Seabury Press, 1975), 6.

22. *Volokolamsk Highway* in *Explosion of a Memory,* trans. and ed. by Carl Weber (New York: PAJ Publications, 1989), 149.

23. Interview with Eugenio Barba, "Anthropology and Theatre," *Performing Arts Journal* 24 (1984): 14.

24. Cf. *Beyond the Floating Islands,* 81. This is my own translation from the Italian and German commentaries that preceded the published English version.

25. Walter Benjamin, *Understanding Brecht,* trans. Anna Bostock (London: Verso, 1984) 84.

26. This return to "life" in performance, Herbert Blau suggests, is one of the crucial transcultural elements of the dance and the theatre that distinguishes them from everyday life because the movement in time that it takes to perform this difference is a measure of the movement's "mastery" over time. Blau links this mastery to Freud's explanation of the differentiating act (the *fort/da* performance of the child) in *Beyond the Pleasure Principle,* the act that rehearses the "representation of a lack which is the recovery of a loss." Cf. "Universals of Performance, or, Amortizing Play," in *The Eye of Prey: Subversions of the Postmodern* (Bloomington: Indiana Univ. Press, 1987), 161–88. For my response to Blau, see "Aversions to the Postmodern," *Theater Three* 6 (1989): 181–87.

27. Tatsumi Hijikata's commentary also appeared in Bonnie Sue Stein's comprehensive introduction to "Butoh: 'Twenty Years Ago We Were Crazy, Dirty, and Mad,' " *The Drama Review* 30, no. 2 (1986):125.

28. Shortly after the workshop Deborah Hay conducted in Houston, I saw her "Letters to My Daughter," in which she writes: "[The body] is changing every moment. One may think one sees an identifiable figure but, in fact, that figure is never the same. This paradoxical reality—that one looks like one is here but here is always in flux—is of crucial importance." Cf. "Playing Awake," *The Drama Review* 33, no. 4 (1989): 70–76.

29. Ibid., 72.

8 ▨ POSTMODERN PERFORMANCE AND TECHNOLOGY

The problematic of postmodernism—and its significance as a cultural struggle over the perception and evaluation of the historical moment in which we live—involves both aesthetic and political questions. These questions can be articulated from various positions across a spectrum of affirmative or critical discourses that may not, at first sight, seem much concerned with the institutional role of theatre in the United States. Much of this discourse and ideological critique, as a repertoire of possibilities for an ongoing inquiry into the social processes of reading and viewing capitalist development and modernization rather than imposing an apparatus of imported and domestic concepts of poststructuralism/postmodernism, are made to converge here on the question of how one might have to rethink the idea of performance in the mid-1980s and after. This is especially true at the level of postindustrial information and communication technology and mass-mediational systems.

A lot of things have changed since Herbert Blau's manifesto for the "Impossible Theatre" in the mid-sixties, including all the good or bad intentions of both the mainstream theatre and the dispersed radical energies of the Judson Church and Living Theatre generation. The changing

This essay was first published under the same title in *Performing Arts Journal* 26/27 (1985).

artistic practices and modes of cultural production—especially visible within an ongoing experimental performance tradition whose irreducibly complex and heterogeneous history is reflected in the critical readings of *Performing Arts Journal* over the last decade (see, for example, the special issue 10/11 on "The American Imagination")—could perhaps be more directly contextualized at the present conjuncture of "discursive formations" and consumptional patterns if we were able to accept the impossibility of speaking about postmodern performance. Included in this view is the conceptual self-understanding of postmodernism as portrayed in recent crisis-theories of knowledge, representation, and performativity by Lyotard, Baudrillard, and Habermas[1], which are impossible to speak of outside of what I shall call the "technological scene": the constructed, technological environment that shapes our vision and embodies our relationship with the life-world. This relationship is nearly totally informed by industrial design, the paradigmatically contradictory and multivalent urban space, and the all-pervasive "supertext" of mass communication and media image production that not only sustains and legitimizes the economic order that has theatricalized itself into a supermarket of spectacles (cf. Guy Debord's *Society of the Spectacle*, 1977) but reinscribes itself as a *technology of viewing conditions* and spectator positions in political and cultural processes.

If one wanted to reactivate the Frankfurt School critique of the repetition compulsion and one-dimensionality intrinsic to culture industrial production, without trying to recuperate Adorno's utopian belief in the radical potential of autonomous aesthetic truth and authenticity, one would need to examine the postmodern "technological scene" in all its pluralistic, heterogeneous, and multidisciplinary dimensions. This, in order to account for a widespread enthusiasm behaving as if contemporary artistic production, its marriage of "high" and "low" and of anything else that is marriageable, had already achieved the reintegration of art and life which the historical avant-garde once considered fundamental to social transformation. It seems perfectly ironic that it is from the present generation of masterbuilders, the heirs of an ideology of integration that espoused the modern architectural utopia of social-*as*-technological transformation, that we hear the most despairing obituaries on the defunct "revolutionary" architecture, on the futile hope for a rehumanizing symbolic praxis within capitalist structures that condition the very function and character of architectural design.

By the time Manfredo Tafuri, in 1973, concluded all that remained in the "drama of architecture" was a flight into pure form, into aesthetic theories or semiologies of its own "language," or into "sublime uselessness,"[2] one could already begin to see the emergence of the new spectacular style-mixing of the postmodernists. Their eclecticism of pastiche, of representational kitsch derived from randomly quoted historical forms, betrays a huge learning process, not only from Las Vegas, but from the recent history of the commodification of early postmodern art (pop, op, conceptual, aleatory art, minimalism, intermedia performance, and so forth), from reified dramaturgies of montage to be found virtually everywhere in cinematic practices, commercial advertising, television programming, exhibitions, sports events, etc., and—perhaps most problematically—from the very theories of reading/writing developed by high academic formalisms (semiotics, deconstruction) that sought to expose and dismantle the dominant system of representation.

All these practices are mutually informing, of course, and although I cannot offer here a detailed analysis of the diversity and dissemination of artistic experimentation in the recent past, it seems important to point out that the overtly radical project of the poststructuralist critique of representation, as well as the provocative polygamy between semiotics, deconstruction, psychoanalysis and feminist theory, ultimately reveals a prefigurative tendency to formalize a new closed circuit of interdisciplinary models of *textuality* that are both totally relevant and irrelevant to the visual and performing arts. They are irrelevant, not because the images, the sound, the scenography, the kinetics, and the text of a performance event should or could privilege the notion that there is one specific language or vocabulary of reading/rewriting it,[3] but because a postmodern critical discourse on performance cannot be satisfied with the increasingly fashionable techniques of an aesthetic theory of textuality at its politically weakest (Derrida, Barthes, et al.), which doesn't acknowledge its involuntary regeneration of the same subject of history, the same family drama of capitalist culture, that it has declared defunct. Nevertheless, what we can deduce from such self-protective formalisms is their repressed fear of irrelevance vis-à-vis a changing public sphere in which we no longer live a part in the drama of alienation that was written into the mise en scène of modernist architecture and exemplified by Beckett's *Waiting for Godot*, our first modern tragedy of the city. Rather, as Jean Baudrillard observes, our lifestyles have grown used to the soft, homogenizing operations of mass communication and commodification forms (with especially high acceleration and self-replication in fashion, entertainment, and art market) which render "real" formal distinctions (i.e., qualitative perceptions of meaning) and the particularity of aesthetic objects virtually obsolescent categories in view of the emerging noncategorical logic of purely operational surfaces—the logic of "imagogenetics" and "computergrammatics," for example, that was so forcefully captured by Nancy Burson's recent exhibition of "Simulacra: Forms without Substance" (International Center of Photography).

It is the purpose of my following remarks to open up a discussion of the intersections between these impressions of postmodernism, especially as far as social and political dimensions are not abstracted from the lived experience in, and the reception of, the "technological scene," and particular examples of contemporary performance in the city. The larger project for future critical theory that I envision lies in thinking through the whole discourse of publicity or what Baudrillard calls the "limitless seduction and ecstasy of communication" in order to locate particular moments of experimentation where the different parameters of lived experience and desublimated art can reveal cultural tensions in the repetitive spectacle of consumption. I shall argue that we need to look at a great many levels of experimentation in the architecture of perception in our culture so that we can analyze the determining impact of technology (which is not soft but always potentially violent and in support of social control) on viewing formations, and especially on those formations of perception and pleasure related to image, sound, space-time, and the body. Any critical theory of cultural production as viewing formation, in other words, addresses the question of differentiated subject positions in the world of the audience. Another more radical question is that of a possible stage beyond the crucial nexus between sexuality and representation that has been consistently explored in recent feminist theory and artistic practice.[4] Most of the contributions to the exhibition "Difference: On Representation and Sexuality," curated by Kate Linker and Jane Weinstock for the New Museum of Contemporary Art in New York, in fact challenged head-on the economy of passive and active voyeurism, spectatorship and narrative identification by mobilizing the gallery space into a confrontation between feminist film theory and the redeployed codes of image-text montage and cinematic technology on the exhibited phototext works themselves. At the same time, there was a certain incohesiveness in the show's terms of address, with regard to the subject matter and to the screening of the independent films (at the Public Theater, in separation from the videotapes in/and the New Museum installation), which may point to the more general question of difference between the various media and their viewing conditions within the larger public sphere of cultural operation.

I hope it will be understood that my initial reference to the postmodern condition of architecture was meant to suggest the inevitable but largely unspoken interrelationship between our technological environment (including built space) and the structured social space of the theatre itself which, in the earlier moments of its history, used to serve as a concrete and metaphorical site of the perspective representation of power. Today, this interrelationship is most obvious when it is most anxiously denied, as in the case of Robert Wilson's multimedia opera *the CIVIL warS*, which wants to be a pure vision, a pure formal construction of its own space and time with no particular reference to history and the modes and relations of production that enable it. Wilson, our latter-day Fitzcarraldo who brings the new opera to the jungle of cities (the twelve-hour fragment, designed as a collaboration between theatres in Cologne, Rotterdam, Marseille, Rome, Tokyo, and Minneapolis, was scheduled for the Olympic Arts Festival in Los Angeles but failed to secure sufficient sponsorship), is perhaps the most typical example of an emerging elite of designers, composers, and visual/performing artists that meets the interests of major cultural institutions in rebuilding the aura of "avant-garde" performance on a very large scale, involving the glamour of high risks and high budgets and the full range of commodity tie-ins (sale of books, posters, records, videocassettes, T-shirts, touring exhibitions, and so forth) available to efficient "art-world" marketing machinery.

Within the trajectory of the postmodern performance culture in the United States one can recognize an almost cynical shift from the adversary ethos of a lived experience of embattled streets, with popular music, happenings, agit prop theatre, etc., as expressions of the civil rights, antiwar, and sexual liberation movements, to the more recent institutional-ization of the 1980s Next Wave, a wave that brings back the image of high art, and with it the patriarchal mythology of the "masterwork" *(Einstein on the Beach?),* while coopting a host of culture industrial forms into material support for its production. This shift from street and SoHo loft to BAM and Lincoln Center is not even surprising if one remembers that it was in the 1960s when McLuhan envisioned the technological aesthetic of the new television, video, and computer society, and when performance artists within the minimal and conceptual art context began to explore the in-termedial language of the future, the dance of electricity.

Figure 30. *Akhnaten.* Opera by Philip Glass. Directed by Achim Freyer. Staatstheater, Stuttgart, 1984. Photo: Horst Huber.

Today, at a time when so many voices speak of the end of history, one can't fail to see the long-term impact of experimental performance from the earlier days of Judson Church, the Kitchen, the Performing Garage, or Ellen Stewart's Cafe La Mama, even though the current appeal of quasicultic large-scale image spectacles (Laurie Anderson) or high-tech operas (Robert Wilson, Philip Glass) is explicable less in terms of the progression of artistic practices themselves than in relation to changed viewing conditions and new parameters of sensibility dictated by all those institutional practices of constructing, processing, and circulating images of the world for us (network and cable TV, video, cinema, MTV, advertising, the press, and so forth) that overlap with the galleries, the museums, and the stages. Given the constant redistribution and recontextualization of material from one medium to another, with the transposition of the performance-style TV music video of Prince's "Let's Go Crazy" ("live" footage from a concert) to the *Purple Rain* version in 35mm as one striking example that, as far as I can tell, has already influenced a choreography of flashdancing on the stage, it becomes increasingly disingenuous to claim that directors/stage-designers like Wilson have changed the way we see images and experience space-time, light, color, volume, and movement in the theatre. In the promotional footnotes to the Cambridge ART's reproduction of the German section of *the CIVIL warS* we read that Wilson's theatrical techniqe is significantly different from "customary dramatic forms" since, "like a dream or a hallucination, the action of a Wilson 'play' takes shape, dissolves, overlaps, fragments, and reforms. Two or three 'stories' may be told simultaneously." Such dreamwork has been with us for quite a while, on stage and on the screen, and if the habits of seeing were really an issue, one could as well turn to TV advertisements and video simulations as the revolutionizers of our spatial and temporal perception. In fact, one might argue that our access to the slowed-down action, the repetitions, and the structural asymmetry of image, music, sound in Wilson's work is largely determined by the repetitive reformulations (within the endless flow of text) of unfulfilled desire that we often experience in watching the fragmented and interrupted fiction or sports event on television. Furthermore, the representation of representation-as-technological manipulation of image, voice, and music tracks has been second nature to recent video art (cf. Max Almy's *Leaving the 20th Century*), which draws on customary dramatic forms and narrational strategies only to break down all familiar spectator positions (masculine and feminine) by electronically "wiping" away the human body and voice into color blotches, mosaic effects, abstract noise. And that is a radical practice, since the body and the voice of the "star" remain the primary focus in commercial TV and, not surprisingly, in MTV, despite the latter's pseudoanarchic visual styles.

The specific challenge of Baudrillard's view of the media's "limitless seduction" lies in his claim that the automatic self-referentiality of the technological simulation of the world leads to the end of any coherent viewpoint or subjectivity, of any epistemology arranged in spatial terms and dependent on distinctions between subject and object, the real and the imaginary, the body and its projections. I would argue instead that the seductive appearance of endless technological semiosis has certain limits even if it were already possible to assume that the electronic mass media's total penetration of culture not only changes perception and social behavior but indeed creates a new theoretical "space" (contemporaneity, simultaneity) in which everything is subject to simulation. Undoubtedly, that would mean the end of the theatre of representation, as Baudrillard concludes. But among the media that are still bounded by the symbolic markers of "customary dramatic forms" as well as by nonprivate, concrete social viewing situations, the theatre's structural resistance to semiological reduction provides a site for dynamic cultural conflict—especially when its nondramatic, nonnarrative, nonlinear, and "abstract" performances behave as if there were no boundaries. When I say "dynamic cultural conflict" I mean to suggest that the unavoidable commodification of so-called avant-garde performances, and their insertion into a material network of ideological pressures, does not prevent them from showing how the theatre, after its primary social function as the medium of "capitalist realism"[5] has been subsumed by cinema and television, can continue to engage the specific phenomenal presence of its actors, dancers, and singers on the stage without assuming, however (as Walter Benjamin and Antonin Artaud did, and a whole tradition of modernist criticism after them), that the representation of this presence is essentially different from technological representation.

In other words, to use my initial metaphor of the "architecture of perception," postmodern experimental performance generally presupposes our conflicted sensory experiences (which will differ by race and age, class and gender) of the technological scene and mobilizes audiovisual techniques of abstraction against the no longer clearly defined/confined phenomenological reality of the stage. The theatre's social function, therefore, will need to be reconsidered, and its current predilection for myth and science fiction more closely analyzed.

When Achim Freyer, whose recent works include a "scenic interpretation" of Händel's oratorio *The Messiah* (which had never been theatrically performed), directed and designed the Stuttgart premiere of Philip Glass's new opera *Akhnaten*, he used a huge cubical holograph for the funeral scene and, at the end of the last act, placed the group of present-day tourists, which wanders across the excavation site of the ancient Egyptian city, behind a blue gauze that made the performers appear like figures in an aquarium. Throughout the Stuttgart performance, Freyer's scenic design set its tableaux or moving pictures (reminiscent of the idea of the stills "concert" built on the score Glass wrote for *The Photographer*) into metaphorical spaces whose grandiose and unreal architecture seemed to come alive purely through the light and the music. Within the dark blue and bright yellow spaces behind the transparent screen, the constitution of perceived presence—the presence of human figures or plastic objects—was

Figure 31. Meredith Monk and Ping Chong. *The Games.* Brooklyn Academy of Music, 1984. Photo: Ruth Walz.

largely a composite effect of the light and sound modulations. I felt that the sensuous flow of Glass's repetitive polymelodic music very nearly dissolved the spatial boundaries with which Freyer's "landscapes" of Egyptian myth framed the actors. The actors themselves assumed a plasticity that made me think of Artaud's "animated hieroglyphs." And these hieroglyphs seemed to float in an unmeasurable aural-temporal dimension where the ecstatically visible is no longer recognizable.

This may sound paradoxical. But I consider the spectacular performance of *Akhnaten* a significant experiment to the extent that it demonstrated the destructuring power of endlessly reproducible, omnipresent music/noise, its problematic relationship to the production of regressive fantasies, and the theatre's ultimately self-destructive denial of the spatial/perceptual limits that are its specific conditions of communication. The crucial limit or out-line in the theatre used to be, and still is, the actor's body—the source of action, the place of articulation, where language, history, the world outside (bodiliness) is incorporated, where something will be shown that the spectator can perceive in reciprocal relation to the scale of proportion offered by the body. The performing body, however subjected to conventions of viewing and to the discursive and representational structures from within which it speaks, is the primary physical condition for a shared experience of the social relations of theatre. The recent history of postmodern experimental performance suggests that the cultural determinations of the boundaries of (shared?) experience have been transformed, and that the spaceship theatre (e.g., Meredith Monk/ Ping Chong's sci-fi opera *The Games*) is ready to leave the twentieth century after having dislocated the human actor into technologically abstracted totalities, or "hyperreal" spaces, that are beyond and above a spectator's particular moment of viewing.

In the case of Wilson's *CIVIL warS* one can almost speak of the *architecturalization* of the body: androgynous actors, hanging from the ceiling behind—or standing motionless in front of—the proscenium-sized scrim on which overdimensional images of human faces are projected, appear as surface material, as if built into the space. The total design-in-motion, with its multiple stage pictures, constantly changing screen projections, text-collages, and soundscapes, cannot be perceived coherently or logically. One feels overwhelmed, oppressed, excited, perhaps less by the incoherent visual scale than by the disjunctions between different time scales (filmic time, real time, musical time) that directly affect the way one perceives the actors *temporally*, separate from their bodies, separate from the voices that trickle from the loudspeakers scattered around the auditorium. One can no longer speak of actors, then, but perhaps it is not possible either to go so far as to compare their demotivated "presence" to the electronically constructed nonsexual human images in recent videos, or to the "replicants" and clones that turn up in new sci-fi films *(Blade Runner)* which seem to deal less with the future than with the present, with Los Angeles and Hollywood, for example.

And yet, all these emerging viewing formations (including the slick androgyny promoted in MTV) must be considered in relation to the dislocation of the actor-in-performance that I have described, since it is quite likely that the idea of live performance in the theatre, after the general invasion of technological "access codes,"[6] will be consumed by postmodernist space operas in which the "role" of the performer can be randomly reproduced, recorded (filmed), and distributed across the entire image/ sound apparatus—inviting the spectator's ear to identify with the spectacle. (This is not paradoxical as far as I can judge from my observation of the consumption of MTV, which is one of listening, not watching, as well as from my recent experiences in the New York "Danceteria," where cult films, such as *The Road Warrior*, are shown without sound on more than two dozen video screens that nobody watches, while everybody seems immersed in listening to the various rock/new music concerts that are going on simultaneously on several floors. In any case, the silent images of *The Road Warrior* in a totally dominant sonic environment that strongly suggests the obsolescence of language and communication in the tradition-al sense, demand analysis in a separate essay.) While this emphasis on the ear might imply the construction of a feminine spectator position of in-teriority and regression (a problem of much concern to film critics at present), it describes, perhaps more generally, an infantile scenario, far removed from the collective critical activity Brecht expected in response to the new epic opera that would abandon the "witchcraft" of the old, and equally far removed from Heiner Müller's political idea of the theatre as a laboratory of the social imagination. And yet, the question of how one listens to Wilson's architectural abstractions is redeterminable (and not determined) precisely through the obvious ideological contradictions built into the scenario of *the CIVIL warS*, into its imaginary "Prussian history" that ends with a hysterical epilogue on the History of Mankind during which we are offered *undifferentiated* images of mythical, anthropomorphic, historical, and literary figures. Sound begins to fill the air, furiously, signifying nothing. The "Snow Owl" screeches (Hopi prophecies, as the program indicates), the "Earth Mother" mutters a Grimm fairy tale, "King Lear" quotes himself, speaking to the blind ("Look with thine ears . . ."), and a tall black shape that looks like Abe Lincoln recites Ecclesiastes in Latin: "tempus est." Black out.

It is impossible not to notice the strange disproportion between the technical design of this "holographic" scene and the total emptiness of its content. The recovery of a social content implies reconceiving the ambiva-

Figure 32. Robert Wilson. *the CIVIL warS*, Act IV A. American Repertory Theatre, 1985. Photo: Richard Feldman.

lent relationship between the theatrical body of the actor and the technological representations by which it is hollowed out. One form of critical engagement with this ambivalence was demonstrated by Falso Movimento, one of the three "post-avant-garde" groups that performed at La Mama's New Italian Theatre Festival in 1984. Their multimedia work *Otello,* directed by Mario Martone with a music score composed and rearranged by Peter Gordon, had little to do with Verdi's nineteenth-century opera or with Shakespeare's tragedy, but they used its movement of ironic allusions back into the drama of jealousy and passion as a kind of musical/rhythmical passage through technologically simulated urban landscapes (projected against movable screens as well as actual painted backdrops). It was also a voyage through time, imaging the transformations of Otello's "passion" in changing relationships between the choreographed movement of the three main characters (Otello, Iago, Desdemona) and the different semantic contents of the architectural designs. The performers themselves had each designed a specific gestus or outline (geometric phrases) for their movement and dance interpretation of that voyage, and their most striking physicalizations occurred when the extensions of the body-in-space melted into the shadows their silhouettes cast on the moving screens. The slide projections of luminous cityscapes would often seem to penetrate their bodies, but one could not lose sight of the difference between the physical body and the fabricated illusionistic surfaces of reality, although that "exterior" design was shown to be already always informative and impressive on the social "character" of the body.

This architecturalization of the body, revealing the metainstitutional power of the city/public space as a social technology, stood in a complicated dialectical relationship to the erotic, sensual contact between performers and audience, mirrored in the almost wordless sexual power shared by Desdemona, Otello, and Iago. If the sadomasochistic exchanges between the three, which led to the predictable (but melodramatically exaggerated) murder, meant to suggest the larger psychosocial dialectic of power within which they are bound, the performance sought to allegorize an imagined source of "passion" (in the real body? the images? the spectator?) by the use of an extraordinarily aggressive and dissonant sonic environment. Gordon's score, mixing electronically distorted recordings of the Verdi opera with overdubbed acoustical and electronic instruments, was so powerfully dominant that the illusion of one's individual resistance to it became part of *Otello,* and perhaps I can say that we became witnesses/victims of something very real—some phantom fear that Otello must strangle—that is part of our projections, our desires, and our deathly confusion in the kind of society we live in. We understand the fascinating violence of the reproductive system, although we may not always hear/see as clearly as in this performance, how the false movements and lines of aggression are "built" into our libidinal and political economy.

If the theatre cannot complete the avant-garde project and change the historical subject for whom, at this point, it can only represent the technological destructuration of "aesthetic-communicative rationality" (Habermas), it can at least explore the critical limits of simulation and perception in the sense in which the "post-avant-garde" performances at La Mama searched for symbolic relationships between the energies of the body and the theatricality of architecture. Furthermore, the dislocation of the actor—perhaps a specific phenomenon of the Next Wave in the United States—needs to be seen in the context of a postmodernist trend toward a fetishization of surfaces that "wipes" the critical and social relations to the specific historical conditions of the production of a work. I suggest, therefore, that we need to give more attention to those postmodern performances that do not let the multimedia apparatus represent itself to itself, but react against that mise en abyme by foregrounding, and experimenting with, the transformable theatricality of body and voice in real space-time—and thus addressing the actually changing conditions of representation *for* social subjects that we experience today.

These conditions, as I have tried to argue here, may turn us more and more into the automatized somnambulists and designed objects that people Wilson's affirmative postmodern spectacles. But they can be engaged differently by collaborative artistic practices (e.g., in the increasingly popular dance-theatre and music-theatre performances) that care about the context-specific, social, and ethnic identities of the body and the subject of performance, and that—even more anachronistically—insist on an ethics of (re)productive choice. Such insistence stands in contradiction to the globalizing or "intertextualizing" abstractions of advanced technologies that are themselves forms of patriarchal power, as feminist critics rightly point out.[7]

Among the most significant compositional and choreographic experiments that were staged in New York in the course of only one year (1984–85) I would count the Odin Teatret's archaeology of a very specific, grown relation to an acting tradition (i.e., a political tradition) in *Brecht's Ashes 2* (La Mama), Martha Clarke's and Richard Peaslee's musical dance interpretation of a Bosch painting in *The Garden of Earthly Delights* (St. Clement's), Sankai Juku's Butoh-inspired body transformations in *Kinkan Shonen* (City Center), Meredith Monk's vocal concert at Carnegie Hall as well as the revival of her theatre work *Quarry* (La Mama), and the Wuppertaler Tanztheater's carnivalistic "rehearsal" of childhood memories in *1980* (BAM). It is hardly accidental that the most consistent and organically grown exploration of the theatricality of expressive performance, showing us a possible future stage for the "postmodern condition," comes from women artists, among them Meredith Monk, Pina Bausch, and Martha Clarke. All three have used technological media in various ways, only to discover that the medium is not the message, and that if theatre wishes to survive as a social institution, it may have to resist the masculinist aesthetic dream of a new "technological sublime" (Lyotard) that would manifest the unpresentable (the immaterial) not just as form without substance, but as form without form. Lyotard's dream was exhibited under the name "Immatériaux"—a theatrical installation presented by the "Centre de création industrielle" at the Beaubourg in Paris. L'effet Baudrillard? Both the exhibition and Baudrillard's theories have obviously influenced my thinking in the 1980s, and they have made me more aware of the implications of the "technological sublime." Whether and how they can be contested by the theatre and the evolving body of work in dance-theatre and performance art remains to be seen.

The undiminished range of possibilities for postmodern performers to light out for new political territories stretches from the very real and presentable world of continuing discoveries that Meredith Monk unearths in her vocal and ritual memory plays *(Dolmen Music, Quarry)*, or that Pina Bausch's dancers retrieve from the underground of self-repression and social instrumentalization *(Kontakthof, 1980)* to the electronic display world ironically displayed by Laurie Anderson *(United States)*. Unearthing and retrieving performance modes already beyond the coordinates of technological representation may be one way the theatre of the 1980s will help us to see and hear our own conditioning. Another way to recover a dislocated audience would be the "Trojan Horse strategy" that the new director, Peter Sellars, of the new American National Theatre has proposed during his short-lived term of residency: "Re-invent the world. . . . ANT will present Shakespeare. And musicals. Late-breaking developments from Ancient Greece. Little family plays. Ravishing and empty spectacles. . . . Mysteries, romances, and the heroic." This "re-invention" of the world, however, may be another technological dream we are already familiar with.

NOTES

1. Cf. Jean-François Lyotard, *The Postmodern Condition: A Report on Knowledge* (Minneapolis, Univ. of Minnesota Press 1984); Jean Baudrillard, *In the Shadow of the Silent Majorities or the End of the Social* (New York, Semiotext(e), 1983) and *Simulations* (New York, Semiotext(e), 1983); Jürgen Habermas, *Theorie des kommunikativen Handelns* (Frankfurt, Suhrkamp, 1981).

2. See Manfredo Tafuri, *Architecture and Utopia: Design and Capitalist Development* (Cambridge, The MIT Press, 1976), ix; 150ff.

3. Cf. Bonnie Marranca's claim that we should develop a "performance *language* that is specifically theatrical, that is not anthropological, not literary, not filmic, not psychoanalytic, not philosophical," In "The Politics of Performance," *Theatrewritings* (New York, PAJ Publications, 1984), 132.

4. Cf. Alice Jardine, "At the Threshold: Feminists and Modernity," *Wedge 6* (Winter 1984): 10–17.

5. I borrow this term, with its obvious allusion to a very different context of cultural politics (and sublime contradictions, as in the case of GDR playwright Heiner Müller who, after a long struggle with Brecht's production aesthetics, has found a way to collaborate with Robert Wilson), from Botho Strauss' play *Trilogy of Recognition*.

6. Cf. Joshua Meyrowitz, *No Sense of Place: The Impact of Electronic Media on Social Behavior* (New York and Oxford, Oxford Univ. Press, 1985), 73ff.

7. See the recent issue of *Diacritics* on "Nuclear Criticism" (14, no. 2 [1984]), especially Zoe Sofia on the "Sexo-semiotics of Extraterrestrialism," 47–59.

We already live out the "aesthetic" hallucination
of reality. Today, the real and the imaginary are
confounded in the same operational totality, in
the black box of the code.
Surely this must mean the end of the theatre of
representation - the space of signs, their conflict, and their silence.

Jean Baudrillard

9 ■ THE AVANT-GARDE MACHINE

In a culture with nearly invisible boundaries separating theatre performance from dance, music, film, television, video, and the various performance art "disciplines," the function of performance criticism itself—
especially in light of a changing public sphere and postindustrial context
for the "avant-garde"—needs to be reconsidered if it wants to engage the
changes and the questions raised by the current role performed by the arts
in the cultural market.

A few years ago Bonnie Marranca suggested that late capitalist
bourgeois culture *is* the avant-garde and that the visual and performing
arts are inevitably tied into the exchange mechanisms and economic values
that the culture produces for them. The question of avant-garde
fashionability, therefore, has become a serious problem, since it is no
longer possible to review aesthetic practices and their meanings separate
from the institutional (publicity, promotion, funding, production) and
technological environment in which they are sold to the public as "new."

The last Next Wave Festival of the experimental performing arts at the
Brooklyn Academy of Music (October through December 1984), or perhaps I should say the last one of these annual festivals that I attended with
a critical and historical concept of the "avant-garde" in mind, offers a good
example of the collusion of advanced art with an even more advanced
technology of cultural promotion. The Next Wave also reminded me of the

organizational and promotional structure of the massive Olympic Arts Festival held in Los Angeles during the same year, and it seems to invite critical analysis precisely because such large-scale events demonstrate how a powerful culture industry privileges diverse interdisciplinary artistic practices. Such an experience tests our critical language, since the avant-garde's often aggressively affirmative embrace of new "waves" and styles of high-tech performance complicates our perception of its changing political, aesthetic, and conceptual investment in postmodernism. These changes cannot be separated from changes in the social organization, in the new postindustrial order that Jean Baudrillard has described as a scenario of limitless seduction.

On the stages of our theatres we occasionally see an event that makes us pause and think, but these are atypical instances. I'm thinking of the New York appearances of the Living Theatre, the Odin Teatret, Pina Bausch's Wuppertal Dance Theatre, Sankai Juku, or the controversy surrounding the Wooster Group's *L.S.D.*, which will perhaps be remembered as technological accidents in an otherwise well-oiled machinery of closed-circuit ideological repetition. The BAM Festival made it clear that the embarrassing end of the "impossible theatre" (if we think of the short-lived return of the Living Theatre as symptomatic) directly reflects the extent to which the radical politics and utopian energies of the sixties have become anachronistic. Clearly we are now meant to celebrate the grand elaborations of an avant-garde aesthetic aligned with late capitalism that defends the new perceptual freedom achieved by nonnarrative, nonrepresentational multimedia spectacles. This aesthetic has evolved from the crisis that the "theatre of images" and formalist art supposedly brought about in relation to language and narrative. But it thoroughly contradicts the idea of a crisis insofar as it enforces spectacular consumption that sustains our artificial sense of freedom and pluralism and at the same time reproduces the conditions for experimentations of the avant-garde itself.

Inserted into this circle is the question of how the avant-garde wants to be perceived by the public. If it were possible to quote Brecht in this context, one might reread his poignant "Notes on the Opera" with respect to the increasingly efficient "homologation of cultural products" (Baudrillard) that today threaten to mock any dialectical thinking. One might also argue, with Herbert Blau, that the (im)possibility of interrupting the conditioned reflexes of consumption has something to do with the general indifference to *meaning* that has developed over the years when the avant-garde was busy experimenting with minimalism, serial repetition, and the random play of surfaces.

At the BAM Festival program of collaborative productions (three concerts, seven dance/opera/multi-media works) I was struck by the cheerful rhetoric with which the organizers discussed their views of the domestic avant-garde. The experimentalists wound up being compared to both Brecht and Wagner and to a concept of large-scale, multimedia performance that, according to the Festival catalog of theoretical writings, is based on an "opera-tic" model of American technology ("the model for the world," according to Howard Klein) that has successfully achieved the "integration of a visual arts sensibility into the stage picture at the expense of language" (Robert Marx).[1]

Paradoxically enough, the catalog does not so much construct the myth of the "model" as try to legitimize the idea of a continuing Next Wave technology, a technology of style, a style machine operating on a commodification principle ("visual arts sensibility"?) perfectly in support of the dominant capitalist relations of reproduction. It is an insidious but predictable idea that tells us exactly what structures of expectation it believes exist in the audience. It is not surprising, therefore, that the chosen works were mostly by artists who have already established a reputation in the art industry.

If the remembrance of the Living Theatre must be repressed[2], this is obviously not the case with the return of *Einstein on the Beach* (now considered "legendary," in reference to the two sold-out performances at the Met in 1976 and its impact on the "theatre of images"). It cost $1 million, equalling the expected gross of the 1984 Next Wave Festival and, incidentally, the missing amount of funds that led to the cancellation of Bob Wilson's new multinational opera, *the CIVIL warS*, originally scheduled to be the main attraction of the Olympic Arts supermarket.

Some of the critical assumptions that surfaced in BAM's festival catalog seemed to relate to content (cf. Marcia Pally, "The Rediscovery of Narrative: Dance in the 1980s"), to the formal contradictions between opera and dance performance (within a larger frame of reference linking Next Wave Collaboration to the "model" of a distintegrated *Gesamtkunstwerk*), to the promotional image of the individual artist-as-collaborator, and to the structures of audience perception in general. All of these relationships merit analysis if we care to entertain a meaningful dialogue with avant-garde performance in the future.

Having said this, my first suggestion would be to rethink the way we think of "relationship" (or "collaboration") itself; i.e. develop a new prepositional thinking that can grasp the heterogeneous collage styles of the postmodern avant-garde without taking for granted the "return" of older representational categories (neo-narrative, neo-expressionism, etc) to the performance, and to the relationship between performer and audience. The festival catalog's biographical effusions about the individual artists and their intentions notwithstanding, we cannot tell what the performances are *about* until we have clarified *how* they wanted to be seen, and how we position ourselves as viewers in relation to them.

Although one assumes that the poststructuralist critique of representation must have affected the avant-garde's use of the available, hierarchical arrangements and limits of theatre space, none of the ten works seemed primarily interested in the problem of frontal vision. One exception was Remy Charlip's perplexingly simple gesture of inviting us to sit *behind* the dancers onstage, looking at the empty theatre where we normally sit. The reverse angle allows us to see more intimately both the tender and sensuous movements in "Ten Men" and the overtly ironic display of the dancers' innocent poses in "Flowering Trees," which reproduce those sketched out on a diagram distributed to the audience. Charlip's play with the ironies of the pose in fact opens with a little mock ballad that he performs with his voice and fingers in a single spot of light: "Every little movement has a meaning all its own." The opening song is called "Opening," but that is of course not what he means. Charlip's ten male dancers strike a number of sweet, erotic poses, which, if anything, are about posing/imposing itself and about the pleasure of being watched closely, which complicates the reductive logic that arrests the psychosexual relations between objectifying look and exposed body. On the other hand, I felt uncomfortable about the invitation to view a performance of mimetic rivalry during which "femininity," by being projected as a synonym for "posing," is impersonated through a patriarchal logic that makes the "feminine" available for parody. Such a parody posits the feminine position as surface, as spectacle, fixed into hierarchical oppositions that revalidate the old symbolic arrangements and apparatuses of representation. The nostalgia for a reassuring narrative trajectory of desire became more embarrassingly obvious when Charlip asked Lucas Hoving, a veteran modern dance star, to present a biographical solo about his performance career ("Growing Up in Public") that turned out to be as regressive as our most recent actor-president's continuing recollections of the American Dream.

The choreography of Charlip's dances appeared as complacent and unchallenging to me as Steve Reich's new composition, *The Desert Music*, which, somewhat surprisingly, shifts his earlier minimal style of endlessly repeated, interlocking structural patterns into the direction of more traditional large-scale concert music, using more instrumental colors and polyrhythmic pulses within clear harmonic cycles. The staccato rhythms enforce the very powerful emotional effect achieved by the overlapping, dissonant parts of the chorus built around repeated "sound-interpretations" of poetic fragments from William Carlos Williams's "The Orchestra," including such ominous lines as "It is a principle of music to repeat the theme. Repeat and repeat again, as the pace mounts. The theme is difficult but no more difficult than the facts to be resolved."

With this awkward text in the center of the orchestration we have very nearly returned from the desert of serial music to the theatre of memory and depth illusion where the ear waits for the "facts" of dissonance and repetition to be "resolved." We hear Reich's harmonic ambiguities (appearances of decentered harmony) in their repeated distance from perfect consonance.

Moderate
    Well, shall we
think or listen? Is there a sound addressed

not wholly to the ear?
We half close
our eyes. We do not
hear it through our eyes.
It is not
a flute note either, it is the relation
of a flute note
to a drum. I am wide
awake. The mind
is listening.

Williams, "The Orchestra"
2nd Movement, *The Desert Music*

Such music, in other words, remains caught in its logic of contradictions (between words and sound, meaning and pure rhythm, dissonance and harmony, D dorian minor and F major, and so forth). Blau might argue for its entrapment in the Law of Eternal Recurrence; i.e., the closed, rhythmic construction whose chordal and pulsional cycles create a predictable pattern of permutations, a displaced continuity of desire for harmonic resolution: a resolution that can be *thought*. Even when the words disappear into syllables, into pure sound, we have heard too much. Contrary to what the avant-garde may claim, we are not in the realm of unbound intensities where, as Artaud had imagined, we would become oblivious of the apparatus of language/thought and, instead, participate in the phantasmatic circulation of figures of desire. That particular Artaudian dream, too, uses the same language that our minds do. I am not sure to what extent the idea of speeding up or slowing down the orchestration of pure (unmediated) sonic images or visual images (in Wilson's operas) perpetuates the illusion that the political economy of signification could be replaced by affective experiences on a tactile and musical level. I suppose Reich wants us to read the poem and then listen to the music without thinking.

But to claim that we need a highly "energetic theatre" (Lyotard) that can extend the boundaries of sense perception does not resolve the problematic status of image-movement and image-perception in our culture. The noise *and* the silent domination of a landscape of consumption generally produces either affective recognition or passive indifference in the viewer, whose expectations are themselves the product of what Roland Barthes has called the *déjà vu*, the already-seen and already-heard.

They may also achieve both effects at the same time. Avant-garde performers operating in this space of deoriginated spectacularity must ask themselves how they can self-critically disrupt the arrangement and composing of the *same* divisions and meaning-effects, and remobilize the traps in the visual field. The ideological repetition of "theatre" within a social structure of spectatorship has been expected to produce the coherence of view and viewer, i.e. the customer who willingly pays for a performance during which he or she will be held in place and confirmed.

The return of the "legend," *Einstein on the Beach,* for a two-week sold-out run at the climax of the festival, destroyed its own myth while capitalizing it, posing as the museum of Wilson's tableaux and Glass's recorded-live music, with revised choreographic "Field (Space Machine)" sections by Lucinda Childs. As presented on the Opera House stage, the mise en scène resembles a monumental kinetic sculpture carefully lit from all sides. As a proscenium vision it looks like a bizarre collection of heterogeneous, disconnected parts, fragments, quotations - distensions of space-time into musical and electronic media superimposed upon the sculptural body of the work. The body of scenic imagery, in its spectacular visibility, both attracts and decenters audience attention through its repetitive movement, incantatory musical rhythm, patterned spinning (in the dance), and murmuring nonsense recitations. The fascinated lingering attachment to the images frozen in repetition frees the performance from linear narrative, from temporality, from rhetorical functions, from structurable scenes of desire, from recognizable references to history ("Einstein"?), from anything in particular. Dehumanized and geometrical dancing alternates with endlessly reciting, amplified but expressionless voices ("These are the days my friends, and these are my days my friends"). The flashing light patterns on a huge panel, in the spaceship scene, simulate the gestural patterns performed by Sheryl Sutton and Lucinda Childs in the five "knee-plays" that disconnect the ongoing keyboard and woodwind riffing of the Glass music with its vocal texts based on numbers and solfège syllables. In the apparent center of these multiple surfaces and polyphonies, a long phallic rectangle of light rises slowly from horizontal to vertical and vanishes.

My description of the five-hour production could go on endlessly, into an overstimulating ensemble of pseudo-performances that no longer follow a perceivable logic of "theatre." *Einstein's* posing of familiar images of technology (train, elevator, spaceship, typewriter, machine-gun, and so forth) "quotes" an older futurist or modernist aesthetic only to reveal the complete effacement of its thematic content. Equally effaced is the logic of representation through which we are used to make sense of theatrical performances on the basis of our body's perception of scale, proportion, "real" time. With the highly complex structural geometry of several visual, musical, verbal, and vocal scores, bringing the work of Wilson and his technicians much closer to the "language" of architectural space-concepts (cf. Charles Jencks's *The Languages of Postmodern Architecture*), we have entered a newer cultural logic that seems to render the construction of space incompatible with the representation of the body and, by producing an unrepresentable "total-theatre" effect, makes any sense of *critical distance* a contradiction in terms. The reviewer can no longer coherently interpret the overcoded "scene." And if the mind can no longer listen to, or find a point of view for, the hyperproduction of images and signifiers, canceling a hermeneutic space, in a strict sense, would equal the abolition of theatre.

In contrast to Blau's idea of theatre as a space of memory and recollection, the "revival" (all these terms will soon become obsolete) of the *Einstein* opera indicates that such productions compete with other emergent forms of high-tech cultural "styles" (another self-contradictory term if applied to what was once considered as the artist's unique, personal expression) that surround us with a new kind of "hyperspace" for which we may not yet possess the perceptual equipment, as Fredric Jameson has argued.[3] Jameson also advises us to think dialectically and grasp the frightening *and* positive aspects of this new postmodern organization of total space. His own example, somewhat reminiscent of Baudrillard's *l'effet beauborg,* is the spectacle of John Portman's Bonaventure Hotel in Los Angeles, which I discussed in the chapter 1.

Baudrillard's radically apocalyptic theory of late capitalism's transfiguration of all familiar categories of representation (*for* a subject) reflects back upon my opening questions about the possible impact of the snychronization and modelization of visuality in postmodern image production. If we can begin to discuss the abolition of theatre in the traditional sense, it is because effacing critical distance and meaningful content in the material structure of spectatorship marks the end of the social function of "live" theatre performance, insofar as Baudrillard thinks of representation or production themselves as outmoded categories since "the social only exists in a perspective space, it dies in the space of simulation . . . and accelerated recycling" that abolishes the difference between the real and its representation.[4]

At the same time, I think it is also possible to argue that the current crisis in our relationship to the avant-garde's hyperproduction of multimedia images arises more directly from the real contradictions in both the more sophisticated and the unreflexive attempts among our next wave collaborators to pose the body of the performer as a part of the new totalizing, technological space. While *Einstein* and comparable large-scale works produced by Wilson, Foreman, Chong, Rauschenberg, and others since the 1970s seem to have pushed architectural and sculptural space construction toward a form of heteroperspectival scenography that treats the performer's body as just another plastic sign in larger configurations, the BAM collaborations between visual technicians and composer-choreographers usually run into trouble as soon as the actual (foregrounded) presence of dancers and singers onstage contradicts the projection of flat, abstract picture planes.

Tim Miller's *Democracy in America,* which involved a cast of twenty-five performers, scenic design by painter Mike Glier, slides by photographer Dona McAdams, and a complex video and projection environment by Greg Miller, failed largely because its picture show, a veritable junkyard of stereotypical images and snapshots of *USA Today,* was presented as if it could complement the live performers. The dancers themselves, however, looked like caricatures that continually stumbled over the platitudes that Miller tried to extrapolate from his TV guide to America ("I believe it's important to find a way to keep going, to do something that makes sense"). His attempt to sound like a straightforward version of Laurie Anderson's electronically distorted speech performance (in *United States Live*) only heightened the viewer's sense of emptiness.

A very different attempt at exploring the new conceptual space of multiple media through the explicit structural interference of musical and choreographic forms was made by Meredith Monk/Ping Chong's *The Games*. Although this production, in contrast to Miller's, did not pretend to be anything other than abstract science fiction, it asked challenging political questions of representation and reproduction. The ironies of reduced human language (voice/body) were deliberately played off against the projections of a dystopian space. That space, lit by Beverly Emmons and designed by Yoshio Yabara, clearly resembled the science-fictional landscape derived from *Star Trek* movies and recent scenarios of the nuclear holocaust, although Ping Chong's elliptical computer graphics, slides, and voice-over effects created a rather more frightening sense of indeterminacy and invisible totality (totalitarianism) than we would normally think possible in the theatre. This simulated hyperspace was a designed *copy* of the Berlin Schaubühne cyclorama with its gigantic concrete walls where the work was first performed, and the connotations of its English-German Newspeak necessarily produced a "third meaning" unavailable to the New York audience. The five "players" and the chorus members of Meredith Monk's vocal ensemble performed a very nearly anachronistic *ritual* of incompletely remembered actions and gestures of the human body, which once may have known how to dramatize emotional self-expressions in dance, mime, movement, rhythm, vocal sound, speech, and intonation.

Diametrically opposed, therefore, to the mesmerizing adult-children games that Pina Bausch's highly individualistic dancers enacted in *1980* a few months earlier, with the BAM stage covered in living lawn grass, *The Games* (subtitle: "Erinnerung an Heute") suggested that the "first generation" of survivors after some vaguely imaginable apocalypse (postmodernism, in fact, seems to be unthinkable *without* the anticipatable nuclear Revelation) will have a difficult time remembering any reasons for any vocabulary of expression, or what the word "IBM" or "sidewalk" stood for. The way in which Monk and Chong imagine the retrogressive stimulation of an apparently erased collective unconscious reveals the inherent thematic contradictions of the postmodern avant-garde, although I would argue that the hackneyed rhetoric of survival and recolonization, which Chong's image texts project onto the huge suspended screens (framed by blue light), creates its powerfully ironic effect precisely because the slogans

> The Games which had
> Come to us from our past
> Were a good candidate
> For form and we the
> People began to construct
> That which might be necessary. . . .

We the people had construed
That form is good
That form is reason
That reason is truth
That it is self-evident
That The Games institute harmony

bear only a highly distorted relationship to the various aborted "post-Olympic" disciplines that the players are forced to rehearse. These vary from innocent-looking children's games (collages of Musical Chairs, Freeze, Blindman's Buff, and so forth) to the more sinister "Migration" and "Memory" exercises and, finally, to "Spiel Vier," a fearful, phantasmagoric version of the competitive athletics of our late capitalist culture.

The performers' struggle to find a ritualistic Form to perform *in*, at the same time, raises the question whether we can reconcile the rigidly diagrammatic spatial design of interlocking planes (the framed movie screen was matched by a lit rectangle on the stage floor that enclosed the players) with the multidimensional tapestry of melodies and sounds that Monk has scored for sixteen voices, synthesizer, keyboards, Flemish bagpipes, violin, and Chinese horn. My first reaction to the performance made me think that to survive avant-garde theatre cannot continue to reproduce images of structural indeterminancy (what are the rules of the game?) within the framing power of the visual apparatus. As *The Games* imagery indicates, the apocalypse is a self-fulfilling prophecy, and in the collapsing of future, present, and past, the real and the imaginary become interchangeable. The human figure in such a visual field will always look like a spatial attachment, a casualty of synthesized time.

But Monk's music, and her own performance of the sexually unidentifiable role of the "Gamemaster," confounds almost everything in these visual formations. Her unpredictable crisscrossing of and tiptoeing around the stage, and the constantly drifting positions that she assumes along the dissonant clusters of choral sound and the oscillations of the keyboards, throws our focused "reading" of Chong's scenography off key. Although the structural power of the music extends over the entire perceptual space, it is perhaps more precise to say that the differences of harmonic movement, texture, tempo and pitch within the collage of vocal, instrumental, and electronic sounds fragment what is happening in front of our eyes as much as they relate a complex sense of scale, form, and emotional weight to the stage movement, i.e. to the demotivated bodies of the players.

The most frightening and exhilarating dimensions in this dialectical interaction are opened up by Monk's voice (live, miked, prerecorded?) itself. We cannot see it, of course, and since we are never sure how to hear these idiosyncratic vocal chants, sighs, wails, shrieks, and cascades as a *voice-body*, Monk's private performance seems to escape our normal theatrical perception. This performance creates an invisible but audible subjective space that embraces us. For me, *The Games* production addresses the crucial question, not only of the representability of the human body within such visual-aural collages, but also the spectator's or auditor's relationship to the competing audiovisual languages or "synthesized fragments" (as Heiner Müller would call them) that take place, that take the place before me but not for me.

It is unnecessary, in this respect, to be reminded that "it is impolite to stare!" This reminder, shouted repeatedly by one of the singers of Peter Gordon's Love of Life Orchestra during the premiere of *Secret Pastures*, a new dance piece by Bill T. Jones and Arnie Zane and Company, merely heightens the already unbearable sensory tension produced by the plural new music/rock/jazz scores that split the ear and (almost) prevent the eye from recognizing the joke—the patently absurd MTV-video scenario that serves as a backdrop for a "full-evening narrative work about an expedition to an uncharted continent" (program). *Secret Pastures*, among other things, is an experimental dance work, and among all the Next Wave productions it probably comes closest to creating the overstimulated, hallucinogenic "euphoria" that Jameson associated with postmodernism. With the dysynchronous comings and goings on the stage, the choreographers play with the audience's perception of the hilarious narrative (the "libretto," printed out in the program) that the dancers propose as they leap, jump, and fly across an entirely inconclusive "expedition" into fantasialand. We witness scenes on the "beach," in the "desert" or the "rainforest," with a mad Professor (Mr. Zane), a Fabricated Man (Mr. Jones), several urban punks named the Young Male Assisant, the Blonde Assistant, the Tall Handsome Reporter, and four "others" that are "purely imaginary," like those monkeys, I assume, that emerge at one point to perform an uncontrollably wild sexual orgy in front of huge cartoons that look like transistor radios.

Less imaginary and more than real are the various stylistic incongruities of the production that foreground all sorts of fashionable camp designs against the pseudonarrative. These designs, from Willi Smith's loose baggy shorts and pulled-up trousers to Marcel Fieve's punk haircuts and makeup to Keith Haring's graffiti decor, create a new wave *tone* as electric as the bizarre, punchy disco patterns that the dancers enact. Eventually their movements begin, paradoxically, to look more flat and "fabricated" than the eccentric and uncoordinated movements of the Fabricated Man who is forced to learn the rules of the game. During the disco orgy, with Gordon's saxophones at their "most frightened state" (composer's notes), these rules are represented as a series of blatant, brutally provocative freeze poses, as if the dancers' acrobatically angular gestures, leaps, and spins ultimately belonged to the pornographic landscape of Haring's subterranean graffiti.

Jones's and Zane's choreography deliberately teases the viewer into recognizing the new "visual arts sensibility" (avant-pop?) that has invaded the academy. Their work gleefully plays around with its serious experimental ethics, not without suggesting, of course, that this new collaboration between SoHo "head design," WilliWear, and video techniques may very well have a future in a new, different kind of theatre. What may go out of fashion is the function of criticism *of* the theatre, although I am not yet prepared to agree with music critic John Piccarella, who recently listened to the recordings of Laurie Anderson's two-evening BAM performances of *United States* in 1983 and concluded:

> But most of all this works as well on record as it did on stage, where the slides, films and lighting effects can just as easily trivialize as amplify the drama of her language and music. Just as the sounds of her performance translated well to records, the visual display of *United States* would probably look more properly conceptualized if scaled down to video. Given current marketing trends, it's surprising that all this dance/music/theatre stuff isn't being offered as commercial video, where it would probably find the same audience. For the price of the orchestra seats at BAM we would have *Einstein on the Beach* or Pina Bausch or Laurie Anderson on the VCR.[5]

This beautifully casual statement is another example of the kind of postmodern euphoria that needs to be analyzed in its connection to the commodification of criticism. I would more than disagree with Piccarella's supposition that all this "stuff" can be miniatuarized into video clips. Some of the works I have discussed here no doubt tend toward cinematographic space or the video-fantasy style of "Flashdance" and "Thriller." It is quite impossible, however, to imagine Meredith Monk's or Pina Bausch's struggling representations of the voice and the body in space outside the theatre.

We cannot be too sure of an audience accustomed to the VCR and a reduced sight of real space and time. But this reduction of cultural consumption is not recognized by the producers of the Next Wave avant-garde as a problem that is in any sense related to the specific aesthetic criteria of experimental art. Or it is recognized too well, which might explain why the future of BAM's festival is almost completely tied up with the accessibility and trendy exchangeability of avant-garde *styles* that can be sold on the stage and translated into success (and into copies for the video market). The work that cannot be translated or adapted to these conditions of the postmodern avant-garde status will disappear from the scene.

NOTES

1. References are to Howard Klein, "The Value of the Valuer," and Robert Marx, "New Music Theater and the Next Wave," *Next Wave Festival Catalogue* (New York: Brooklyn Academy of Music, 1984), 4–10.
2. Cf. Gerald Rabkin's penetrating analysis of "The Return of the Living Theatre: Paradise Lost," *Performing Arts Journal* 23 (1984): 7–20. My views of the "impossible theatre" and the radical potential, whether illusory or not, of the experimental avant-garde of the 1960s implicitly refer to Herbert Blau's work. See his recent "The Impossible Takes a Little Time," *Performing Arts Journal* 24 (1984): 29–42.

3. Cf. "Postmodernism, or the Cultural Logic of Late Capitalism," *New Left Review* 146 (1984), 53–92.

4. Jean Baudrillard, *In the Shadow of the Silent Majorities, Or, The End of the Social,* tr. Paul Foss, Paul Patton, and John Johnston (New York: Semiotext(e), 1983), 83–85.

5. John Piccarella, "Laurie Anderson Goes Down Easy," *Village Voice* (January 22, 1985): 91, 118.

21 yeah on the surface (small laughter) was the
 8 did I say something to offend you
16 maintain
 5 what are you referring to
23 a very effective picture
21 seen

> from: "Morning before Battle"
> R. Wilson, *the CIVIL warS* III.E

10   KNEEPLAY: CAN WITCHES FLY?

In his operas, Texas-born stage director/designer Robert Wilson claims, the audience is presented with pure visions and pictures, not with the interpretation of a text or a story. The performances are "constructions in space and time" that first of all invite a new and different perception of theatrical space-time itself. The audience is free to pick up and put together the many "stories" it may imagine having seen. Or heard. Or not. (Small laughter.)[1]

After watching the Cambridge ART's American premiere production of Act III E and Act IV from the Cologne segment of Wilson's uncompleted twelve-hour multinational opera, *the CIVIL warS*, I had a recurring nightmare in which Frederick the Great dances with two polar bears and a dead dog while reciting Kafka's letter to his father set to music of Schubert's "Erlkönig." Where to begin interpreting this dream? First, I intend to use the materials of the nightmare opera in order to make a critical transition from myth (*the CIVIL warS*) to history (postmodernity under late capitalism) in order to more fully link Wilson's theatre to the occasion for which it was produced (the theatre of the 1984 Olympics). One awakens from one's nightmares by awakening *to* them.

Second, in granting Wilson's performance theatre an exemplary place in my essays on theatre and postmodernism, I want to emphasize the connection between an aesthetics of the technological sublime and the

spectacle of advanced capitalism. As a tendency in the postmodern mentality of the 1980s, Wilson's colossal image theatre represents a simulacrum
of the mass-produced Image World of capitalism pervaded by theatrical
hyperboles and metaphors standing in for the experience of lived reality.

Undoubtedly Wilson's image theatre, with its provocatively mixed
baroque minimalism traceable from *The Life and Times of Sigmund Freud*
(1969) to *Einstein on the Beach* (1976) to *the CIVIL warS* (1984) and on to the
truly astonishing output of the last few years (*Alcestis, Hamletmachine,
Quartet, Death, Destruction & Detroit* II, *Le Martyre de Saint Sébastien, The
Forest, Parzival, Doktor Faustus, Orlando, The Black Rider, King Lear*), has had
a major influence on most of the established categories and concepts we
use to describe drama, opera, music theatre, and dance. We have to keep
in mind, of course, that the experiments of avant-garde theory and practice
over the past decade cannot be separated from larger changes in the form
of cultural production in postmodern capitalism. I insist on seeing these
changes in their mutual interdependence, since it is in light of globalized
image production (and its attendant industries of mass circulation) that we
perceive the conditioned and conditional freedom of Wilson's seemingly
unlimited and unending theatre spectacles, whose mythico-ritual *and* technological logics perform a strange, contradictory dance across a stage once
considered a closed space of representation. That space, primarily constructed by words and the logocentrism and anthropocentrism of drama, is
now conceivable as an open laboratory of image associations, sci-fi simulations, polyphonic sound landscapes, abstract sculptural designs, un-
interpretable and self-recursive signs. Like a true postmodern architect,
Wilson draws, builds, assembles, and designs a new space-in-motion
whose decorative, superficial violence fascinates precisely because it seems
to have made the question of reference, content, and value forever un-
decidable and anachronistic.

In other words, speaking of interpretation, how can one review an
epilogue that presents undifferentiated images of mythical, anthropomorphic, historical, and literary figures, together with fragmented words
(Hopi Indian prophecies, a Grimm fairy tale, Ecclesiastes, *King Lear*, a
Heiner Müller text) and sound filling the air and floating in it like audible
but invisible bodies? Did I see a tall, black shape that looked like a top-
hatted Abraham Lincoln, or was that another unredeemed fiction of the
mind, analogous to the nonexisting Cordelia whom the words recited by
the King Lear actor (Jeremy Geidt) simultaneously evoke and deny: "Now
she's gone forever. . . . Look on her. Look there, look there"? In his hands
Geidt is holding a crumpled newspaper.

When I referred to a certain violence in Wilson's laboratory of the
imagination, I was thinking of the numbing entropic structure of Wilson's
opera in relation to the chain of motifs that links the haunting opening
movement, evoking the horizon of a battle during the infinitely slow
waking up of a band of American Civil War soldiers, with complex super-
positions of abstract stage pictures in Act IV. All of these ostensibly create a

way of looking at the eternal recurrence of conflict, family romance, historical struggle, natural disaster, and death. Crucial to Wilson's theatre is the
abandonment of a dramatic action that would seek to establish an internal
continuity or linear sequence or any kind of mimetic representation of
cause and effect. On the contrary, the montage performance disperses or
blends its multiple images, screen projections, texts, sounds and gestural
movements in order to achieve a visual-musical rhythm that can no longer
be perceived coherently or logically. On the surface, such a metamorphic
space-time does not allow a meaningful differentiation between subjective
and historic "scenes," between imaginary projection (the film images operating as an allegory of phantasmatic construction) and symbolic order
(with its iron Prussian Law of the Father).

The figure of Frederick the Great, the effeminate son-turned-military-
despot (played by Priscilla Smith), is exemplary in this respect, since at no
point do we associate the woman performer with a historic character.
He/she has no reality other than, literally, a position in the painterly,
two-dimensional space (structured primarily through Wilson's and Jennifer Tipton's extraordinary lighting design), shifting into and out of the
architectural and rhythmic relationships organized by Wilson's visual
score. The musical-acoustical score, which combines compositions by Hans
Peter Kuhn, Philip Glass, Bach, Schubert, as well as the disembodied,
overlapping text recitations issuing from speakers scattered around the
auditorium, simulates a fourth dimension that I experienced as a kind of
tonal and phonic modulation of time. In other words, I listened to and
watched abstract configurations of shape, color, sound, volume, scale,
tempo, and duration. The power of the gigantic tableaux vivants, precisely
because they insinuate nothing but immanent presence, inevitably mysti-
fied the random sketches of Prussian life, civil and military. Heiner Müller's oblique texts were treated as plastic material, they gained a graphic
texture similar to the "quoted" filmic images (from *Koyaanisqatsi*, for example) or to those effects that looked like gratuitous quotations from the
circus and vaudeville (the laughing woman, the polar bears, the "smilers,"
the horse). Some of these effects are so grotesque that one cannot understand how Wilson wants them to be seen in conjunction with the cool
formalist beauty of his architectonic choreography. Surely the image of the
"king" riding on the hobby horse cannot be an interpretive reference to
Frederick or the Erlkönig? This choreography of stasis, movement, light,
and sound in overlapping spaces can create surreal effects of multi-
perspectivity that put our normal synchronic vision to a severe test. These
impressions, however, in their polyvalence and pseudounconscious, sensual force, tend to regress into trancelike repetitions of the theme. At no
point does Wilson seem to be aware of the naive pretentiousness of the
"archetypal" images (the Earth Mother, swimming turtles, flying eagles,
and so forth) he conjures up with such extensive technological effort.

Far from offering "pure visions" without interpretation, the nonnarrative intermediate structure of *the CIVIL warS* cannot but remind us that its

material form of selection and construction already belongs to a pre-interpreted domain. Although Wilson's "theatre of images" (with its unmistakable Eastern influences) strives toward an irrational, mystical syntax, its psychoperceptual processes are firmly grounded in a bourgeois ideology that seeks to displace its actual civil wars by imaginary flights into transcendent and mythical realms. Wilson's universalized, sublimated Prussian "history" is such a flight from history, and the aesthetic beauty of the images is troublesome because we are expected to believe that it is uncoercive and purposeless.

In the opening evocation and immediate mystification of the American Civil War, however, we can locate a microstructural model of the Wilsonian "sublime" that allows us to reinterpret the actual banality of the sound tapestry ("Morning before Battle") woven into the surreal beauty of the mise-en-scène of the soldiers' camp. The random sound bites reflect the murmur of everyday talk, and the landscape of the soldiers' camp itself, slowly awakening to the light of dawn, is elevated into an almost cosmic dimension, as if the dawn of warfare were meant to symbolize the consumption of Time as such. The space in this landscape is undefined, unbounded, unreal; but is it "unpresentable" in the sense in which Lyotard redefines the Kantian sublime for postmodernism? Lyotard believes that in postmodern aesthetics the unpresentable, the infinitely powerful and awesome, can be inscribed in presentation itself to the extent that the latter

Figure 33. Robert Wilson, *the CIVIL warS,* Act V, Prologue. Teatro dell'Opera, Rome. 1984.

emphasizes incommensurabilities. If we remember Kant's distinction between the sublime and the colossal, however, it may be more appropriate to speak of the postmodern technological sublime as a distortion, a gargantuan and grotesque version of the spectacle of immense nature that Kant originally analyzed in *Critique of Judgment*.

In Wilson's mise-en-scène of the "civil war" as unpresentable Idea, cosmic nature, literary and fairy-tale worlds, sonic noise, American and Prussian "history" and "culture" are all synthesized into a colossal hologram whose underlying imagination seems derived from the commodified versions of the Big American Landscape and the overexposure of a mythic America in the culture industry. I find it significant, therefore, that Wilson's projected twelve-hour multinational opera was chosen to be the artistic superpresentation in the 1984 Olympics at Los Angeles, linking the first fully aestheticized spectacle of athletics (edited and controlled by American corporate capital) with a gigantic festival of performing arts to be staged and cosponsored simultaneously. I will never forget the successful choreography of the total event. The colossal distortions, however, that took place in the meeting of economic, cultural, and political interests, warrant a brief reexamination of the theatrical metaphors that were circulated in the service of ideology.

"It's an immense project, demanding extraordinary performance from our people and equipment. We're happy to accept this challenge [the Olympics], because it gives us an opportunity to show the world how good we are at what we do."[2] The rhetoric of the advertising sponsors, in its endless, anticipatory rehearsals of the imminent success of its productivist "aesthetic," had already mapped out the glittering surfaces and triumphant colors of the "greatest show on earth," as Peter Ueberroth and Hollywood producer David Wolper would later describe the opening ceremony of the XXIII Olympiad in Los Angeles.

The opening performance at the Coliseum was staged with a cast of thousands of musicians (including 170 piano players on 74 grand pianos), dancers and actors, with then President Reagan inaugurating the show as his oversized image was beamed onto the electronic billboard of the stadium and, via satellite, onto the millions of TV screens of the world that was watching. In the center of the colossal ceremony was a D. W. Griffith-like pageant of the "Birth of a Nation," a rapidly edited, postmodern Hollywood version of the Old West and the Frontier. The stage sets and cardboard desert towns were rolled in; the pioneers and cowboys danced on the trail, and after the Goldrush we were even permitted a few glimpses of the exotic tepees and igloos of an aboriginal population. Wolper's show was a dazzling tour de force of star-spangled kitsch and mythic ornamentalism; its focus was not at all the trivial content of a universal myth called "America" but rather the immediate worldwide visibility of the ultimate technological production of the staging itself—the perfected marriage of spectacle and technology in which the American conquest of the West was ideologically reaffirmed as the triumph of commodity capitalism. One could argue that the show was staged for the commercials and the titanic revenues they generated. Simultaneously, however, television's domination of the event turned the Olympics into a postmodern performance of heroic conquest: the conquest of the world as picture.

The Games themselves, perfectly commercialized and controlled by a multimillion dollar corporate sponsorship, appeared already "written" before they started, including all the dramas that the sports events are supposed to create. After the boycott of the socialist countries had cleared the stage for the uninhibited and cynically honest display of capitalism's superior fabrication of effects, it was not only the pictures of athletic heroics, the grace, speed, and power of the winners or the tears of the fallen Mary Decker that dominated one's impression of the spectacle, but also the "surprises of the American spirit" *(Newsweek)* or, in Reagan's words, the "newly discovered pride in our great nation" presented by ABC's cameras as the unifying, cathartic principle of the action. This model has almost nothing to do anymore with the ritual of sport and its former meanings embodied in the idealistic ethics of values symbolically communicated through competitive performances of skills based on a shared social and cultural understanding of fair play, justice, and merit.

In its current commodified and degraded version, sport has been completely functionalized by the commercial and sensationalist mechanisms that the broadcast media and entertainment industries use to advance their market principles and investment interests. The market mentality in sport, in turn, reproduces the general canons of entertainment on which it depends by stimulating the mass consumption of its star cults and the cult of winning, which in the case of the Olympic Games played into resurgent patriotism as well as the nationally approved military oneupmanship promoted in the era of Reagan's aestheticized politics.

Reagan's observation of the "newly discovered pride in our great nation," however, is not fully explained by the conjunction of sport, entertainment, politics, and aesthetics. Rather, that observation mostly resulted from the masterfully choreographed televised images of the Olympic spectacle (ABC invested $225 million to broadcast the games) sold to the viewing world as a package that glued ideology ("showing the world how good America is") to the commodity.

This packaging is the model of advanced technological entertainment industries, and we can hardly pretend to ignore the *blind discipline* required of a mass-reproduced spectacle, a discipline once linked to the staging of a collective imagination that produced both the aesthetic fantasies and the brutal realities of fascism. (It helps to review the television footage of the 1984 Opening Ceremony in comparison to Leni Riefenstahl's *Triumph of the Will* and her film of the Berlin Olympic Games in 1936.)

The packaging of aestheticized sport under late capitalism is rarely questioned because the visual disciplines of our technological culture are so totally consumed by the mass audiences that the displacement of sport and politics onto the aesthetic product is no longer even recognized in the unifying perspective of the American cameras. The extensibility of the packaging becomes a measure of present-day cultural engineering, and there is no reason to assume why athletic culture should be any different from artistic culture. The *model,* i.e., the overintensive repetition of spectacular forms and fashions served equally well as the organizing principle of the ten-week Olympic Arts Festival (June 1–August 12, 1984) that was officially announced as a "joyous marriage of art and sport." In this marriage the arts were scheduled to provide a "universal language, a bridge of illumination that connects all members of our increasingly multi-cultural society." This slogan, reinvented by the main sponsor—the Times Mirror Company—of the 12-million-dollar festival, could be heard in conjunction with one of the many advertisements that sang this epitaph for the Games, this first entirely uninhibited commercial festival of the Olympic Spirit, before a flag-waving patriotism had even begun to take hold of the country: "We're insuring the Olympic Games because our business is ensuring people's dreams."[3]

And to round off the fantasies of this midsummer night's dream, festival director Robert Fitzpatrick confidently announced to the world that this extensive arts event was to be the largest and most diverse in modern history. Its array of more than four hundred performances and exhibitions—a potpourri of dance, theatre, opera, concerts, exhibits, film and other events by artists from eighteen countries—was certainly mind-boggling. For a short while Los Angeles, a city that not only combined the superlatives associated with Hollywood and Disneyland but dispersed its festival audiences into geographically quite separate and distanced areas of the basin, could consider itself the cultural capital of the world.

Not all the world had been invited, however. The Polish theatre group Cricot 2, which presented Tadeusz Kantor's *The Dead Class* and *Wielopole, Wielopole,* was the only ensemble from a socialist country; the international poetry festival was cancelled because the expected UNESCO grant did not arrive. The artistic bridge of illumination for the multicultural audience was apparently only a dream. It turned out to be a vehicle primarily for the import of established master productions (Giorgio Strehler's *Tempesta,* for example, goes back to the Piccolo Teatro's 1977 revival of an even earlier production of the Shakespearean play in 1948) and famous ensembles (RSC, Théâtre du Soleil, Royal Opera Covent Garden, Ballet Folklorico de Guadalajara, Grupo de Teatro Macunaima, Tadashi Suzuki's Waseda Sho-Gekijo, Royal Winnipeg Ballet, and so on) that seemed to rule out any risks or the kind of political complications the organizers so desperately wished to dissociate from their own reappropriation of cultural capital. While the shipload of French Impressionist masterpieces from the Louvre safely arrived at the Los Angeles harbor, the sharp protests of the local Odyssey Theatre, one of the leading experimental groups in Los Angeles, brought attention to the fact that the multinational festival program had excluded the nearly 150 community theatres, fringe companies, and the various ethnic/cultural centers that explore both new and traditional artistic projects in Los Angeles.

An interesting mixture of both could be seen in some of the productions that were eventually allowed to join the festival. Laura Farabough's Nightfire almost literally recreated the "marriage of art and sport" by transforming a high school gym into a swimming pool as their stage for an aqueous drama of mime and acrobatics (entitled *Liquid Distance/Timed Approach*). Less ambitious and more ironic, the Groundlings invited audiences to their tiny Hollywood theatre for an evening of improvisational farce-making, their specific brand of Californian commedia dell'arte (*Olympic Trials, a Chick Hazard Mystery*) which joyfully parodies the conventions of detective melodrama and emplots, following audience cues, every conceivable stock character out of the film industry nearby. Immediately sold out, the eight performances in the Groundling Theatre actually encouraged the audience to participate and have fun—an idea that Fitzpatrick had cautiously hinted at on the eve of the festival's gala opening, before he unveiled Robert Graham's sculptural dedication to the Olympics and welcomed a capacity audience to the American debut of Pina Bausch's Wuppertaler Tanztheater at the Pasadena Civic Auditorium. Graham's tribute to the Attic ideal of proportions or to the classical sculptures on the Parthenon turned out to be two gigantic, headless bronze figures. The decapitated torsos of Athletic Man and Woman appeared to be an appropriate, solemn joke, a joke on the body about which I shall have more to say in my last chapter.

What kind of fun Fitzpatrick had in mind when he said "Bausch should be some indication this isn't business as usual," or what audience he sought to address never became quite clear. The opening night audience in Pasadena had apparently come to see a ballet and was completely unprepared for the unsettling effects of the often violent physical images of self-inflicted pain in Bausch's work. Unlike the heated critical debates that followed the Bausch troupe's appearances at the Brooklyn Academy several weeks later, the shocked response in Pasadena was stifled and diluted by the immediate measures the organizers took to reintegrate the disenchanted audience into the on-going cocktail party atmosphere of the festival (free champagne and chocolate cake after the show).

There was a greater willingness to endure and confront defamiliarized or non-Western theatre styles during the performances of the butoh dance cycle *Jomon Sho* by Sankai Juku (during an outdoor performance in a downtown business district one could see the white, naked bodies of the dancers slowly float down from the roof of a bank building), or the Japanese interpretation of *The Trojan Women* by Tadashi Suzuki's company, or the unusual French-Asian Shakespeare interpretation of the Théâtre du Soleil (*Richard II*, 1 *Henry IV*, *Twelfth Night*). These performances, at the same time, redirected attention to the more conveniently "universal" and spectacular "interculturalism" of Shakespearean drama—that many-headed master paradigm of cultural capital that has become infinitely adaptable and redistributable, mirroring the profitability of the system of commutation and exchange itself. Shakespeare brought alive in four different languages! The idea was greater than faith in the audiences (plot summaries in English provided), although the Goodman Theatre of Chicago & The Flying Karamazov Brothers' version of *The Comedy of Errors*, in any case, played across the boundaries of translation by indulging in the purely farcical games of jugglers, circus clowns, and acrobats—wildly conventional cousins of the Marx Brothers. The sheer brilliance of their controlled errors of juggling, at the same time, can open up new perspectives on the dramatic construction of twin identities on the stage of a popular theatre which, in Shakespeare's time as in ours, needs the confusion of reality in order to dream of its possibility.

It is more difficult to apprehend Ariane Mnouchkine's suggestion that we have lost the "true" sense of Shakespeare's theatre. How do we know what we have lost? The Théâtre du Soleil plunders the Asian performance styles, including the use of extremely stylized make-up, quasi-oriental costumes, accompaniment of percussive instruments, and a stage design that looks like a cross between the Noh's entrance walkway and the Kabuki *hanamichi* ramps. Such a pillage extends their basic use of popular theatrical elements into a very rich physical vocabulary of gestures that question precisely those conventions of psychological realism with which we have modernized and domesticated the language of the Shakespearean plays. As an alternative, using the huge, Cartoucherie-like playing space of a rebuilt television studio, Mnouchkine's troupe translated the relations of power and the relations between lovers, fathers, and sons in Shakespeare's drama into the very different rhythms and physical movements of Kabuki and Kathakali techniques while returning the sources of dramatized human conflicts to clearly recognizable, stylized gestures of emotional expression.

The deliberately shrill monotony of the play of power in *Richard II* between these samurai-style warriors in masks and the insistent urgency of their explosive vocal delivery offered an unexpectedly thorough critical perspective on the smooth, perfectionist, and inherently shallow Royal Shakespeare Company's production of *Much Ado About Nothing* shown in Royce Hall at UCLA. Its beautiful stage designs and richly costumed actors (with Derek Jacobi as Benedick and Sinead Cusack as Beatrice), fully met the audiences' expectations. There was very little in this production (directed by Terry Hands) that made you think about the play or the actors' work, since the consuming eye was mainly directed at the surface theatricality of the opulent plexiglass designs and the play of reflected light, colors, and fancy dress in this supermarket of fabricated atmospheres.

These juxtapositions on the festival agenda between the shimmering synthetics of the Royal Shakespeare Company's conventional modern Shakespeare and the demystifying rituals of primitive power in the revisionist French adaptation of historical tragedy in fact raised the question of how one is to study the intercultural collision of production and acting styles without merely succumbing to the fascination of the otherness of "Asian" gestures, especially when those gestures, as in the Théâtre du Soleil's *Twelfth Night,* tend to be further mixed up with a thoroughly French expression of the kind of humor and clownery we identify with Italian commedia dell'arte. In other words, the loss of specificity in these combinations of historically and culturally disparate performance traditions indicates the cost of simulating the abstract "universality" of Shakespearean drama on a Californian stage that does not know its audience. Theatre's easiest solution has often been not to ask such questions but rely on what is left of its magic to captivate whatever audience it plays to. The best example may very well be Giorgio Strehler's insistent reproductions of Prospero's dream in the Piccolo Teatro's *Tempesta,* an Italian storm of images that is "untranslatable" because it is so intensely in touch with its native operatic and comedic traditions that the grand effects of baroque illusionism (as in the opening shipwreck scene), like the drunken Pantaloons Stephano and Trinculo, or like the magician-director Prospero himself, become a very particular vision of the power of the "great theatre machine" (Strehler) that makes its Ariels fly through the air and—Caliban-like—is stripped naked when the illusions come to an end.

The Olympic Arts Festival needed its Shakespeare, even if only to distract us from the power of illusion in the global agenda of the festival itself. No one ever mentioned or critically addressed the articulation of real cultural and artistic differences but, instead, proclaimed its promotional concept through infantile slogans such as Fitzpatrick's promise of a "return to the spirit of ancient Greece." The slogans, of course, substantially facilitate the dream-logic of self-confirming power—showing the world how good they are at what they do—in the programming of consumption.

The symbolic violence these slogans do to the "universal language" of the arts must be resisted at the level of theatrical reception where the structures of expectation, political and aesthetic, are reproduced as habitual reflexes-in-performance, once the houselights go off. At the level of production, we can be sure that accidents will happen. It is a peculiar and puzzling coincidence that the festival planners' most cherished and specially commissioned superevent, Wilson's *the CIVIL warS,* did not in fact take place. Ironically, those sponsors who turned out to be "too hesitant to pay for something they can't imagine" (Fitzpatrick), did not realize that the beautifully seductive and mystifying parade of images and pageants Wilson had created for the *warS* would have been the perfect match for Hollywood's production of the opening ceremony of the Games. It is tempting to think of Wilson as our postmodernist Shakespeare, our designer-as-Prospero making the Ariels of the most advanced audiovisual, lighting, and laser technologies fly through the myths of our civilization that are founded in the repression of the Calibans and in the forgetting of civil wars. The distortion and reduction of history is the main principle through which the spectacle of capitalism universalizes its image movement and absorbs the contradictions and accidents it produces.

NOTES

1. References to Wilson's comments are taken from German and English editions of the program book published for the Cologne segment of *the CIVIL warS.* See especially *"the CIVIL warS:* Constructions in Space and Time. An Interview," program book, ed. Jan Graham Geidt (Cambridge: American Repertory Theatre, 1985), 13–22. Quotations from Wilson's text collage are also taken from this program book.

2. "We're giving it our best," advertising slogan by Motorola, Inc. The Text I quoted is from the company's description of its vital sponsorship role in "making the 1984 Los Angeles Olympics the smoothest run and best coordinated in history." Motorola provided communications and electronics equipment. The ad was published in *Time* magazine, August 20, 1984, 42–43. See also "What Price Prestige," an in-depth analysis of the various Olympic goals of corporate sponsorship, which followed *Newsweek's* full-blown coverage of the American Olympic team's "Surprises of the Spirit," August 20, 1984, 20–29.

3. The statement by the Times Mirror Company is quoted from the introduction to the 1984 *Olympic Arts Festival Catalog* (Los Angeles: Los Angeles Times Syndicate, 1984). The insurance slogan was created by Mutual Life Insurance Company and broadcast on national television. The connection between insurance and dream caught on, and the Southland Corporation ran a double-page ad for Seven-Eleven that showed a victorious American athlete next to a caption that read "Being in the Olympics is the stuff dreams are made of. . . . The dream begins with freedom." See for example *Time* magazine, August 20, 1984, 2–3.

One's own body—that most forgotten land

Walter Benjamin

11   THE POSTMODERN BODY
IN PERFORMANCE

The following reflections and commentaries concern themselves with contemporary "productions" of the body. A familiar term in the language of theatre, production refers to the technical and aesthetic process of staging a performance. I also use it here to address cultural practices that intersect and overlap with constructions and images of the body in performance. The choice of this subject, and the montage character of my observations as they move across the material and metaphorical differences in the appearance of the body in art, performance, the media and the promotional industries, are motivated by the dramatic turns that I believe the role of the body has taken since it was rediscovered as a site and pretext for recent debates about representation and gender, about history and postmodern culture, and about theory and its vanishing point or referent.

My fragmentary remarks treat the body as a referent of certain discursive, aesthetic and technological productions; as a performance always threatened by its disappearance; and as a model for the volatile operation of ideologies and symbolic productions within an economy of reproduction. The theatre itself, of course, seems modeled on such an economy, but it too has undergone changes as well as a loss of cultural significance. We could perhaps better understand these changes if we examined the topicality and diffusion of the notion of "performance" in Western societies. We have experienced a similar diffusion of the postmodern body, insofar as there has been such an outpouring of discourses on the body (especially the female body), that we must assume the current perception of the body to be a completely problematic issue.

In asking how the body is perceived and constructed today, I will focus attention on the advanced technical modes of production that have become available, as well as on the contradictory positions for the performance of the body within the fully technological culture of late modern societies.

The body is the inscribed surface of events (traced by language and dissolved by ideas), the locus of a dissociated self (adopting the illusion of substantial unity), and a volume in disintegration. Genealogy, as an analysis of descent, is thus situated within the articulation of the body and history. Its task is to expose a body totally imprinted by history and the process of history's destruction of the body.[1]

One cannot understand a body. It cannot be analysed. One perceives it. That's why I am increasingly interested in ballet, because there's nothing to understand in it. . . . Grotowski says that the problem for an actor is to find his degree-zero. In the same way, theatre has to find its degree-zero again and again.[2]

The Overexposed Body

For several months during the 1988 fall exhibition at Houston's Contemporary Arts Museum, five headless figures stood silently and motionless in front of the metallic wall of the museum, with their truncated, bulging bodies turned toward the noisy rush of cars that constantly cross the intersection of two busy streets. The frozen postures of the huge headless *Bodybuilders* (constructed by sculptor Paul Kittelson of steel armatures and foam rubber) created a strange contrast to the flow of the traffic: a scene of powerful if monstrous disablement against the speed of automobilized bodies in constant transit, the smooth functioning of the movement of metabolical vehicles.[3] Like bodyguards posted along the metallic wall of the museum, the figures both belonged and did not belong to the exhibition inside, even though their public display, perhaps unwittingly, performed a rather complex and ironic "writing on the wall," a suspended joke on the public function of the museum itself as the institutionalized place in which the portraits and studies of the human body are preserved, aesthetically defined, categorized, and incorporated into art history.

However, the provocative positioning of the *Bodybuilders* outside and in front of the institutional domain of high art did not merely serve to critique artificial distinctions between "inside" and "outside," between aesthetic and popular representations of the body. Rather, the figures escape a logic of opposites as such, which reduces bodies to fixed positions (of interiority/exteriority, masculinity/femininity, subject/object), precisely because they are posed in between existing or evolving cultural

Figures 34, 35, 36. *Bodybuilders/Mindless Competition* by Paul Kittelson, 1988. Foam rubber, steel, approx. 120". Installation for First Texas Triennial, Contemporary Arts Museum, Houston, 1988.

categories of art, performance, sport, exercise, fitness, health, or beauty through which models and images of the body are produced. As figures of monstrosity they may appear transparent; but if bodybuilding is *in excess* of the body proper, if it transgresses proper limits and plays havoc with the very notion of "the proper" to construct a *corps étranger* (Bataille's "strange or foreign body"),[4] then it can only be read allegorically and in its fluid intersections with other cultural constructions and exhibitions of the body.

The exhibition of the *Bodybuilders* thus is not immediately understandable in terms of the poses that crave attention or reflect an image of narcissistic obsession with the body. But the question of whether (and whose?) obsession is imaged in these sexless, oversized and deformed bodies, and whether such a deforming obsession reflects particular social conditions or cultural fantasies at this historical stage of late modernity, becomes more urgent once we actually see these "foreign bodies" as museum pieces or aesthetic objects placed into an urban space of circulation. In this space of consumption, the body and representations of it are inseparable from the multiple economies of the city: from the circulation and exchange of money and desire, fashion and technology, power and information, and from media-incited cultural fantasies that fluctuate between repulsion, fear, and fascination over the destiny of the body.

One local newspaper review responded with a foreboding narrative: "These towering black hunks glisten seductively in the hot Texas sun. At night their distorted forms rise from their pedestals like dense black smoke from an oil well explosion or apocalyptic nuclear mushrooms."[5] Other responses to the *Bodybuilders* included descriptions of them as armor, walls, and intimidating body-machines. A medical student I interviewed expressed her disgust about such a "parody" of the human body's "natural beauty." One can imagine any number of rhetorical projections, which indicates how the figures become receptors of cultural symptoms, and how the body-as-metaphor is marked with and processed through technical, medical, military, and aesthetic discourses. The processing itself, whether it produces a "seductive" or an "apocalyptic" image (or one that is both at once), refers us to the *technology of bodies* and the formation/dissolution of subjects examined in Foucault's micropolitical studies of disciplinary power.

In the wake of Foucault and French poststructuralism, current critiques of the postmodern condition have even more strongly emphasized the processing and commodification of the body through all the signs and rhetorical reductions manufactured in the fashion and consumer culture, in art and science, and in the political economy of crisis-regulation. The current fear about the breakdown of the body's immune system has already produced new media hysteria about the contaminated body (comparable to the Chernobyl syndrome). The invasion of privacy, the surveillance and policing of bodies, and the appropriation of traumatized bodies (suffering from mental illness, eating disorders, cancer, AIDS) by medical, psychoanalytic, political, and fundamentalist discourses only increase the production of new mythological figures at the horizon of postmodern cultural fantasy. These figures, and especially the social roles and performances imaged and mirrored through model-bodies of the sports, fitness, health, food, beauty, and entertainment industries, have invested the biological body with fictions of self-expression, freedom of choice, success, perfection, and eternal youth that function obsessively as a simultaneous denial of death and imperfection. The fantasmatics of this denial surface across all "futuristic" reconceptions of the human body in science fiction, in medical, biogenetic and cybernetic engineering, in the technoparanoia of postmodern literature (Pynchon, Burroughs, Vonnegut) and postmodern theory (cf. the organless bodies/desiring machines in Deleuze and Guattari's *Anti-Oedipus*).[6]

The artificial reconception of bodies has been historically based on the myth of the human automaton, but as the dream of autonomous systems underwent changes from the mechanical age to the electronic age, so did the progressive abstraction and transmutation of body models into the cyborgs and clones of our advanced technoculture lead to more obvious contradictions. The artifactual body, made-up, designed, perfected, and thus absorbed into innumerable, contradictory cultural codes of performance, style, and wholeness ("total design"), is an alien body, displaced from the subject that seeks to match a model not of her or his own production.

Paradoxically, the reconstruction of the body, so excessively promoted through the contemporary mass media, appears to be the counterpart of the literally destructive violence and vulnerability experienced at the level of the body as well as in our psychic dispositions. This interiorized violence finds it fantasmatic expression in the general fascination with the fragmented and disfigured body that one would call obscene if it did not so transparently expose the dissolution of the cultural boundaries of subjectivity. Today's screen image of a fuzzy, schizoid subjectivity is emblematized in the digitalized and fractalized body in video art and MTV. And that body, after its disappearance into the electronic and computerized imaging processes, is perhaps no longer even a scene of phantasms and a metaphor of the decentered subject at all.

Rather, the carnival of body parts and special effects in video art has already broken beyond the theatricalized frame of desire, the *theatrum analyticum* (Lacoue-Labarthe) of psychoanalysis, in which the real (body) itself is missing yet returns to "speak" and "(dis)figure" itself through the unconscious. But the discourse of the body, or the discursive sexuality privileged in poststructuralist theory (cf. Roland Barthes's extended search for the body in *Pleasure of the Text*), could not blissfully recover the body except as an "intractable referent" or a simulacrum of the "degree zero"— that transgressive break or gap where the body might have appeared. When it appears in the writing, as exemplified by Barthes's progressively fragmented texts (*A Lover's Discourse*) and his final turn toward the photograph (*Camera Lucida*), its ecstasy is a maddening afterimage, and a temporal hallucination: "That has been. . . . It is not there."[7]

The photograph can capture the body, guaranteeing its absence as presence. "The presence of the thing (at a certain past moment) is never metaphoric." Curiously, Barthes's description of the body-as-pose (at a certain past moment) then slides to the body-as-corpse: "the photograph then becomes horrible . . . because it certifies, so to speak, that the corpse is alive, as *corpse*: it is the living image of a dead thing."[8]

The late Barthes here anticipates the posttheatrical hologram of a hypermodern society, sketched out in Baudrillard's theory of the digital space of a culture dissolved into "tactical hallucinations" perfectly designed to bury us alive since "the real is not only what can be reproduced, *but that which is always already reproduced*."[9]

We can think of the total theatre of Artaud only with black humor, his Theatre of Cruelty, of which this spatio-dynamic simulation is only an abject caricature.

This also means the collapse of reality into hyperrealism, in the minute duplication of the real, preferably on the basis of another reproductive medium— advertising, photo, etc. From medium to medium the real is volatilized; it becomes an allegory of death, but it is reinforced by its very destruction; it becomes the real for the real, fetish for the lost object—no longer object of representation, but ecstasy of denegation and of its own ritual extermination: the hyperreal.[10]

In a culture of afterimages, with collective life following the death lying at the heart of simulation, the electronic imaging process—in extension of the whole spectrum of audiovisual media (photography, film, television, radio, graphic design, etc.)—epitomizes the potential for an endless circulation of fetishized lost objects. It is significant for our understanding of postmodernism that today's mediated bodily practices, and all models of the body, can be said to await their own negation or reversal in an infinite referral process resembling the design logic of video technology. The latter's technical range of image manipulation, modification, and recomposition is almost limitless, while the materiality of video (invisible electro-magnetic charges) is elusive. Video is literal and actual in its immediate recording of surfaces; its computerized control systems simultaneously allow distortions and synthetic effects. The specificity of video art is blurred because its technology can effectively reproduce the systems of signification, styles, and modes of address of film and television, and in turn is usable by other tape media (music), performance mediums (dance, theatre, music), and any promotional, educational, or instructional industries.

The reconstruction of the body, which we have observed in commercial culture and in theory, thus has been taking place during the emergence of video as the postmodern technology *par excellence* and as the most paradigmatic operational venue for the exchange of simulacra "from medium to medium." It is the production of exchangeable and commodifiable bodies that concerns us here as a phenomenon of continuous displacement along a chain of competing and often contradictory cultural and aesthetic "poses" that become figures or technological ghosts for the postmodern body. In this sense we could also call the body a medium for its own *dépassement*. In an advanced capitalist and technocratic culture where we see everything fetishized and commodified, men's and women's bodies can only be body doubles, overexposed on the surface, everywhere visible and in performance, producing their multiple identities.

Self-reproduction as the reproduction of meaning, of expression, of bodily articulation. Yet "it must simulate, after a fashion, the absolute risk [of death], and it must laugh at this simulacrum . . . in the comedy that it thereby plays for itself."[11]

But what if "self" and "body" have lost their meanings or their (illusionary) reciprocity?

What is there
to perform?
What "reality"?

Performance Models

The spectacle is the moment when the commodity has attained the total occupation *of social life.*

Not only is the relation to the commodity visible but it is all one sees: the world one sees is its world.[12]

Society cannot be a disembodied spectacle, and the tangible world cannot be replaced by images. So even if we followed Debord's hypothesis made in the 1960s that the social formation of late capitalism would be marked by the equal visibility of all things and by the conversion of all activities into the pure exchange of performance signs and commodity displays, the "reality" of the body-in-performance will have to be examined much more deeply in order to speculate on the displacement of theatre over the last two decades. When I refer to this particular displacement of an older model of production (involving texts, actors playing characters on a stage, and a mise-en-scène based on conventional techniques of theatrical illusion), I want to suggest that the changing role of the physical body in performance art, dance-theatre, postmodern dance, multimedia and conceptual art emerged simultaneously with the increasingly globalizing technology of the electronic media and the promotional industries' commodification of all spheres of culture. In contrast to the plastic arts, film, and television, the concrete material presence of the body in the performing arts has always been taken for granted. It would require extensive historical research to delineate the changing codes and conventions by

means of which the actor's or dancer's body (as presence) has been produced and received as a distinguishing sign in a particular aesthetic and
cultural sign system throughout the history of performance. In this sense,
historical semiotics and structural anthropology today, supported by a
Lacanian psychoanalytic theory of the psyche as representation or a kind of
generalized sign economy that only touches upon the physical body at
points where it is socially coded and gendered, would confirm our suspicion that *the* body, or a "natural" body, never existed. Performers have
always only performed representations of bodies inscribed by language,
theatrical codes, and gestural/corporeal stances, and imprinted by history.

The most interesting archaeological and genealogical studies of the
imprinted body (preceding and following Foucault's pathbreaking *Discipline and Punish),*[13] however, would also seem to press inevitably toward
Debord's "Society of the Spectacle" and Baudrillard's posthistorical,
cybernetic universe where bodies, together with history and the social,
have disappeared into the highest degree of abstraction. This inevitability
and finality, ironically, make contemporary revivals and recuperations of
the body synonymous with the fashionable, eclectic "historicism" of postmodern art and, for example, postmodern architecture's fascination with
mannerism and the baroque. Most of these playful historicist quotations
and random appropriations (e.g. neo-geo painters repainting older abstraction; neoexpressionist painters repainting the visceral gestures of the older
expressionism) produce empty aesthetic effects, which are for the sake of
gesture only.[14] Or they confound themselves in an ostensibly critical or
cynical but also quite literal simulation of serially produced consumer
products, images, and photographs.

Figure 37. Barbara Kruger,
Untitled, 1987.

In the process of copying commodification and the spectacle itself, neoconceptual art merely accelerates the effects of implosion and transparency, and the reproducibility of the same renders such art indistinguishable from commodity fetishism and the ecstatic performances of fashion and advertising. This is tantamount to erasing history by continuously recycling new images of the same. Fashion reinscribes the body with every imaginable and "unimagined" version of the total body or of the perfection of body parts, as if imperfections, differences, and mortalities could be effaced or edited out by the perpetuation of this recursive loop of stylistic madness.

Interestingly, in their reach toward pure spectacle, recent photo ads of Calvin Klein's "Obsession for the Body" no longer even show the product (a scent, perhaps) but only the nude breasts and headless upper torso of a woman. The naming of the anonymous model body, "Obsession for the Body," repositions the body (along the chain of Klein ads and all other photos of nude models) as a pure fetish of desire (desire for desire), another doubling effect that is fast approaching its terminal point. But this degree zero has not been reached yet, since the image has a potential for multiple and ambivalent meanings that play, in excess, across the surface encoding of the feminine, eroticized, and seductive body.

Who does this fetishized female image perform for? Does it simultaneously satisfy male and female narcissistic-voyeuristic fantasy? Why does the focus of the grey, shadowy, and ghostly image—the breasts, erect nipples, and raised arms—raise the issue of the fetishized female body (the headless upper-body part erotically substituted for the whole) without manipulating the gaze in the obsessive manner in which previous Calvin Klein ads played with androgynous and sexually ambiguous appearances? And why do the raised and extended arms evoke an image of the arrested movement of a dancer? Wings of Desire?

The image for "Obsession for the Body" seems both more obscure and less transgressive than Klein's earlier sleepwear ads or the extravagant video commercials that introduced the perfume and its name. At the same time it is particularly noticeable that the shadowy image not only abandons the look of the model altogether but also diffuses the distinctions between the body and space (place, location). In this sense, the model appears to float in a kind of phantom space, everywhere and nowhere, thus increasing the obsessional search for multiple meanings that may not take us anywhere. Or does it increase our indifference?

In the light of what I have examined through this book, the problem of the "floating models" in our culture finally assumes a crucial significance for all our attempts to locate a body and a practice that could contest an aestheticized culture reflected in its fashions having nothing to do with any real body but remaining entirely closed and ritualized inside the "model effect" of indeterminacy and indifference.

My questions in response to "Obsession for the Body," however, were meant to indicate an equally insistent desire, on part of postmodern critical (especially feminist) practices, to subvert such "model effects" and to search for possible gaps and ruptures in the recursive scenario of the spectacle: for example, in the forced exhibition of the female body taking place in all the media. Notwithstanding the ironies and overdeterminations in the movement of postmodern theory itself, the most provocative questions in regard to the obsession for the body are derived from the intensive investigation of the inscription of desire, and of the economy of exchange between performer and spectator elaborated mostly in feminist film theory.[15] Any intervention into visual representation today will need to take into account the problematics of voyeurism, fetishism, scopophilia, and the gaze—woman as the object of male pleasure and the bearer of male lack—developed by feminist theory and extended into a larger cultural critique.

My own interest in the displacement of theatre, and the dislocation/reconstruction of the body in performance, was originally inspired by my experience of the disparate developments in performance art and multimedia performance theatre over the last two decades. To a certain degree, my reflections today are also influenced by the theoretical deconstruction of theatrical representation and the "recovery" of the body's *presence* in performance art, where this presence is foregrounded and validated. Before I finally turn to the paradoxical history of recent live performance, I will continue, for a moment, to place performance in close, complementary relation to the production of the body in other visual media.

In what direction does the model's headless torso (in "Obsession for the Body") float or move? Although it may seem perverse, there is an obvious relationship between the model body in the photo ad and the headless sculptures of the *Bodybuilders* in front of the museum. If we connect Barthes's notion of the body-as-pose or corpse with the question of fetishism and erotic substitution, then both images could be described as "stills" that, like the fetish, result from a look that has isolated or frozen a fragment of the spatiotemporal continuum. In the case of the *Bodybuilders*, we can see the interrupted sequence of poses, since the sculptor places five "freeze-frames" next to each other, thus creating a tableau-like dance of mortification and death. The fashion model in "Obsession for the Body" dissolves into another image in the instant we turn the page. What is disturbing about both productions, however, is the absence of the face. A fascinating and threatening lack, like a mask, arrests visual exchange and parodies the "blind" model of specular identification (central to male/female subject positions) that need the body as a prop.

"Discover how beautiful you can be," promises world champion bodybuilder Rachel McLish in her new *Perfect Parts* guidebook.[16] Together with its deliberate blindness towards the masculinizing performance of bodybuilding, McLish's guide constructs a completely contradictory ideal whose cosmetic, feminized appearance, as a seen body, does not mirror the sculpting process as a fragmenting and dissociating technology. During a recent self-exhibition at one of Houston's President and First Lady health clubs, McLish autographed photographs of her body for a massive audience of men, women, and children who had come to scan their role model and witness the postmodern Pygmalion come to life. This image of a self-consciously produced female physique reflects a novel condensation of cultural contradictions (the thin, muscular, tough, curvaceous and powerfully sexy body). At the same time the image depends on a machinated body controlled by very precisely repeated exercises and poses, comparable, in a way, to Craig's idea of the "Über-Marionette" as an instrument of calculated design.[17]

This dependence on repeatability and arrested movement finds an even more paradoxical form in the aerobic body's brutal struggle against its own immobilization, performed in one place at full speed. Designed almost exclusively for female consumers, aerobic dance-exercises became hugely popular after the Jane Fonda work-out techniques in bestselling made-for-video productions provided the image support for the mass dissemination of a new body-in-motion structured around a self-determining, self-assertive ideal (and, in Jane Fonda's case, a cult figure). The electronically disseminated body model choreographs a cultural scene of instruction/mimicry that promotes an exercise of subjective and corporeal self-transformation while masking the ritualized submission of the body to serial, monotonous, and stationary motion. In her willful self-production of an actively new feminine body, the woman participant misrecognizes the mirror structure in this performative exchange, aligned as it is around persistent cultural/hierarchical oppositions between mobility/immobility, seeing/being seen, and so forth. She is drawn into a phantom interaction with the two-dimensional, depthless and absent body of the video image that simulates an actual relation between body model and "real" performance in "real" time.[18]

The impossibility of being at one with one's own body image or with the videated body that reflects back a culturally constructed mirror image generates the typical repetition compulsion that has become the mark of all postmodern performance. These include performances predicated on breaking away from the theatricalized body to the degree zero—where Artaud's Theatre of Cruelty might have taken place before its hypostasized autonomous materiality became propped up with an essentializing metaphysics.

The question of the body (Who is posing? What is being posed?), then, cannot be answered except by taking into account a long history of "propping" and repositioning the subject/body relation, and by observing how reconstructions of the body in postmodern performance have become subject to the enormous pressures of constantly multiplying screens and false mirrors. I would go so far as to argue that the performing body as a self-reflexive, aesthetic production (in theatre, dance, and so on) has lost its privileged position or separate autonomy (its "resistance" to the repetitious Spectacle)[19] largely because the ideological encoding of the body slides across all the media of American pop art culture and makes it nearly impossible to locate or reclaim *ruptures* in terms of oppositions between "truth" ("authenticity") and "spectacle" ("surface").

To use an example, we could think of Madonna and read her representation of pop culture in the light of the Andy Warhol effect that has already preempted any controversy about authentic and artificial art. Imitating and repeating David Bowie, Madonna has pushed the manipulation of the surface to the point where her career has become a continual performance art piece. ("What I do is total commercialism, but it's also art. I think I have a very healthy point of view about myself," she said in a recent interview on MTV.) Since "Like a Virgin," she has controlled and produced her images, reconstructed her personae of the good/bad/vamp-ingenue/punk/technogirl several times through albums, music videos, concerts and endless photographs. She promoted her latest concept ("Like a Prayer") with a global strategy of releasing the music video before the album as a Pepsi commercial watched the same night in forty countries, by just about 300 million people.

Her newly rediscovered Catholicism is as much a reversal and simulation as the prior concept switches from virgin to material girl, and her ironic, carnal evocations of her body pose as semiological masquerades that play with the crucifixes, opera gloves, corsets, chains, and rosary-beads as if these props had any representational meaning or fetishized value. Her doubling as a sexual icon (Marilyn Monroe) was ghosted by the same deliberate artificiality as her exaggerated body flailing and sultry pouting on stage and on video, and her synthesized pop-rock now copies the sleekly glamorous and aerobicized look of her body movements. After watching the uncannily edited narcissistic fantasies of her Pepsi video (a vertigenous dreamscape of burning crosses, stigmata, miscegenation, miracles, and a doubled child/Madonna reversal of the gaze in the video-within-the-video), and after listening to an ostensibly "confessional" album that examines her origins and her broken marriage, her performances only yield a sense of the polymorphous perverse, multistylistic simulation that knows when to insert a throbbingly sincere cello or piano line or a hallucinatory cross-fade.

After the video images of interracial love and religious ecstasy were denounced by the American Family Association and various Catholic groups, "Like a Prayer" even received a retroactive effect of taboo-breaking shock. This misreading of Madonna's confessional/blasphemous *poses* will heighten the rhetorical blurring of self-images she has constructed. The duplicity of her signals, like the crucifix dangling over her exposed breasts, derives its significance from such misunderstandings of the artificiality of Madonna's titillating persona, which cannot be "freeze-framed" or identified since it is in constant movement, spreading out, multiple, fluid. Her image of herself as not-yet.

That has been. It is not there.

Re-modeling

The theater event must be tactile, corporeal, carnal even: the actor materializes in the flesh. But any way you look at it, the theater is a play of mind. An abstraction, blooded, spilling over the empty space. And the mind moves in and out of the space, keeping its eye on those dead bodies.[20]

As we increase our efforts to think beyond or below the surface of the Spectacle, we come to remember that the theatre, perhaps to a greater extent than we can imagine today, had always been troubled by its appearance as spectacle. Unlike a more innocent and unreflexive tradition of dance that claimed the performing body as a natural medium for intuitive or unconscious human feelings, the theatre has had to face a consistent antitheatrical tradition that saw the actor as a masquerade and the play of characters as a source or condition of ambivalence. This playing of the self as a persona, a role, or a representation complicates the perception of who or what is speaking or playing, and how the signs of inner feeling are displayed, concealed, or counterfeited. The actor complicates the surface, as well as the depth and perspective created by the corporeality of the body that cannot be reduced, even though the anxious perception of the *illusory presence* of the body—our play of mind—is a problem that has radically affected the theory and practice of theatre only during this century's slow disintegration of the Cartesian self.

When Foucault wrote of the body as a "volume in disintegration" gradually destroyed by history, he was not necessarily thinking of the panopticon of the theatre and the convoluted subjections of the *discursive body* in Western drama. From these subjections the European and American avant-garde tried to salvage the "event," the manifestation of something that was not already obeying the disciplines and technologies of production.

It is interesting to remember that a marginal tradition of speculative thought (Kleist, Craig, the Bauhaus experiments by Schlemmer) had theorized the artificial-mechanical body-figure (in ballet), and the perfected repeatability (in the Über-Marionette) of autoreferential, nonmimetic body movement or bodily play, with the paradoxical intention of liberating the body from any constraints of emotional or physical representation. In view of such theories of abstraction, one can perhaps better place the critical significance of Artaud's challenging and intensely complicated vision of a pure theatre entirely severed from the principle of repetition governed by texts, symbolic narration, or the ideological productions of representation. Artaud's rejection of psychological theatre and the textually inscribed body (never itself but always other, in imitation of a model) makes him invent a series of metaphorical substitutions, away from and beyond the existing dramatic theatre and the entire Aristotelian tradition, in order to posit and envision the spatial, kinetic, and polyphonic performance of a body that *is*, and that can breathe and intone the affective topography of its somatic and psychic totality. Between the concrete physics and the magical alchemy of this theatre, the body dances. (No-thing but making use of everything.)[21]

We may very well agree with Baudrillard that postmodern performance has only created "abject caricatures" of Artaud's impossible vision of a total theatre. This was perhaps unavoidable since the exploration of the body, *after* Artaud, could only begin with interpretations of the metaphor of "cruelty" that hovers over Artaud's projected "metaphysics-in-action" seizing the theatre like a plague, like a "whirlwind of higher forces."[22]

Already with Grotowski's "holy actor" we not only encounter a more literal emphasis on the symbolic body as a corporeal presence "revealing" itself (its human condition) in an act of extreme self-confrontation, but also the quasimystical asceticism of a highly disciplined bodily technique that essentializes the authenticity of the individual actor's self-purifying work (variously described as self-penetration; trance, sacrifice; removal of psychic or physical blockages; total organic awareness of body-life; fusion of discipline and spontaneity, and so on). Since Grotowski's Laboratory Theatre experimented in relative isolation in Poland, the highly charged, ritualistic, and cathartic experience of the physical performances only achieved their wide-ranging impact after the international presentation of *Apocalypsis cum Figuris, Akropolis,* and *The Constant Prince* in 1969–70, at a time when Grotowski was about to abandon theatre and begin his trans-cultural, paratheatrical research.

We noted that when we eliminated certain blocks and obstacles what remains is most elementary and most simple—what exists between human beings when they have a certain confidence between each other and when they look for an understanding that goes beyond the understanding of words. . . . Precisely at that point one does not perform any more. One day we found it necessary to eliminate the notion of theatre (an actor in front of a spectator).[23]

Although Grotowski had always stressed that his essential concern was to push the human confrontation between actor and spectator to such an extreme that a *shared* authenticity at an unconscious, nonverbal, and corporeal level could be achieved, his ideal of a collective ritual remained elusive. It was, consequently, replaced during the 1970s and 1980s by a kind of global search for elementary and archaic pretheatrical "sources," conducted with a carefully selected and elitist team of researchers (interconnected with Eugenio Barba's cross-cultural studies of the physical body and psychophysical act-in-performance).[24] I find the trajectory of Grotowski's work, and the nomadic character and global dispersion of his continuing search for the body "in the beginning,"[25] rather fascinating for two specific reasons. First, the sincerity of Grotowski's search for a total and authentic act of the present body, during which the actor breaks the shell of his or her social identity and the *mask* of representation, involved a humanist ethics and an ethos of sacrificial redemption practiced and performed within a technically constructed artistic framework. When it became clear that such an act of *directed* spontaneous presence (i.e., directed, structured, and prepared for performance in front of an audience) could not break the divisive play of mirrors within the theatrical structure of performance, abandoning performance itself was only logical. Grotowski's posttheatrical search for the degree zero led to a dispersion of increasingly vaguely defined cultural activities that dissolved the notion of performance into process-oriented exercises exploring the "sources of life" and the direct, primary perception of "existence, of presence."[26] This ostensibly pluralist, pancultural exchange of experience was mimicked, in the 1980s, by the differently motivated, ideologically reactionary production aesthetics of Peter Brook or Robert Wilson, who in their separate ways began to cultivate a syncretic, intercultural vision of shared experience. For Brook, the incorporation of "other" materials, experiences, and "other-cultural" body techniques into his epic performances seem obviously intended as a renovation of Western theatre, in the "universal" spirit of Brook's definitive model (Shakespeare, not Grotowski). In Wilson's case, one cannot be too sure what it means.

Second, dislocating the body from textual theatre, and Grotowski's abandonment of the formal structure of theatre as such, can be seen now in its full significance as an epistemological rupture converging with the revolutionary impulses of the 1960s toward liberating the entire body politic that collapsed under the weight of its own internal contradictions. The dissolution of Grotowski's "holy actor," and of the theatrical search for an authentic, participatory event, meets its ghostly double in the slow demise of the Living Theatre and the gradual exhaustion of the utopian energy that inspired American experiments in the 1960s and 1970s. On the one hand, such experiments sought to theatricalize and transform life itself, like a revolution, like Paradise Now. But the uncritical immersion into a kind of ontological hysteria, acted out in innumerable action events, happenings, chance events, nonart art events, rituals and auto-performances, was bound to disperse itself into various optical illusions of the liberated body. Instead of being able to break the mask of representation, some of the more radical and dangerous body art events (e.g. the self-mutilations of Gina Pane and Chris Burden) only reconfirmed the limits of transgression that were soon reached in the ritualized exhibitions of literally naked, vulnerable bodies.

As in Hermann Nitsch's orgiastic, bloody crucifixions of animals, or Vito Acconci's solipsistic rite of masturbation, the whole mimicry of archaic rituals (whether communal or "private," as they were sometimes called by women artists who explored their bodies as "sacred beings") reached a dead end by breaking down into parody, a histrionic footnote at the margins of late capitalism's technological simulation and cynical exchange of ritual violence in the social body. On the other hand, we can now see that another very heterogeneous complex of experimental work was developing out of this profusion of transgressive energy. Although it is important for our perspective on postmodern performance to perceive the close relations and interconnections between the emergence of postmodern dance (with its beginnings in the Cunningham/Judson Church experiments), dance-theatre (the expressionist-realist antiaesthetic de-

veloped by Pina Bausch and other European choreographers), performance art (with its direct links to minimalism, and conceptual art experiments in sculpture, film, video, new music, painting and dance), and
formalist multimedia performance theatre (Robert Wilson, Ping Chong,
Wooster Group, Richard Foreman), I want to ask whether we can distinguish two main directions into which the performing body has been
moved.

I do not want to engage in the impossible task of sketching a history of
influences and of clearly marked or distinct reconceptions of the body in
performance over the last two decades. Instead I propose to foreground
two apparently disparate attempts, among these movements of postmodern performance, to renegotiate the place of the body and the subject
within formal structures of performance, and within reflexive modes exploring the productions of the body or the exchange between performer
and spectator under the concealing "mask of representation."

Grotowski discovered that this mask conceals the illusive play of mind
and perception that makes a body seen, regardless how extreme the effort
to separate it from its roles, its mediated presence, and from being watched. The body is not just there, the performer his or her own object,
self-explanatory, a three-dimensional volume in real space and real time,
more or less existing in front of an audience without any props (the old
drama, with its plot, actions, characters, and stage sets referring to another
reality) to hold on to. Early conceptual performance art wanted to challenge and expose the unself-conscious repetitions and reifications of cultural stereotypes in traditional drama. All the early performances were
thus explicitly antithetical to theatre. But with the pressures of the Pleasure
Principle behind them (the ecstatic 1960s), and the new medium of a
liberated body in mind, most of the formal or informal performance art
experiments of the 1970s assumed too easily and too quickly that the
presentness of the body, once the performer works with it, "explores it,
manipulates it, paints it, covers it, uncovers it, freezes it, moves it, cuts it,
isolates it, and speaks to it as if it were a foreign object . . . a foreign body
where the subject's desires and repressions surface,"[27] was guaranteed as
an immediate act-in-itself, the source of its own production and displacement.

That particular illusion of a continuous present was entangled from
the start with the deconstructive impulse of the performer wanting to
expose the theatrical machinery of mystifications in the theatre but mis-
understanding the "reality" of the *demystifying gestures.* They were always
quite theatrical, of course. If performance art wanted to dissolve the body
and reconstitute it, move it across and away from the "scene" of theatricality that reinscribes the codes of representation through the gaze of the
audience, it had to continuously disrupt the conditions of its own specular-
ity. Instead of abdicating performance, as Grotowski did, performance art
performed the abdication, fragmentation, dispossession, slippage and

blurring of the subject of performance. Its conspicuous body hurled through the more or less excruciating tautologies; its narcissistic recursiveness remained undiminished by the endless rehearsals of the failure to understand the political uselessness of self-deconstruction (a later version of Grotowski's extreme emphasis on the suffering, sacrificial body).

Aesthetically and theoretically, the overexposure of the literal body and the self-abusive display of emotional fantasies and aggressions in some of the autobiographical and confessional performance art and in early feminist body art gradually exhausted itself, and its limiting effects became apparent. As we moved from the 1970s into the 1980s, we gradually lost faith in the literal and semiotic manipulation of the body language: the screams, whispers and silences, the gyrations and frantic repetitions, in the body, of reflexes that also showed up, as depletions of the imagination, in the inconsequential chatter and improvised murmuring.

For a theory of postmodern performance art constituted after the fact, it is also quite characteristic to say that the performance events themselves were deliberately ephemeral. What has survived are images in our mind, or photographs that have resurfaced in the discourse and documentation, our Camera Lucida of the postmodern. As a form of cultural production, the textlessness of performance art generally shifts critical attention toward the visual, or toward the perceived relationship between body, space, sound, light, and objects. This attention to the visual construction of the performances, and the functional relationships between the manipulation or display of the body and the manipulation of space, must be considered crucial in terms of the historical trajectory of performance art. Not only did it take place in a predominantly visual arts context (galleries, art spaces, studios, lofts, and the music club scene), it also operated in a much closer formal interrelationship with experiments in new music (industrial music, punk, electronic music), video art, film and dance.

I would argue, then, that the initial, reductive focus on the physical body-in-performance was gradually superceded both by a more critically reflexive formalist exploration and a more commercially oriented, popular embrace of the multiple, artistically challenging crossovers between the visual media and the new possibilities of technological intervention.

I cannot do justice here to the distinctive developments of so many artists such as Laurie Anderson, Yvonne Rainer, Meredith Monk, Marina Abramovic, Karole Armitage, Valie Export, Dara Birnbaum, Nam June Paik, David Byrne, Robert Longo, Michael Smith, Spalding Gray. It is hardly surprising that some of them, after having drawn on cabaret, musical, and entertainment techniques for their solo work, eventually made their own crossover from experimental performance to mass culture. If this is the "emblematic fulfilment of the postmodern in its movement from the sixties to the eighties,"[28] it can only be understood in the context of the cultural hegemonic of the spectacle discussed earlier.

It will then become necessary to ask whether self-exposure and self-manipulation in performance are subsumed by the spectacle, or whether there is a degree or quality of difference in the control and manipulation of image entertained by Madonna and, say, Laurie Anderson. The narrative, acoustic, and visual management of Anderson's image as performer is a fascinating case of simulation having superseded the idea of a literal, "real" presence or identity altogether. Anderson's identity is forever displaced and delayed. Like the vocal "delays" and electronic distortions of her voice, her own body and gender identity are set afloat in the multitrack audiovisual "choreography" to which she (ironically) refers as the "Language of the Future" in Part I of *United States:*

> Current runs through bodies
> and then it doesn't.
> On again.
> Off again.
> Always two things
> Switching.
> One thing instantly replaces
> another.
> It was the language
> of the Future.

Her performance of this language as a kind of electronic closed-circuit transvestism is both tongue-in-cheek and disturbing, since the brave new world she sees and sings about, these "United States," appears as a completely artifactual, digitalized space/surface/map of ready-made signs. Can her perception be explained as symptomatic of the total inscription of the body/map under the conditions of postindustrial culture that have effected the "unification and minimalization of experiential states" and the "neutralization of apprehension"?[29] As one of her critics suggests, in her reperformance of the "condition of woman," in particular, we see the postmodern space of the "United States" as a female space of "tautological, minimal existence" insofar as the hegemonic structure forces her to copy, imitate, borrow, assimilate, appropriate, and take on styles and attitudes of this monitored space. Anderson, in this fashion, plays the "answering machine" within her own electronic circuits that also replicate the no longer distinguishable relations between elite and vernacular cultures in a "presentation of the now which is inaccessible to critical consciousness." This postmodern reading of Anderson's reperformance is seductive and problematic because it posits a totally closed universe in which Anderson's deconstruction of any stable identity is not seen as a critical act of representation but as a powerless internalization of the pervasive flow of simulacra. One could also argue, however, that Anderson is in control of the technological manipulation of the various (gender) identities constructed on the surface. These identities are not the same. However, the question of whether the presentation of "woman" and "female" space can be forever delayed in such ironic projections of the homeland *(Home of the Brave)* will be answered very differently by those performance artists who have not entered into the exchange between subculture and mass culture, and whose work and continuing focus on the politics of the body (the social construction of gender identity) have marginalized them. I am thinking, for example, of the solo, group, and communal performance experiments developed by feminist, lesbian, gay, and transvestite artists, of the work you would not see at the BAM Next Wave Festival but in clubs such as 8BC, the Pyramid, the WOW Café or P.S.122 (New York) or in alternative cabarets and galleries across the country, or on the beach in California (cf. Suzanne Lacy's *Whisper, the Waves, the Wind* and *Dark Madonna*).[30]

The particular dissimilarities of scale, performance site, and anti-hegemonic content of these works would require a lot more attention than I can give them here. I want to conclude my observations with another suggestion, however, that will reconnect the trajectory of performance art with the simultaneous and parallel development of formalist multimedia performance theatre (Wilson's "theatre of images," but also Foreman's later work, and the cinematic theatre experiments of Squat or the Italian "Nuova Spettacolarita" groups such as Falso Movimento and La Gaia Scienza). The differences in scale between performance art and performance theatre are considerable, and it is still significant, I believe, that at the current stage of these two antithetical models of production I would see Rachel Rosenthal perform at the Kitchen, or find Karen Finley scare the hell out of a bunch of rednecks in a Dallas punk-rock club. I would have to fly to La Scala or the Berlin Schaubühne to attend Robert Wilson's latest baroque, multinational high-tech opera.

In between those differences, however, one could trace the encroaching impact of image and reproductive media technologies on the visual structure of recent performance art that has begun to reconstruct the images of the body in ways paradoxically comparable to Wilson's more recent down-scaling and retextualization of his abstract, architectural, and presentational theatre.[31]

The demateralization of language and of the actor's body in Wilson's most remarkable work (the operas of the 1970s and the incomplete Gesamtkunstwerk of *the CIVIL warS* that was shown in segments between 1983 and 1986) was a formidable attempt to abolish textual-discursive theatre and replace it with a highly formalized and stylized scenography of geometrical construction and aesthetic calculation. The artificial mathematical composition of his slow-moving visual tableaux reduces the performers' bodies to figures or signs in the larger scenic architecture. There is an obvious difference, for example, in the way in which Laurie Anderson can be said to "embody" her electronic body mutations and communicate her "playing" to the audience (in *Home of the Brave* she plays on herself as a percussion instrument, a musician of the body), and the way in which Wilson's actors don't communicate with the audience. Perhaps comparable to Schlemmer's apparently mechanical marionettes in the *Bauhaus Dances*, in which he experimented with the abstraction of the body's relationship to space, Wilson's performers are both abstracted—they are pictorial lines drawn onto the surface, moved, and then frozen to be redrawn—and presented as positions or numbers within a visual and auditory configuration. (Wilson often multiplies the figure of a woman into "Woman 1," "Woman 2," "Woman 3," and so forth) In this sense, Wilson's theatre effects a radical repositioning of the human body: within the multiple transparent superimpositions of images, the body is not privileged but treated as one material, one cipher, among others.

At the same time, the mutations between these elements, i.e., the syntheses of sound, light, motion, bodies, and objects (with a predominantly lateral movement, parallel to the stage apron), create a dream-like sense of unreality that allows the spectator to free-associate anything with everything, consume the idealized surface of the spectacle. The pictorial, flattened surface-in-motion offers some excruciating paradoxes that are further complicated by the use of the proscenium space as an amalgamation of quasipainterly, cinematic, architectural and trompe l'oeil spaces. The *constructedness* of "time" and "space" is so overbearing that it is hard to know whether Wilson's posthistorical conception of his archetypal, nonnarrative, and nonlinear pictures is derived from a completely uncritical reverence for the primacy of the image, or whether his deployment of the aesthetic surface as "mask" redirects attention to the perfected falseness of the construction of apparency.

It's like the Greek theatre in that when the Greek actor was on stage he wore a mask, which presented an image that was different from what he was saying. It's in this way that what I'm trying to do is similar to Greek theatre—the entire stage is a mask. That's one reason I use microphones—to create a distance between the sound and the image.[32]

In his refusal to discuss meanings, or to mention the human actor in his architectural equations of images and sounds, Wilson rather perversely fetishizes the surface and the technological control over the surface. "As far as I am concerned the best way to achieve this is with something mechanical that offers total control. Then we have freedom. The ideal solution would be to become a machine."[33] With this remark (made in reference to *the CIVIL warS*), Wilson may unwittingly echo Kleist's theory of the marionette theatre. More insidiously, he also rehearses the equation of technology and freedom now beginning to haunt American postmodern culture with its fully vacant look and its seductively designed surfaces barely masking the deprivation and abandonment of the social body. Unlike Edward Hopper's deeply haunted paintings, Wilson's trompe l'oeil pictures seem completely unconscious of the dehumanized presence/emptiness of the designed transparence. His aesthetic equation of technological perfection and freedom, especially in the denial of its ideological function, is symptomatic of "male fantasies"[34] about mastery and control. His reduction of human consequence to neutral manipulable elements in the landscape conceals the absolute, ahistorical function ascribed to the body-as-sign.

It remains to be seen whether contemporary performance art has the nerve and the power to rehistoricize the images of the body that are currently faded out and imploded into the technological halls of mirrors of the video theatre (cf. John Jesurun's *Deep Sleep* and *White Water*) that copies both Wilson and Laurie Anderson. In the video theatre, the body disappears into a communications language; it keeps returning as a coded signal subservient to no particular message except the one we already know (the media/TV are more real than the real).

Originally a filmmaker and sculptor, John Jesurun brings to his theatre a special sensitivity to the space of images; he manipulates the powerful presence of a technologically constructed reality to highlight the precarious nature of human language and expression. His recent works have played into the fear (and the conspiracy theory) that our lives are sucked up by the pervasive reality of screen projections. In *White Water* he seems to push beyond the idea that we are engaged in a struggle to assure or maintain an identity that is not already mediated and projected in advance. When I saw the work at the Kitchen, the space of images in *White Water* was relentlessly

Figure 38. John Jesurun's *White Water.* The Kitchen, New York City, 1986. Photo: Massimo Agus.

closed circuit: the rectangular, raked stage was surrounded on all four sides by the audience which, in turn, was surrounded by sixteen video monitors on high pedestals. Four monitors sat in the corners of the grey-carpeted floor, surrounding the cool geometry of the furniture—two tables and two chairs arranged in a parallelogram. When the lights went down, the pale white light of the TV screens glowed as we observed the perpetual motion of talking heads (on stage and on the screens). Their dialogue appeared to revolve around the story of a miraculous phantom-apparition a boy claimed to have had. The boy was interviewed, in turn, by a man and a woman playing several roles (psychiatrist, priest, lawyer, talk-show host), and by a producer played by the boy himself (his "other" image on video).

The interrogations had a hallucinogenic quality, enacted in an extremely rapid, fragmented, and nonsequential manner: a kind of assembly line or machine of quotations, puns, malapropisms, and bizarre excursions into the Old Testament and pop music. At the same time, there was a clear, almost clinical attitude toward the logic of this language collage. It partook of the same reality or unreality transmitted through the video images (still shots of a lake, a window frame, or close-ups of the actors' faces). We were in the land of Magritte, but also made to feel the desperate insistence with which the boy clung to his phantasm of a disembodied woman with healing powers.

But this insistence was purely an effect of Jesurun's hyperreal language. Characteristically, the actors spoke a kind of "live," accelerated version of the disembodied language in Wilson, in intense rhythms that created a sense of temporality and speed very different from any emotional or psychological realism of acting. Our seeing and hearing were forced into complex contradictions by Jesurun's electronic theatre. The increasingly violent scene of interrogation became a search for the truth of what really happened to the boy. But the longer we listened to the conflicting descriptions of his vision of the disembodied goddess (mother figure), the more we became aware of the stasis within this network of information overload and language babble. The closed-circuit channels of the video monitors, as environment for the actors and the audience, allowed fantasy constructions to be tied into a narcissistic loop. Predictably, the boy ended up confessing that there might be "nothing outside him" at the end of the performance.

On the other hand, in Karen Finley's solo performances of *I'm An Ass Man* and *The Constant State of Desire*, which I saw at the Dallas Theatre Gallery (1986) and at P.S. 122 (New York City, 1987), her body is visible everywhere and exposed to the extent that her confrontational, frontal display—obscene, vulgar, threatening, scatological, pornographic, ironic, seeing and seen—accelerates and pushes the technical idea of "overexposure" (an error of the camera) toward the edge where we can experience the limit. Look, see, here it is—now you can see it. But can we really *see* the body on the edge, traumatized yet aggressively phallic, abjected yet excessively vituperative in its constant rehearsal of sadistic fantasies of objectification, a body voicing the cross-gendered languages of the unconscious and becoming the "sight" of patriarchal fear and loathing? Seductive and exhibitionistic, Finley shows her body as the site of traumatic fantasies, infantile desires, masochistic dreams, sexual practices and biological processes, celebrating perversely the missing reality of the *grotesque body* (inescapable matter: urine, feces, sperm, menstrual blood, vomit, tears) obscured in our culture. "You leather kind of folk with your spiked hair, I love to think about you masturbating!" I remember Finley's direct and calculated provocation of the (predominantly male) audience on a late night in Dallas as a symptomatic strategy which, in the longer and metaphorically denser performance of *The Constant State of Desire*, came to function as a continuous translation of the body-in-pain and of the relations between flesh and language. Above all, her translation ("You make me sick!") is brutally ironic in the reversal of the traditional relationship between the masturbating voyeurs or fetishists and the overexposed woman's body on

Figure 39. Karen Finley, *The Constant State of Desire*. P.S. 122, New York City, 1987. Photo: Dona Ann McAdams.

the stages of male violence (the theatre, the family home, the workplace, the doctor's office, pornography, the dominant heterosexual institutions and media that produce their images of desirable bodies).

The reversal remains powerfully ambiguous. Finley humiliates and taunts the audience with its spectatorial desire for her body while her body (re)produces a grotesque mirror of abusive power in the multiple, disjointed subject positions from which she speaks (vilifier and vilified; victimizer, victim, and voyeur) and from within which she seeks to unleash a transgressive force of disgust, of physical and emotional unease. It is symptomatic, in this respect, that she literalizes the metaphors of incorporation and ingestion (eating, sucking) in her "improper" mixing of food and body parts (sexual orifices), and in her refusing to keep it all in, to keep silent about incestuous secrets and the effects of abuse on the body. Her incantatory whirlwind monologues push the exposed body—violated, vulnerable, colonized, desired, rejected, idealized, objectified, exploited, pathological—to the other side of the mask, where it perhaps can no longer be looked at, desired or penetrated or controlled, where it might confront the spectator with a horror version of his or her own body. In perverting the desire to watch her, Finley's body returns like a revenger, speaking with a postmodern accent and unmitigated rage. But she can speak her self as something other, naming the places of the "unspeakable" (not in the official code), the censored, and the "most foreign" (not mapped), laughing at the aggravated, guilt-ridden audience who had come to see the spectacle of woman.

Finley's intensification of the grotesque body, and her refusal to take part in the neutralization of difference and of the theatre, offers another point of departure for our return to the critical questions that were raised in the previous essays. I don't think there are any conclusions I want to draw. But the practices and countermodels I have described allow us to think that the theatre cannot be absorbed by the Spectacle of a technological culture of violence as long as it can still experience and reperform the contradictions produced by this culture. Such performances are the rehearsals for which we are responsible.

NOTES

1. Michel Foucault, "Nietzsche, Genealogy, History," in *Language, Counter-Memory, Practice*, ed. Donald Bouchard (Ithaca: Cornell Univ. Press, 1977), 148.

2. Heiner Müller, "A Talk beneath Language," *ballett international* no. 12 (1984): 24.

3. In Paul Virilio's view of modern progress, the accelerated production of speed has created technical bodies/technological vehicles whose movement approaches the point of exhaustion at which it breaks down into inertia (death). See his *Speed and Politics*, trans. Mark Polizotti (New York: Semiotext(e), 1986), 75–95.

4. Cf. Georges Bataille, *Visions of Excess: Selected Writings*, 1927–39, trans. A. Stoeckl with C. R. Lovitt and D. M. Leslie (Minneapolis: Univ. of Minnesota Press, 1985), 94.

5. Gregorio Salazar, "First Texas Triennial," *Public News,* 28 September 1988, 7.

6. Cf. David Porush's illuminating study of the relationship between post-modern technological culture and fiction, in *The Soft Machine: Cybernetic Fiction* (London and New York: Methuen, 1985). See also *The Technological Imagination: Theories and Fictions,* ed. Teresa de Lauretis, Andreas Huyssen, and Kathleen Woodward (Madison: Coda Press, 1980); and *The Myths of Information: Technology and Postindustrial Culture,* ed. Kathleen Woodward (Madison: Coda Press, 1980). The current overproduction of critical and theoretical analyses of the "History of the Body" (cf. the 3-volume edition of essays published in the journal *Zone* in 1989) and of cultural constructions of the gendered body in relation to the problematics of subjectivity, voyeurism, fetishism, and scopophilia in visual representation (cf. the violently polemical issue of the *Canadian Journal of Political and Social Theory* on "Body Invaders: Panic Sex in America," ed. Arthur Kroker and Marilouise Kroker, in 1987, and a host of other essays published in *Representations, Cultural Critique, October, Screen, Sub-stance, The Drama Review, Diacritics, Social Text,* etc.) is in itself a fascinating symptom of the stakes of the body at this historical juncture of postmodernity.

7. Roland Barthes, *Camera Lucida,* trans. Richard Howard (New York: Hill & Wang, 1981), 115.

8. Ibid., 78–79.

9. Jean Baudrillard, *Simulations* (New York: Semiotext(e), 1983), 146.

10. Ibid., 141–142.

11. Jacques Derrida, *Writing and Difference,* trans. Alan Bass (Chicago: Univ. of Chicago Press, 1978), 256.

12. Guy Debord, *Society of the Spectacle* (Detroit: Black and Red, 1983), #42.

13. Foucault's progressive investigation of "corporal powers," in his studies of madness, the medical gaze, the prison, and sexuality, traces the evolution and elaborations of the *technology of bodies* from a determinist perspective that reaches its limit in the postmodern conception of a purely relational and abstract power, a symbolic medium of exchange. As studies of the ideological and political history of the body that trace (beginning with the late Middle Ages) its dislocations and relocations (cf. from spectacular, public punishment, and corporal pain to modern forensic psychiatry and penology), Foucault's work bears interesting comparisons to Mikhail Bakhtin's cultural analysis of late medieval carnival, the "grotesque body," and the significant differences between the human body as represented in popular festivity and as represented in classical statuary or high culture (*Rabelais and His World,* trans. H. Iswolsky [Cambridge: MIT Press, 1968]). See also Norbert Elias's comprehensive study of the social control of body functions and manners, and the progressive public regulation of the body through restructuring and internal coding of personality (*The Civilizing Process,* 2 vols., trans. E. Jephcott [New York: Pantheon, 1978/82]). Francis Barker, in his study of the privatization and subjection of the body, speaks of an increasing "de-realization" of the body beginning with the seventeenth century and its transition from the feudal to the capitalist mode of production. Cf. *The Tremulous Body: Essays in Subjection* (London: Methuen, 1984). For a brilliant example of radical feminist interventions into these historical and sociological theories of subjectivity and the body, see Teresa de Lauretis, *Technologies of Gender: Essays on Theory, Film and Fiction* (Bloomington: Indiana Univ. Press, 1987).

14. See Hal Foster, *Recodings: Art, Spectacle, Cultural Politics* (Port Townsend: Bay Press, 1985), 41.

15. I am indebted to Peggy Phelan's suggestive essay on "Feminist Theory, Poststructuralism, and Performance" *The Drama Review* 32, no. 1 [1988]: 107–27), which engages the crucial texts of recent feminist film theory and criticism (Johnston, Mulvay, Doane, Kaplan, Silverman, de Lauretis) but offers a sig-

nificant departure for the less-developed theoretical praxis in theatre, dance, and performance art studies. Her choice of Yvonne Rainer's work (in both dance and film) as a case study offers many challenging insights while managing to include a critique of what she perceives as the essentializing and apolitical weaknesses in Eugenio Barba's theatre-anthropological studies of the actor's "physiological body."

16. The guide book is a fine example of the instrumentalization of body parts in the service of a perverse redesign of a body ideal ("for a sleeker, stronger, sexier, fitter, healthier, totally perfect you") that thrives on and reaffirms an almost medievalized guilt, shame, and hatred about one's depraved body. Cf. *Perfect Parts* (New York: Warner Books, 1987). The Guide is dedicated to Jesus.

17. "If you could make your body into a machine, or into a dead piece of material such as clay, and *if* it could obey you in every movement for the entire space of time it was before an audience, and *if* you could put aside Shakespeare's Poem, you would be able to make a work of art out of that which is in you. For you would not only have dreamt, you would have executed to perfection, and that which you had executed could be repeated time after time . . ." We need to see Craig's theory of the performance machine ("The Actor and the Über-Marionette," originally published in *The Mask* [1908]) both in its intertextual relations to the baroque (geometrically perfect court dance), Diderot *(Paradoxe sur le Comédien)*, and Kleist's marionette-*Kunstfigur*, as well as to postmodern revisions of the mechanical or abstracted body in earlier avant-garde practices (in futurism and surrealism) and especially the Bauhaus experiments (cf. Schlemmer's allusion to the masquerade, dissimulation, and artificiality of the baroque as a major influence on his choreography of "precision mechanisms"). Cf. *The Theater of the Bauhaus*, ed. Walter Gropius (Middletown: Wesleyan Univ. Press, 1979). For an excellent discussion of these interrelations, see Mark Franco, "Repeatability, Reconstruction and Beyond," *Theatre Journal* 41, no. 1 (1989): 56–74.

18. Cf. Elizabeth Kagan and Margaret Morse's challenging critique of the spatiodynamic organization of the aerobics ritual in "The Body Electronic. Aerobic Exercise on Video: Women's Search for Empowerment and Self-Transformation," *The Drama Review* 32, 4 (1988): 164–80.

19. I am using the formulation in reference to Adorno's dialectic. The case for a "resistant" postmodernism and committed, political theatre praxis has recently been made by Philip Auslander, "Toward a Concept of the Political in Postmodern Theatre," *Theatre Journal* 39, no. 1 (1987): 20–34.

20. Herbert Blau, *Take Up the Bodies: Theatre at the Vanishing Point* (Urbana: Univ. of Illinois Press, 1982), 7.

21. Cf. Antonin Artaud, *The Theatre and Its Double* (New York: Grove Press, 1958), 12.

22. Ibid., 83.

23. Jerzy Grotowski, quoted by Richard Mennen in "Grotowski's Paratheatrical Projects," *The Drama Review* 20, no. 3 (1975): 60.

24. The recent controversy over Barba's anthropological study of pancultural "energy" and "pre-expressive presence" in performance raises the issue whether such practices are mystifying and symptomatic of the more conservative and apolitical tendencies among theatre practitioners who try to sublimate the failure of the Western avant-garde. See Philip Zarilli's critique of Barba's research in "For Whom Is the 'Invisible' Not Visible? Reflections on Representation in the Work of Eugenio Barba," *The Drama Review* 32, no. 1 (1988): 95–106, and Barba's response in *The Drama Review* 32, no. 4 (1988): 7–14.

25. Grotowski, "Wandering towards a Theatre of Sources," reprinted in Jennifer Kumiega, *The Theater of Grotowski* (London: Methuen, 1985), 228–30.

26. Grotowski, quoted in Kumiega, 203.

27. Josette Féral, "Performance and Theatricality: The Subject Demystified," *Modern Drama* 25, no. 1 (1982): 171. See also Chantal Pontbriand, "'The Eye finds no fixed point on which to rest . . .'", *Modern Drama* 25, no. 1 (1982): 154–69. The special issue of *Modern Drama*, in which these essays on performance art and theory appeared, marks the belated point of recognition in the American academic theatre culture that something like "performance art" had happened and actually disturbed or contested the conventions of theatre/drama.

28. Herbert Blau, *The Eye of Prey: Subversions of the Postmodern* (Bloomington: Indiana Univ. Press, 1987), xvi.

29. Herman Rapaport, "'Can You Say Hello?' Laurie Anderson's *United States*," *Theatre Journal* 38, no. 3 (1986): 339–54. Rapaport's critique of Anderson's acquiescence to mass-cultural hegemony and to direct reproductions of the dead language of "pastiche" is indebted to Fredric Jameson's influential assessment of postmodern "blank parody" in "Postmodernism and the Cultural Logic of Late Capitalism," *New Left Review* 146 (1984): 53–92.

30. For an extensive critical discussion of the significance of Lacy's large-scale collaborative rituals (involving the performance of socially marginalized/ "minimalized" older women), see Moira Roth, "Suzanne Lacy: Social Reformer and Witch"; Diane Rothenberg, "Social Art/Social Action"; and Lucy R. Lippard, "Lacy: Some of Her Own Medicine," in a special section of *The Drama Review* 32, no. 1 (1988): 42–76.

31. For a strongly affirmative interpretation of Wilson's work in Europe, see Hans-Thies Lehmann, "Robert Wilson: Scenographer," *Parkett* 16 (1988), 44–53. See also Bonnie Marranca's poetic and ecological response to Wilson's recent stagings in her "The Forest as Archive: Wilson and Interculturalism," *Performing Arts Journal* 33/34 (1989): 36–44.

32. Robert Wilson, in reference to his *Alcestis* production and the emplacement of Heiner Müller's text, *Description of a Picture*. The performance was first shown at the ART (Cambridge) in 1986, and subsequently in Stuttgart, West Germany, where Wilson directed both his adaptation of Euripides and Gluck's opera *Alcestis*. Quoted from "Alcestis: A Casebook," *Performing Arts Journal* 28 (1986): 102.

33. Quoted from the German edition of the program book for the Cologne segment of *the CIVIL warS*. The interview with Wilson is printed in "*the CIVIL warS*—a construction in space and time. Ein Gespräch," 41–55.

34. Cf. Klaus Theweleit's psychocultural study of fascism as desiring production/death production in *Male Fantasies: Women, Floods, Bodies, History* (Minneapolis: Univ. of Minnesota Press, 1987).

Index

Abstraction, 22, 47, 223–24
Acconci, Vito, 219
Acting, 3, 43–44, 55, 61, 83, 85, 94, 104–10, 149–53, 159, 180, 217
Adorno, Theodor, 50n, 170
Aerobics, xii, 141, 215
AIDS, 23–24, 123, 130, 208
Alienation effect, 41, 57, 61–62, 104, 114, 148, 155
Anderson, Laurie, xii, 29–30, 46, 61, 64, 174, 221–23, 225. Works: *United States*, 29–30, 180, 189, 192, 222; *Home of the Brave*, 46, 222
Architecture, xiii, 4–12, 35–41, 125, 170–75, 212
Art, postmodern, xiii, 3, 11–14, 22, 122–31, 212
Artaud, Antonin, xi, 35, 42, 44, 47, 58, 81, 85, 92–93, 95, 98, 114–15, 148–49, 175, 186, 215, 217–18
Auschwitz, 18, 50n
Avant-garde, the, xi, 12, 18, 25, 42–47, 52, 55, 57, 67, 85, 91, 93, 115, 133, 147, 154, 163, 170, 179, 182–83, 189, 192, 195, 217

Bakhtin, Mikhail, 74n, 155
Barba, Eugenio, xii, 29, 151–59, 161–63, 218, 230n. *See also* Grotowski
Barthes, Roland, 42, 83–84, 171, 186, 209–10
Bataille, Georges, 8, 56, 208
Baudrillard, Jean, xiii, 8–9, 18, 20–23, 36, 48n, 50n, 56, 79, 114, 117, 147, 171, 182, 210, 212, 217. Works: *America*, 1, 20–22; *Forget Foucault*, 9, 67, 83; *L'effet Beaubourg*, 49n; *In the Shadow of the Silent Majorities*, 21, 50n, 188; *Simulations*, 21, 50n, 79, 174–75
Bausch, Pina, xii, 45–46, 97, 132–45, 163–65, 180, 192, 201, 220. Works: *Arien*, 137–40, 142; *Bandoneon*, 164; *Bluebeard*, 132; *Cafe Müller*, 132; *Carnations*, 164; *Don't Be Afraid*, 133; *Kontakthof*, 136–37, 142; *On the Mountain a Cry Was Heard*, 140, 143; *Rite of Spring*, 138; *Victor*, 164–65; *1980*, 138, 189. *See also* Wuppertaler Tanztheater
Beckett, Samuel, 57, 64, 84, 89, 91, 111,

149, 171. Works: *Footfalls*, 91; *Ohio Impromptu*, 91; *Rockaby*, 111; *That Time*, 111; *The Unnamable*, 114
Bender, Gretchen, 126, 128
Benjamin, Walter, 6, 52–53, 58, 65, 67, 93, 157, 159, 163, 175, 205. Works: *Illuminations*, 74n; *The Origins of German Tragic Drama*, 52, 74n; *Passagenwerk*, 6, 76n
Benmussa, Simone, 93
Berkowitz, Terry, 122, 127–31
Berlin Wall, the, 2–3, 48n, 52, 89
Beuys, Joseph, xi, xiv, 12–15, 20, 126
Blade Runner, 5, 41, 177
Blau, Herbert, xiii, 29, 80, 169, 183, 187; and KRAKEN, xiii, 83, 87, 90–91, 93–95, 97. Works: *Blooded Thought*, 80–92; *The Eye of Prey*, 221; *Take Up the Bodies*, 80–96, 216–17
Boal, Augusto, 29, 146
Body, the, xii, 28, 31, 33, 45–47, 68, 114, 120, 133, 149, 159–66, 176–81; dispersion of, 6, 117, 120, 206, 218; manipulation of, 45, 120, 174–76, 185, 190, 221; as postmodern body, 6, 19, 23, 205–31 *passim*; "writing" of, 46, 61, 166
Body art, 44, 221
Body building, xii, 141, 149, 206–208, 214–15
Bogosian, Eric, 46
Bonaventure Hotel, 5–10, 21, 25, 188
Brecht, Bertolt, x, xi, 29, 42, 52–53, 56, 61, 83–84, 88, 96, 98, 148–49, 153, 156–62, 183; and Berliner Ensemble, 58; and learning play, xii, 53, 60, 62, 76n, 160; and tanztheater, 134, 136; and "theatre of the scientific age," 29, 53, 149. Works: *A Man's a Man*, 53; *Fatzer-Material*, 160; *The Measures Taken*, 60
Breton, André, 12
Breuer, Lee, 44
Brith Gof, 98
Brook, Peter, 29, 82, 149, 154–55, 167n, 219
Brown, Trisha, 44
Burden, Chris, 219

Caffarena, Attilio, 29, 36–38
Calvino, Italo, 33

JOHANNES BIRRINGER is Professor of Performance Studies at Northwestern University. He is a theatre director who has created experimental work in performance, dance, and film/video in the United States and Europe. His most recent works include *Invisible Cities*; a concert-exhibition on the AIDS crisis titled AD MORTEM; a new dance-opera, *Orpheus and Eurydike*; and two documentary films, *Memories of a Revolution* and *Border-Land*.